iPad®

PORTABLE GENIUS
2nd EDITION

Paul McFedries

iPad® Portable Genius, 2nd Edition

Published by
John Wiley & Sons, Inc.
10475 Crosspoint Blvd.
Indianapolis, IN 46256
www.wiley.com

Copyright © 2014 by John Wiley & Sons, Inc., Ind

Published simultaneously in Canada

ISBN: 978-1-118-70872-9

Manufactured in the United States of America

10 9 8 7 6 5 4 3 2 1

No part of this publication may be reproduced, stored in a retrieval system or transmitted in any form or by any means, electronic, mechanical, photocopying, recording, scanning or otherwise, except as permitted under Sections 107 or 108 of the 1976 United States Copyright Act, without either the prior written permission of the Publisher, or authorization through payment of the appropriate per-copy fee to the Copyright Clearance Center, 222 Rosewood Drive, Danvers, MA 01923, (978) 750-8400, fax (978) 646-8600. Requests to the Publisher for permission should be addressed to the Permissions Department, John Wiley & Sons, Inc., 111 River Street, Hoboken, NJ 07030, 201-748-6011, fax 201-748-6008, or online at http://www. wiley.com/go/permissions.

Limit of Liability/Disclaimer of Warranty: The publisher and the author make no representations or warranties with respect to the accuracy or completeness of the contents of this work and specifically disclaim all warranties, including without limitation warranties of fitness for a particular purpose. No warranty may be created or extended by sales or promotional materials. The advice and strategies contained herein may not be suitable for every situation. This work is sold with the understanding that the publisher is not engaged in rendering legal, accounting, or other professional services. If professional assistance is required, the services of a competent professional person should be sought. Neither the publisher nor the author shall be liable for damages arising herefrom. The fact that an organization or Web site is referred to in this work as a citation and/or a potential source of further information does not mean that the author or the publisher endorses the information the organization of Web site may provide or recommendations it may make. Further, readers should be aware that Internet Web sites listed in this work may have changed or disappeared between when this work was written and when it is read.

For general information on our other products and services or to obtain technical support, please contact our Customer Care Department within the U.S. at (877) 762-2974, outside the U.S. at (317) 572-3993 or fax (317) 572-4002.

John Wiley & Sons, Inc. also publishes its books in a variety of electronic formats and by print-on-demand. Some content that appears in standard print versions of this book may not be available in other formats. For more information about Wiley products, visit us at www.wiley.com.

Library of Congress Control Number: 2013949526

Trademarks: Wiley and the Wiley logo are trademarks or registered trademarks of John Wiley & Sons, Inc. and/ or its affiliates in the United States and/or other countries, and may not be used without written permission. iPad and iPad mini are trademarks or registered trademarks of Apple, Inc. All other trademarks are the property of their respective owners. John Wiley & Sons, Inc. is not associated with any product or vendor mentioned in this book. iPad® Portable Genius, 2nd Edition is an independent publication and has not been authorized, sponsored, or otherwise approved by Apple, Inc.

Credits

Acquisitions Editor
Aaron Black

Project Editor
Katharine Dvorak

Technical Editor
Paul Sellars

Copy Editor
Lauren Kennedy

Director, Content Development & Assembly
Robyn Siesky

Vice President and Executive Group
Publisher
Richard Swadley

About the Author

Paul McFedries is a full-time technical writer. Paul has been authoring computer books since 1991 and has more than 85 books to his credit. Paul's books have sold more than four million copies worldwide. These books include the Wiley titles *iPhone 5s & iPhone 5c Portable Genius*; *Macs Portable Genius, Third Edition*; *MacBook Air Portable Genius, Fourth Edition*; *Switching to a Mac Portable Genius, Second Edition*; *Teach Yourself VISUALLY OS X Mavericks*; and *The Facebook Guide for People Over 50*. Paul is also the proprietor of Word Spy (www.wordspy.com), a website that tracks new words and phrases as they enter the English language. Paul encourages everyone to drop by his personal website at www.mcfedries.com, or to follow him on Twitter at www.twitter.com/paulmcf and www.twitter.com/wordspy.

Acknowledgments

Being a technical writer is an awesome vocation: You get to work at home, you get to set your own schedule, and you get to help other people understand and use technology, which is a big warm-fuzzy-feeling generator. But perhaps the best part of technical writing is getting to be among the first to not only use, but also really *dive into* the latest and greatest software and hardware. The hardware side is often the most fun, because it means you get to play with gadgets, and that's a gadget geek's definition of a dream job. So, to say I had a blast researching and writing about the latest versions of the iPad and iPad mini redefines the word *understatement*. What self-respecting gadget guy wouldn't have a perma-grin while poking and prodding these devices to see just what they can do?

And what self-respecting technical writer wouldn't be constantly shaking his head in admiration while working with the amazing editorial team at Wiley? Skip back a couple of pages to see the complete list of the team who worked so hard to bring you this book. The people I worked with directly included Acquisitions Editor Aaron Black, who brings professionalism and smarts to every project; Project Editor Katharine Dvorak, whose enthusiasm made her a pleasure to work with and whose idea-generating brain made this a much better book; and Copy Editor Lauren Kennedy, who exhibited a gasp-inducing eye for detail and who came up with an awe-inspiring number of really great suggestions that make me look like a much better writer than I am. My heartfelt thanks to all of you for your outstanding work on this project.

Contents

chapter 6

How Do I Make the Most
of E-mail? 114

chapter 7

How Do I Manage My
E-book Library? 140

chapter 8

How Can I Have Fun with Photos? 162

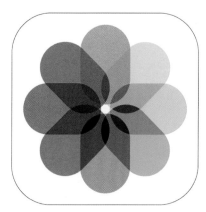

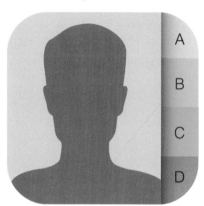

Thursday

12

chapter 13

How Can I Navigate
My World with iPad?   272

chapter 14

How Do I Protect or Fix
My iPad or iPad mini?   292

Introduction

There are many reasons behind the success of the iPad and the iPad mini, as well as their smaller cousins, the iPhone and iPod touch. However, if you polled fans of these devices, I bet one reason would quickly bubble up to the top spot: the touch interface. It's slick, elegant, and just so easy: a tap here, a tap there, and away you go.

Using the iPad or iPad mini touch interface is like playing in one of those seaside areas where the water is only a couple of feet deep no matter where you go; you can still have all kinds of fun, but you never have to swim hard and there's little chance of drowning. However, if you walk out far enough in many of those ocean areas, you suddenly come to the edge of an underwater shelf, where the sandy bottom gives way to the inky ocean depths.

Your tablet, too, has its unexplored depths: hidden settings, obscure features, out-of-the-way preferences, and little-known techniques. The usefulness of some of these features is debatable, at best, but many of them can help you work faster, more easily, and more efficiently. Rather than swimming blindly through the murky waters of your tablet's deep end, you might consider making an appointment with your local Apple Store's Genius Bar. More often than not, the on-duty genius can give you good advice on how to get more out of your iPad or iPad mini investment.

The Genius Bar is a great thing, but it isn't always convenient. You usually have to make an appointment, drag yourself down to the store, perhaps wait for your genius, get the advice you need (or the problem looked at, or whatever), and then make your way back home. In some cases, you may need to leave your device for a while (the horror!) to get a problem checked out and hopefully resolved.

What you really need is a version of the Genius Bar that's easier to access, more convenient, and doesn't require tons of time, or leaving your iPad or iPad mini in the hands of a stranger. What you really need is a portable genius that enables you to be more productive, and solve problems wherever you and your tablet happen to be hanging out.

Welcome to *iPad® Portable Genius, 2nd Edition*. This book is like a small-scale Genius Bar all wrapped up in an easy-to-use, easy-to-access, and eminently portable format. In this book, I cover how to get more out of your iPad or iPad mini by accessing all of the really powerful and timesaving features that aren't obvious at a casual glance. I also explain how to avoid the tablet's occasional annoying character traits and, in those cases where such behavior can't be avoided, how to work around it.

Finally, this book tells you how to prevent iPad and iPad mini problems from occurring and, just in case your preventative measures are for naught, how to fix many common problems yourself. This edition also includes updates on the most important and useful new features in iOS 7, such as Control Center, Activation Lock, Twitter links, AirDrop, iTunes Radio, and much more.

This book is for iPad and iPad mini users who know the basics, but want to take their education to a higher level. It's a book for people who want to be more productive, more efficient, more creative, and more self-sufficient (at least as far as their tablet goes). It's a book for people who use their iPad or iPad mini every day, but would like to incorporate it into more of their day-to-day activities. It's a book I had a blast writing, so I think it's a book you'll enjoy reading.

How Do I Start Using My iPad or iPad mini?

5:05

Wednesday, August 21

> slide to unlock

When you first look at your iPad or iPad mini, you probably notice its sleek, curvaceous design. Then, you probably notice what might be its most remarkable feature — no buttons! Unlike your garden-variety tablet that bristles with keys, switches, and ports, the iPad and iPad mini have only a few physical buttons. This makes for a stylish (possibly even sexy) design. However, it leads to an obvious problem: How do you work the darn thing? This chapter gives you the grand tour of your iPad or iPad mini. It covers the few buttons, as well as the real heart of the tablet — its remarkable touchscreen.

Using the Home Button

The starting point for most of your iPad or iPad mini excursions is the Home button, which is the circular button on the face of the tablet at the bottom, as shown in Figure 1.1.

The Home button

1.1 Press the Home button to (among other things) leave standby mode or return to the Home screen.

The Home button has the following main functions:

- When the iPad or iPad mini is in standby mode, pressing the Home button wakes the device and displays the unlock screen.

- When the iPad or iPad mini is running, pressing the Home button returns the device to the Home screen (or, if the Home screen is currently displayed, it displays the Search screen).

- Pressing and holding the Home button invokes Siri, which enables you to control many iPad or iPad mini features using voice commands. (If Siri is turned off, pressing and hold-ing the Home button invokes Voice Control, Siri's predecessor.)

- Double-pressing the Home button displays the multitasking bar, which enables you to quickly switch between your running apps.

If your tablet is in standby mode, press the Home button to display the slide to unlock screen, as shown in Figure 1.2. (This screen appears for up to about 8 seconds; if you don't do anything, the tablet drops back into standby mode.)

1.2 Slide your finger along the screen from left to right to unlock your iPad or iPad mini.

Place your finger on the left side of the screen and slide it to the right side of the screen. This unlocks the tablet and displays the Home screen.

Working with the Sleep/Wake Button

If your iPad or iPad mini is on but you're not using it, the tablet automatically goes into standby mode after 1 minute. This is called Auto-Lock, and it's a handy feature because it saves battery power when your tablet is just sitting there. However, you can also put your tablet into standby mode at any time by using the Sleep/Wake button. You can find this dash-shaped button, shown in Figure 1.3, at the top of your tablet. The Sleep/Wake button has two main functions: Sleeping/ waking and powering on/off.

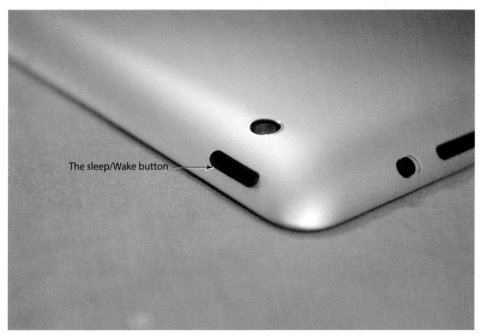

The sleep/Wake button

1.3 Your tablet's Sleep/Wake button.

Sleeping and waking the iPad or iPad mini

If you're currently using your iPad or iPad mini, you can put the tablet in standby mode by pressing the Sleep/Wake button once, which drops the power consumption considerably. You can still receive incoming e-mail messages and texts but the screen powers down. Tap the Sleep/Wake button again to wake your tablet. This is just like pressing the Home button: You're prompted with the slide to unlock screen and you slide your finger from the left side of the screen to the right to unlock the tablet.

Genius

Press the Sleep/Wake button to put your tablet in standby mode whenever you're not using the screen. This not only conserves battery power but also it prevents accidental screen taps. If you have a program (such as the Music app) running, it continues to run even after the tablet is in standby.

Powering the iPad or iPad mini on and off

You can also use the Sleep/Wake button to turn off your iPad or iPad mini so that it doesn't use any power. This is a good idea if your battery is getting low and you don't think you'll be able to charge it any time soon. You might also want to turn off your tablet if you won't be using it for a few days.

To turn off your iPad or iPad mini, press and hold the Sleep/Wake button for 3 seconds. When the slide to power off slider appears on the screen, as shown in Figure 1.4, use your finger to drag the slider all the way to the right. The tablet shuts down after a few seconds.

1.4 Hold down the Sleep/Wake button for a few seconds to see the slide to power off screen.

Note

If you change your mind and decide to leave your iPad or iPad mini on, tap the Cancel button that appears at the bottom of the screen. Note, too, that the slide to power off screen automatically cancels itself if you do nothing for 30 seconds.

When you're ready to resume your iPad or iPad mini chores, press and hold the Sleep/Wake button until you see the Apple icon. The tablet powers up, and then, a few seconds later, displays the slide to unlock screen.

Caution When your cellular-enabled iPad or iPad mini is in standby mode, it still communicates with the nearest cellular network to check for new messages. This isn't a problem at home but it can lead to massive roaming charges if you're overseas. When you travel, you should always power off your cellular-enabled tablet when you're not using it.

Working with the Side Switch

To prevent your iPad or iPad mini from disturbing the people nearby, you can put your tablet in silent mode, which means it doesn't play any alerts or sound effects. When the sound is turned off, only alarms that you've set using the Clock app will sound.

You switch the iPad or iPad mini between normal and silent modes using the Side switch, which is located on the right side of the device, near the top (assuming you're holding the tablet in portrait mode, where the Home button appears at the bottom), as shown in Figure 1.5.

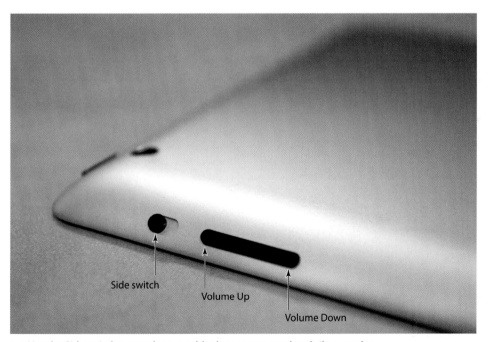

1.5 Use the Side switch to toggle your tablet between normal and silent modes.

Use the Side switch to control the following functions:

- **Put the tablet in silent mode.** Flick the Side switch down. You see an orange dot on the switch and the screen displays a bell with a slash through it.

- **Resume the normal mode.** Flick the Side switch up, toward the top of the tablet. You no longer see the orange dot on the switch and the screen displays a bell and the current volume level.

Operating the Volume Controls

The volume controls are on the right side of the iPad or iPad mini (again, when you're holding the tablet in portrait mode) right below the Side switch. The iPad mini has two separate buttons but the iPad has what looks like a single volume control (see Figure 1.5). However, there really are two buttons on the iPad. On both devices, the button closer to the top of the tablet is Volume Up, and you press it to increase the volume; the button closer to the bottom of the tablet is Volume Down, and you press it to decrease the volume. As you adjust the volume, a speaker appears on-screen with filled-in dashes representing the volume level.

You use these buttons in the following ways to control the volume on your iPad or iPad mini:

- If you're using the Music app, the volume controls adjust the music volume.

- In all other situations, the volume controls adjust the output of sounds, such as alerts and effects.

Getting to Know the Rest of the Tablet

In addition to the touchscreen, there are other physical features of your iPad or iPad mini that you need to get to know. For starters, the tablet's bottom panel has the following two features (Figure 1.6 shows the bottom panel on the iPad mini):

- **Speaker.** The iPad has a single speaker to the right of the Lightning connector, while the iPad mini has a two-speaker stereo system — one on each side of the connector. This is where the sound is broadcast when you listen to music, ask Siri something, or talk to someone over FaceTime.

● **Lightning connector.** This feature is on the bottom panel of the tablet in the center. This is where you connect the USB cable to either charge your tablet or hook it up to a computer.

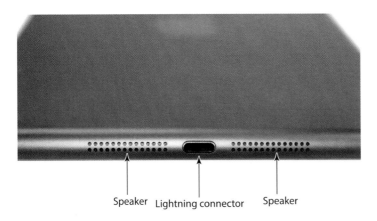

Speaker   Lightning connector   Speaker

1.6 The bottom panel on the iPad mini houses two speakers and the Lightning connector.

Genius

Because the speaker is at the bottom of the tablet, you may have trouble hearing it. In that case, hold the iPad or iPad mini so that the bottom panel is facing you, which should give you better sound quality.

The top panel of the iPad and iPad mini is home to the Sleep/Wake button, as well as the following features shown in Figure 1.7:

● **Headset jack.** The headset jack is located at the left of the top panel of the iPad or iPad mini. This is where you plug in the earbuds that came with your tablet to listen to music. You can also use this jack to plug in any other headset or headphones that use a 3.5mm stereo audio jack.

● **Microphone.** This feature is located on the top of your tablet in the middle of the top panel. This is where the iPad or iPad mini picks up your voice for FaceTime calls and anything else that requires you to speak.

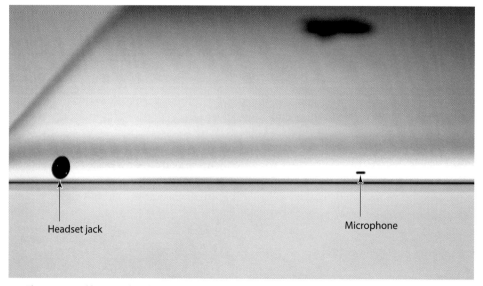

Headset jack

Microphone

1.7 The top panel houses the Sleep/Wake button, as well as the headset jack and microphone.

The front of the tablet holds the Home button, as shown earlier in this chapter, but it also holds the front camera, as shown in Figure 1.8. This is one of two cameras on the iPad and iPad mini. You can use this one to take pictures of yourself (and perhaps a nearby friend or loved one) or to conduct FaceTime video calls.

Front camera

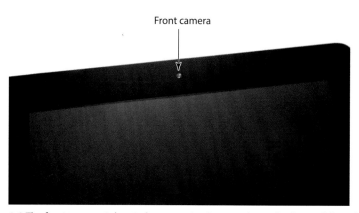

1.8 The front camera is located, appropriately enough, on the front of the tablet.

The back of the tablet is home to the rear cam-era, as shown in Figure 1.9. This camera has a much higher resolution than the front camera, so you'll probably use it to take most of your photos.

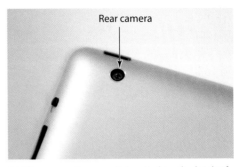

Rear camera

1.9 The second camera is located on the back of the iPad or iPad mini.

Operating the Touchscreen

I can't get enough of the touchscreen on the iPad and iPad mini, and I think it's the tablet's best feature. You can zoom in and out, scroll through lists, drag items here and there, and even type messages. Amazingly, the touchscreen requires no external hardware to do all this. You don't need a stylus or digital pen, and you don't need to attach anything to the tablet. Instead, the touchscreen requires only your finger (or, for some operations, two or more fingers).

As you might imagine, the screen is a fingerprint magnet and it *will* become smeared, so get yourself a polishing cloth to make short work of these smudges. As far as more serious marks go, the screen is made of a chemically treated, optical-quality glass that helps protect the screen from scratches.

Navigating the touchscreen

There are a few maneuvers that you need to be familiar with to successfully use the iPad or iPad mini touchscreen in all its glory. I refer to the following gestures throughout the rest of the book, so play around with them now, and make sure that you understand them:

- **Tap.** This means that you use your finger to quickly press and release the screen where desired. This gesture is what you use to initiate just about any action on the iPad or iPad mini. It opens apps, activates options, accesses text boxes, and much more.

- **Double-tap.** This is what it sounds like: two quick taps with your finger. In apps, such as Photos or Safari, it zooms in on images or parts of web pages. A second double-tap zooms back out.

- **Swipe and flick.** To swipe means to drag your finger across the screen. You use this technique to scroll through lists, drag items to different spots, and unlock the iPad or iPad mini. A flick is just an abbreviated version of a swipe. Flick your finger across the screen and the tablet rapidly scrolls through the list. The faster you flick, the faster it scrolls. Touch the screen to stop the scrolling process.

- **Spread and pinch.** You use these techniques to zoom in on or out of the screen. To spread means to move two fingers apart, and you use it to zoom in; to pinch means to move two fingers closer together, and you use it to zoom out. This is especially useful when viewing web pages because the text is often too small to read. Spread to zoom in on the text for easy reading, and pinch to return to the full screen for easy scrolling and navigation.

Searching your tablet

Parkinson's Law of Data pithily encapsulates an inescapable fact of digital life: "Data expands to fill the space available for storage." So whether you have a basic 16GB iPad or iPad mini or a top-of-the-line 128GB iPad, you will probably fill your tablet with music, photos, contacts, e-mail messages, Safari bookmarks, and on and on.

That's cool because it means you can bring your digital world with you wherever you go, but there's another law that quickly comes into play; call it McFedries' Law of Digital Needles in Electronic Haystacks: "The more data you have, the harder it is to find what you need." Fortunately, iOS rides to the rescue by adding welcome search features to the iPad and iPad mini.

If you use a Mac, then you probably know how indispensable the Spotlight search feature is. It's just a humble text box, but Spotlight enables you to find *anything* on your Mac in just a blink or two of an eye. It's an essential tool in this era of massive hard drives. (Windows users get much the same functionality with Start screen or Start menu searches.)

The size of your tablet's hard drive might pale in comparison to your desktop's drive, but you can still pack an amazing amount of stuff into that tiny package, so you really need a way to search your entire tablet, including e-mail, contacts, calendars, bookmarks, apps, and much more. So Spotlight for iOS is a welcome feature indeed, and it's just as easy to use as Spotlight on the Mac:

1. **Tap the Home button to return to the Home screen.**

2. **Flick down on the screen.** iOS displays the Search iPad box at the top of the screen.

3. **Enter your search text.** Spotlight immediately begins displaying items that match your text as you type.

4. **Tap Search to see the complete results.** If you see the item you're looking for, tap it to open it.

Genius

Spotlight looks for a wide variety of items within your tablet's hard drive. If you find you're getting too many results, you can configure Spotlight to only search selected sources, and you can also change the order in which Spotlight returns the results. Tap Settings, tap General, and then tap Spotlight Search. In the Spotlight Search screen, tap any data type that you don't want to see in the search result. You can also tap and drag the move handle on the right to position each type in the list.

Typing on the keyboard

You can type on your tablet, although don't expect to pound out the prose as easily as you can on your computer. The on-screen keyboard (the iPad's portrait mode keyboard is shown in Figure 1.10) is a bit too small for rapid and accurate typing. However, the iPad and iPad mini do touch-screen typing better than any other tablet out there.

To use the keyboard, tap into an area that requires text input and the keyboard appears automatically. Tap the keys that you want to enter. As you touch each key, a magnified version of the letter pops up. If you touch the wrong key, slide your finger over to the correct one. The keyboard will not enter a key until your finger comes off the screen.

Special keys

The keyboard features the following specialty keys that allow you to do some tricks:

- **Backspace.** This key has a left-pointing arrow with an X inside it, and deletes at three different speeds. The first speed is in response to a single tap, which deletes the character to the left of the blinking cursor. The second speed kicks in when you press and hold the key, which tells the tablet to move backward through the letters, deleting as it goes. The third speed engages if you press and hold the key for a few seconds, and it causes the tablet to delete entire words.

- **Return.** This key moves to the next line or accepts the current input (much like the Return key on a Mac or the Enter key in Windows).

- **Shift.** This key (there are actually two of them) has a little upward-pointing arrow and you tap it once to engage shift. The arrow's outline turns blue, and the next letter that you type will be uppercase. After you type the character, the Shift key returns to normal.

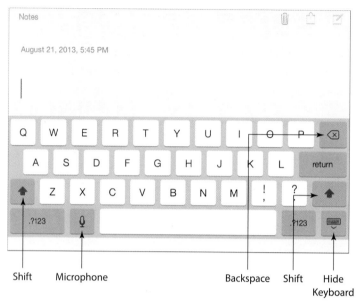

Shift   Microphone   Backspace   Shift   Hide
                                                                    Keyboard

1.10 Trust the touchscreen, even though the keys may be small.

- **.?123.** Tap this key to display the numeric keyboard, which includes numbers and most punctuation marks. The key then changes to ABC, which you tap to return to the standard keyboard.

- **#+=.** This key appears within the numeric keyboard. Tap the key to display yet another keyboard, which contains more punctuation marks as well as a few symbols that aren't frequently used.

- **Microphone.** This key starts the Dictation feature, which enables you to dictate text instead of typing it. I explain how to use Dictation in Chapter 6.

- **Hide Keyboard.** Tap this key to hide the keyboard when you longer need it.

Note The Return key often changes its name depending on the context. For example, if you're using Safari to type a web page address, the Return key's name changes to Go. Similarly, if you're using Safari to search for information on the web, the Return key's name changes to Search.

Editing text

Everyone asks me how you're supposed to move throughout the text in order to edit it. The only obvious option is to delete all the way back to your error, which is impractical to say the least. The solution is, of course, in the touchscreen, which enables you to zoom in on the specific section of text you want to edit. Follow these steps to do so:

1. **Press and hold your finger on the line you want to edit.** The tablet displays the text inside a magnifying glass and within that text you see the cursor. (You might need to angle your tablet just so to see the cursor.)

2. **Slide your finger along the line.** As you slide, the cursor moves through the text in the same direction.

3. **When the cursor is where you want to begin editing, remove your finger.**

Selecting, cutting, copying, and pasting

How you select and then either cut or copy text depends on whether that text is editable or noneditable. The simplest case is noneditable text, which is what you get on a web page. In that scenario, when the text you want to use is on the screen, tap and hold anywhere within the text. After a second or two, your iPad or iPad mini selects the text and displays blue selection handles around it. If necessary, tap and drag the selection handles to select more or less of the text, as shown in Figure 1.11, and then tap Copy.

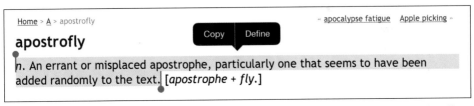

1.11 For text that you can't edit, tap and hold within the text to select it, adjust the selection handles, and then tap Copy.

If the text is editable, such as the text in a note, an e-mail message you're composing, or any text box, then the process is more involved, but only ever so slightly. Follow these steps to cut or copy editable text:

1. **Tap and hold anywhere within the text.** After a short pause for effect, you see a couple of buttons above the text, as shown in Figure 1.12. (If you've previously copied some text, you'll also see a Paste button; more on this below.)

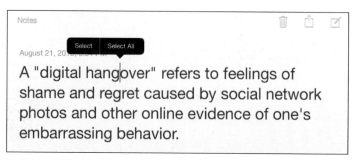

1.12 For editable text, tap and hold within it to see these options.

2. **Tap one of the following options:**

   - **Select.** Tap this button if you only want to select some of the text. You see blue selection handles around the word you tapped.

   - **Select All.** Tap this button if you prefer to select all of the text. You'll then see the buttons shown in Figure 1.13. If you don't need to adjust the selection, skip to step 4.

3. **Tap and drag the selection handles to select the text with which you want to work.** You now see a new set of buttons above the text (see Figure 1.13).

4. **Tap one of the following actions:**

   - **Cut.** Tap this button to remove the text and store it in the tablet's memory.

   - **Copy.** Tap this button to store a copy of the text in the tablet's memory.

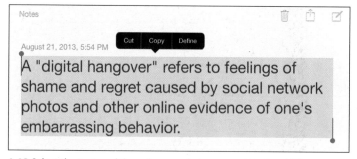

1.13 Select the text, and then choose what you want to do with it.

With your text cut or copied and residing snugly in the iPad or iPad mini's memory, you're ready to paste the text. If you want to paste the text into a different app, open that app. Position the cursor where you want the text to appear, tap the cursor, and then tap Paste, as shown in Figure 1.14. Your tablet dutifully adds the cut or copied text.

1.14 Tap the cursor, and then tap Paste to place your cut or copied text in the app.

If you want to make a copy of a photo, such as an image shown on a web page, the process is more or less the same as copying noneditable text. Follow these steps to copy an image:

1. **Tap and hold the photo.** After a second or two, you see a pop-up menu of image options.

2. **Tap Copy.** The tablet copies the photo into its memory.

3. **Open the app where you want the copy of the photo to appear.**

4. **Position the cursor where you want the photo to appear, and then tap the cursor.**

5. **Tap Paste.** The iPad or iPad mini pastes the photo.

The addition of the Cut, Copy, and Paste commands makes the iPad or iPad mini feel even more like a computer. That's good, but it also means that you can also make the same pasting errors that you can with your regular computer. For example, you might paste the text or photo in the wrong spot, or once you've performed the paste you might realize that you selected the wrong data.

1.15 Reverse an imprudent paste by shaking the tablet, and then tapping Undo Paste.

Frustrating? Yes. A big problem? Nope! Slap your forehead lightly in exasperation, and then perform one of the iPad or iPad mini's coolest tricks: shake it. Your tablet displays the options shown in Figure 1.15. Tap Undo Paste to reverse your most recent paste, and then move on with your life.

Using the suggestion feature

As you type, the iPad or iPad mini provides a suggestion in a little bubble underneath the current word. To accept the suggestion, tap the spacebar or any punctuation. To ignore it, tap the suggested word bubble on the screen. This helps save time when you use apostrophes. Leave the apostrophe out and the tablet recommends the correct word. For example, if you type *shell*, the tablet suggests *she'll* because that's a legitimate word, as well. If *she'll* is what you want, accept the suggestion (again, by tapping the spacebar or any punctuation); otherwise, tap the suggestion to retain *shell*. The suggestion feature also shows up with misspelled words. The iPad or iPad mini guesses the correct word and provides a suggestion. If the suggestion is the word you want, accept it.

Running Your Tablet from the Control Center

As you'll see as you read the rest of this book, your iPad or iPad mini is positively bristling with useful tools. However, sometimes your tablet's tools aren't always readily accessible. Most features and settings require several taps, which doesn't sound like much, but it can get old fast with features you use frequently.

Fortunately, the latest version of the operating system that runs your tablet — called iOS 7 — aims to solve that problem by offering the Control Center. This is a special screen that offers one-flick access to a dozen of your tablet's most useful features. By "one-flick access" I mean just this: from any iPad or iPad mini screen, flick your finger up from the bottom of the screen. This displays the Control Center, as shown in Figure 1.16. To hide the Control Center, either tap the Home button or tap the downward-pointing arrow that appears at the top of the Control Center screen.

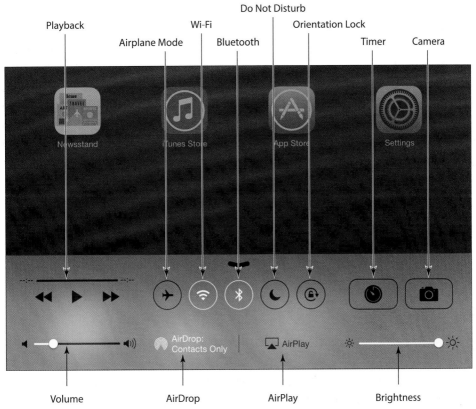

1.16 Flick up from the bottom of any screen to come face-to-face with the Control Center.

How Do I Connect to a Network?

You can do plenty of things on your iPad or iPad mini without having to reach out and touch some remote website or service. You can jot some notes, add appointments, edit contacts, or just play around with the settings. However, I'm willing to bet you didn't fork over the bucks for your tablet just so you could use the Notes app. Whether you want to go on a web surfin' Safari, visit the App Store or iBookstore to grab some content, or use Maps to find your way, the iPad or iPad mini comes alive when it's connected to a network.

Connecting to a Wi-Fi Network

As you see a bit later in this chapter, the cellular-enabled iPad or iPad mini automatically connects to cellular networks. However, things aren't automatic when it comes to wireless network connections — which iOS refers to as *Wi-Fi* connections. As soon as you try to access something on the Internet — a website, your e-mail, a map, or whatever — your tablet scours the surrounding airwaves for Wi-Fi network signals. If you've never connected to a Wi-Fi network or if you're in an area that doesn't have any Wi-Fi networks you've used in the past, you see the Select a Wireless Network dialog, as shown in Figure 2.1.

Select a Wireless Network

LinkF 🔒

LogophiliaB 🔒

LogophiliaR 🔒

Cancel

2.1 If you're just starting out on the Wi-Fi trail, your iPad or iPad mini displays a list of nearby networks.

This dialog displays a list of the Wi-Fi networks that are within range. (If you don't see the Select a Wireless Network dialog, you can still connect to a wireless network; I cover how later in this chapter.) For each network, you get the following three tidbits of data:

- **Network name.** This is the name that the administrator has assigned to the network. If you're in a coffee shop or similar public hotspot and you want to use that network, look for the name (or a variation thereof) of the shop.

- **Password-protection.** If a Wi-Fi network displays a lock icon, it means the network is protected by a password and you need to know that password to make the connection.

Making your first connection

Follow these steps to connect to a Wi-Fi network:

1. **Tap the network you want to use.** If the network is protected by a password, your iPad or iPad mini prompts you to type it, as shown in Figure 2.2.

2. **Use the keyboard to type the password.**

3. **Tap Join.** The tablet connects to the network and adds the Wi-Fi network signal strength icon to the status bar.

To connect to a commercial Wi-Fi operation — such as those you find in airports, hotels, and convention centers — you almost always have to take one more step. In most cases, the network prompts you for your name and either a password or credit card data so you can be charged for accessing the network. If you're not prompted right away, you will be as soon as you try to access a website or check your e-mail. Type your information and then enjoy the Internet in all its Wi-Fi glory.

Enter password for "LogophiliaB"

Cancel	Join

2.2 If the Wi-Fi network is secured with a password, you type it in this screen.

Caution Because the password box shows dots instead of the actual text for added security, this is no place to demonstrate your touchscreen speed-typing prowess. Slow and steady wins the password-typing race (or something).

Connecting to known or hidden networks

If the Wi-Fi network is one that you use all of the time — for example, your home or office network — the good news is your iPad or iPad mini remembers any network to which you connect. As soon as a known network comes within range, your tablet makes the connection without a peep.

Each Wi-Fi network has a name — often called the Service Set Identifier, or SSID — that identifies the network to Wi-Fi-friendly devices, such as your iPad or iPad mini. By default, most Wi-Fi networks broadcast the network name so you can see and connect to it. However, some Wi-Fi networks disable network name broadcasting as a security precaution. The idea here is that if an unauthorized user can't see the network, he or she can't attempt to connect to it. However, some devices can pick up the network name when authorized computers connect to it, so this is not a foolproof security measure.

You can still connect to a hidden Wi-Fi network by manually entering the connection settings. You need to know the network name, its security and encryption types, and the password. To do so, follow these steps:

1. **On the Home screen, tap Settings to open the Settings app.**

2. **Tap Wi-Fi.** You see the Wi-Fi Networks screen.

3. **Tap Other.** The Other Network screen appears, as shown in Figure 2.3.

4. **Type the network name in the Name text box.**

5. **Tap Security to open the Security screen.**

6. **Tap the type of security used by the Wi-Fi network: WEP, WPA, WPA2,**

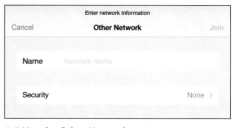

2.3 Use the Other Network screen to connect to a hidden Wi-Fi network.

WPA Enterprise, WPA2 Enterprise, or None. If you're not sure, try WPA2, which is the most common type for home networks.

7. **Tap Other Network to return to the Other Network screen.** If you chose WEP, WPA, WPA2, WPA Enterprise, or WPA2 Enterprise, your iPad or iPad mini prompts you to type the password.

8. **Use the keyboard to type the password.**

9. **Tap Join.** The tablet connects to the network and adds the Wi-Fi network signal strength icon to the status bar.

Stopping incessant Wi-Fi network prompts

The Select a Wireless Network dialog is a handy convenience if you're not sure whether a Wi-Fi network is available. However, as you move around town, you may find that this dialog pops up all over the place as new Wi-Fi networks come within range. One solution is to wear your finger down to the bone with all of the constant tapping of the Cancel button, but there's a better way: just tell your iPad or iPad mini to shut up already with the Wi-Fi prompting. Here's how:

1. **On the Home screen, tap Settings.** The Settings screen appears.

2. **Tap Wi-Fi.** The Wi-Fi screen appears.

3. **Tap the Ask to Join Networks switch to the Off position, as shown in Figure 2.4.** Your tablet no longer prompts you with nearby networks. Whew!

Okay, I hear you ask, if I'm no longer seeing the prompts, how do I connect to a Wi-Fi network if I don't even know it's there? That's a good question, and here's a good answer:

1. **On the Home screen, tap Settings to open the Settings app.**

2. **Tap Wi-Fi.** The Wi-Fi Networks screen appears and the Choose a Network list shows you the available Wi-Fi networks.

3. **Tap the network you want to use.** If the network is protected by a password, your iPad or iPad mini prompts you to type it.

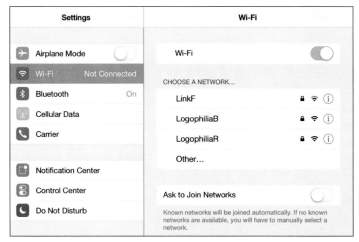

2.4 Toggle the Ask to Join Networks switch to Off to put a gag on network prompts.

4. **Use the keyboard to type the password.**

5. **Tap Join.** The tablet connects to the network and adds the Wi-Fi network signal strength icon to the status bar.

Forgetting a Wi-Fi network

Having the iPad or iPad mini remember networks you've joined is certainly convenient, except, of course, when it's not. For example, if you have a couple of networks nearby that you can join, you might connect to one and then realize that the other is better in some way (for example, it's faster or cheaper). Unfortunately, there's a good chance your tablet will continue to connect to the network you don't want every time it comes within range, which can be a real hassle. Rather than threatening to throw your tablet into the nearest trash can, you can tell it to forget the network you don't want to use. Here's how it's done:

1. **On the Home screen, tap Settings to open the Settings app.**

2. **Tap Wi-Fi.** The Wi-Fi Networks screen appears.

3. **Tap the blue More Info icon to the right of the network you want to forget.** Settings displays the network's settings screen.

4. **Tap Forget this Network.** Settings asks you to confirm.

5. **Tap Forget.** Settings discards the login data for the network and no longer connects to the network automatically.

Turning off the Wi-Fi antenna

The iPad or iPad mini Wi-Fi antenna is constantly on the lookout for nearby Wi-Fi networks. That's useful because it means you always have an up-to-date list of networks to check out and the tablet's location services (such as the Maps app) are more accurate, but it also takes a toll on the battery. If you know you won't be using Wi-Fi for a while, you can save some battery juice for more important pursuits by following these steps to turn off the Wi-Fi antenna:

1. **On the Home screen, tap Settings to launch the Settings app.**

2. **Tap Wi-Fi.** The Wi-Fi Networks screen appears.

3. **Tap the Wi-Fi switch to the Off position.** Your tablet disconnects from your current Wi-Fi network and hides the Choose a Network list.

When you're ready to resume your Wi-Fi duties, return to the Wi-Fi Networks screen and tap the Wi-Fi switch to the On position.

Genius

In iOS 7, you can also toggle the Wi-Fi antenna off and on by flicking up from the bottom of the screen to open the Control Center and then tapping the Wi-Fi icon.

Tethering to an iPhone Internet connection

If you have a Wi-Fi-only iPad or iPad mini, you might think you're stuck if you're out and about, need to use the Internet, and there's no Wi-Fi in sight. If you have an iPhone that's running iOS 4.3 or later, then you can work around this problem by using a nifty feature called Personal Hotspot, which enables you to configure your iPhone as a kind of Internet hub or gateway device — something like the hotspots that are available in coffee shops and other public areas.

You can connect your iPad or iPad mini to your iPhone via Wi-Fi and your tablet can then use the iPhone cellular Internet connection to get online. This is often called *Internet tethering*. This sounds too good to be true, but it's real — I swear. The downside (you just knew there had to be a downside) is that additional usage charges apply. In the United States, for example, as of this writing AT&T only offers tethering with its highest price data plan, which costs $50 per month, $20 more than the next lowest price plan (although you also get an extra 2GB of data). Similarly, Sprint's tethering options start at an extra $19.99 per month for 2GB of tethering data, while Verizon's plans all include tethering and start at $60 per month.

Your first step down the Personal Hotspot road is to activate the feature on your iPhone. Here's how it's done:

1. **On the iPhone Home screen, tap Settings to open the Settings app.**

2. **Tap Personal Hotspot.** Your iPhone opens the Personal Hotspot screen.

3. **Tap the Personal Hotspot switch to the On position.** If you don't have the Bluetooth antenna turned on, your iPhone asks if you want to turn it on.

4. **Tap Wi-Fi and USB Only.**

5. **Personal Hotspot generates a Wi-Fi password automatically, as shown in Figure 2.5.** You can set your own by tapping Wi-Fi Password, typing the new password, and then tapping Done.

2.5 When you activate Personal Hotspot, the iPhone generates a password for you.

Caution Prior to iOS 7, your iPhone generated a tethering password by sandwiching a two-digit number between two four-character words (for example, near77mica). Unfortunately, Apple used only a relatively small set of words to generate these passwords, making them susceptible to brute-force attacks. This isn't a problem with iOS 7 (which generates random passwords), but if you're running iOS 6 or earlier on your iPhone, be sure to change the tethering password to something more secure.

With Personal Hotspot enabled on your iPhone, follow these steps to connect your iPad or iPad mini to it via Wi-Fi:

1. **On your tablet, tap Settings, and then tap Wi-Fi to display the list of nearby wireless networks.**

2. **In the network list, tap the one that has the same name as your iPhone, as shown in Figure 2.6.** Your tablet prompts you for the Wi-Fi password.

3. **Type the Personal Hotspot Wi-Fi password, and then tap OK.** In the status bar, your iPad or iPad mini shows the Personal Hotspot icon, which is two interconnected rings, as shown in Figure 2.7. Your iPhone shows Personal Hotspot: 1 Connection.

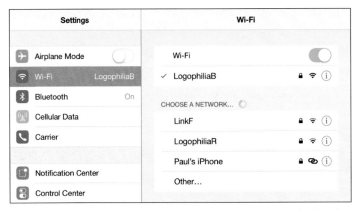

2.6 To make a Wi-Fi connection to the iPhone hotspot, display the list of wireless networks and then select the network with the same name as your iPhone.

Note

If you have a third- or fourth-generation cellular iPad or iPad mini, you can use it as a Personal Hotspot if your data plan allows for Internet tethering. Tap Settings, tap General, tap Network, tap Personal Hotspot, and then tap the Personal Hotspot switch to On.

2.7 When your iPad or iPad mini is tethered, it shows the Personal Hotspot icon in the status bar.

Working with Cellular Network Connections

Connections to a cellular network are automatic and occur behind the scenes. As soon as you switch on your cellular-enabled iPad or iPad mini, it checks for an LTE signal. If it finds one, it connects to the network and displays the LTE (or 4G) icon in the status bar, as well as the connection strength (the more bars, the better).

If your current area doesn't do the LTE thing, your tablet tries to connect to the slower 3G network. If that works, you see the 3G icon in the status bar, as well as the signal strength. If there's no 3G network within range, your tablet looks for an EDGE network instead. If that works, you see the E icon in the status bar (plus the usual signal strength bars). If none of that works, you see No Signal, so you might as well go home.

Tracking cellular data usage

Having a data plan with a cellular provider means never having to worry about getting access to the network. However, unless you're paying for unlimited access (lucky you!), you should be worrying about going over whatever maximum amount of data usage your plan provides per month. That's because going over your data max means you start paying through the nose for each megabyte, and you can run up a hefty bill in no time.

To avoid that, keep track of your cellular data usage by following these steps:

1. **On the Home screen, tap Settings to fire up the Settings app.**

2. **Tap Cellular Data to open the Cellular Data screen.**

3. **In the Cellular Data Usage section, read the Current Period and Current Period Roaming values.**

4. **If you're at the end of your data period, tap Reset Statistics to start with fresh values for the new period.**

Genius

The cellular usage values are meaningful only if they correspond to your monthly data cycle with your provider. Check with your cellular provider to see which day of the month your data resets. On that day, follow the previous steps to open the Cellular Usage screen, and then tap Reset Statistics. When the iPad or iPad mini asks you to confirm, tap Reset.

Disabling data roaming

Data roaming is an often convenient cellular plan feature that enables you to surf the web, check and send e-mail, and exchange text messages when you're outside your provider's normal coverage area. The downside is that, unless you've got a fixed-rate roaming package from your cellular provider, roaming charges are almost always eye-poppingly expensive — they're often several dollars per minute or megabyte, depending on where you are and what type of service you're using. Not good!

Unfortunately, if you have the iPad or iPad mini Data Roaming feature turned on, you may incur massive roaming charges, even if you never use the device. That's because your iPad or iPad mini still performs background checks for things like incoming e-mail and text messages. As a result, one week in some far-off land could cost you hundreds of dollars, even if you never turn on your tablet. Again, not good!

To avoid this insanity, follow these steps to turn off Data Roaming when you don't need it:

1. **On the Home screen, tap Settings to launch the Settings app.**
2. **Tap Cellular Data.** The Cellular Data screen opens.
3. **Tap the Data Roaming On/Off button to change this setting to Off.** Settings disables data roaming.

Turning off LTE

Using the LTE cellular network is a real pleasure because it's so much faster than a 3G connection (which, in turn, is much faster than a molasses-in-January EDGE connection). If LTE has a downside, it's that it uses up a lot of battery power. That's true even if you're currently connected to a Wi-Fi network, because the LTE antenna is constantly looking for an LTE signal. If you'll be on your Wi-Fi network for a while, or if the battery is running low and you don't need an LTE cellular connection, you can follow these steps to turn off the LTE antenna and reduce the load on your tablet's battery:

1. **On the Home screen, tap Settings to open the Settings app.**
2. **Tap Cellular Data.** The Cellular Data screen opens.
3. **Tap the Enable LTE switch to Off.** Settings turns off the LTE antenna.

Turning off cellular data

If you've reached the limit of your cellular data plan, you almost certainly want to avoid going over the cap because the charges are usually prohibitively expensive. As long as you have a Wi-Fi network in range, or you're disciplined enough not to surf the web or cruise YouTube when there's no Wi-Fi in sight, you'll be okay. Still, accidents can happen. For example, you might accidentally tap a link in an e-mail message or text message, or someone in your household might use your phone without knowing about your restrictions.

To prevent these sorts of accidents (or if you simply don't trust yourself when it comes to YouTube), you can turn off cellular data altogether, which means your iPad or iPad mini only accesses Internet data if it has a Wi-Fi signal. Follow these steps to turn off cellular data on your tablet:

1. **On the Home screen, tap Settings to bring up the Settings app.**

2. **Tap Cellular Data.** The Cellular Data screen opens.

3. **Tap the Cellular Data switch to the Off position.** Settings disconnects from your cellular connection.

Controlling cellular data usage

Rather than turning off cellular data completely, as I described in the previous section, you can take a more targeted approach. For example, if you're a bit worried about going over your cellular plan's data ceiling, it makes sense to avoid relatively high-bandwidth items such as FaceTime and iTunes, but not relatively low-bandwidth content such as iCloud documents and Safari's reading list.

You could just police this yourself but, hey, you're a busy person and you might forget the next time a FaceTime call comes in and you're in a cellular-only neighborhood. I suggest that you leave the details to your iPad or iPad mini by configuring it not to allow certain content types over a cellular connection. To get set up, follow these steps:

1. **On the Home screen, tap Settings.** The Settings app appears.

2. **Tap Cellular Data.** The Cellular Data screen opens.

3. **In the Use Cellular Data for section, tap the switch to Off for each type of content you want to ban from cellular.**

Switching Your Tablet to Airplane Mode

When you board a flight, aviation regulations in most countries are super-strict about disallowing not only cell phone calls, but also wireless signals of *any* kind. This means your tablet is a real hazard to sensitive airline equipment because it also transmits Wi-Fi and Bluetooth signals, even if there are no Wi-Fi receivers or Bluetooth devices within 30,000 feet of your current position.

Your pilot or friendly flight attendant will suggest that you simply turn off your device. Sure, that does the job but, darn it, you have an iPad or iPad mini, which means there are plenty of things you can do outside of its wireless capabilities, such as listen to music or an audiobook, watch a show, view photos, and much more.

So how do you reconcile the no-wireless-and-that-means-you regulations with the multitude of wireless-free apps? You put your iPad or iPad mini into a special state called Airplane Mode. This mode turns off the transceivers — the internal components that transmit and receive wireless signals — for the cellular antenna, Wi-Fi, and Bluetooth features. With your tablet now safely in compliance with federal aviation regulations, you're free to use any app that doesn't rely on wireless transmissions.

There are two methods you can use to activate Airplane Mode:

- **On the Home screen, tap Settings and then tap the Airplane Mode switch to On.**

- **Swipe up from the bottom of the screen to open the Control Center, and then tap the Airplane Mode button, pointed out in Figure 2.8.**

Your iPad or iPad mini disconnects your cellular network and your wireless network (if you have a current connection). Notice, as well, that while Airplane Mode is on, an airplane icon appears in the status bar in place of the signal strength and network icons.

Airplane Mode button

Airplane Mode icon

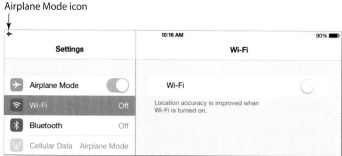

2.8 When your tablet is in Airplane Mode, the Airplane Mode icon appears in the status bar.

Connecting Your Tablet to a Bluetooth Device

Your iPad or iPad mini is configured to use a wireless technology called Bluetooth, which enables you to make wireless connections to other Bluetooth-friendly devices. For your iPad or iPad mini, this includes Bluetooth headsets, keyboards, speakers, and printers.

In theory, connecting Bluetooth devices should be criminally easy: You turn on the Bluetooth feature on each device — in Bluetooth jargon, you make the device *discoverable* — bring them within 33 feet of each other, and they connect without further ado. In practice, however, there's usually at least a bit of further ado (and sometimes plenty of it). This usually takes one or both of the following forms:

- **Making your device discoverable.** Unlike Wi-Fi devices that broadcast their signals constantly, most Bluetooth devices only broadcast their availability when you say so. This makes sense in many cases because you usually only want to connect a Bluetooth component such as a headset or keyboard with a single device. By controlling when the device is discoverable, you ensure that it works only with the device you want it to.

● **Pairing the tablet and the device.** As a security precaution, many Bluetooth devices need to be paired with another device before the connection is established. In most cases, the pairing is accomplished by entering a multi-digit passkey — iOS calls it a PIN — that you must then also enter into the Bluetooth device (assuming, of course, that it has some kind of keypad). In the case of a headset, the device comes with a default passkey that you must type into your tablet to set up the pairing.

Making your tablet discoverable

Your first order of Bluetooth business is to ensure that your iPad or iPad mini is discoverable. It usually is by default, but follow these steps to activate the Bluetooth feature and make sure your tablet is discoverable:

1. **On the Home screen, tap Settings.** The Settings screen appears.

2. **Tap Bluetooth.** The Bluetooth screen appears.

3. **Tap the Bluetooth On/Off button to change the setting to On.** To remind you that Bluetooth is on, your iPad or iPad mini displays the Bluetooth icon in the status bar, as shown in Figure 2.9.

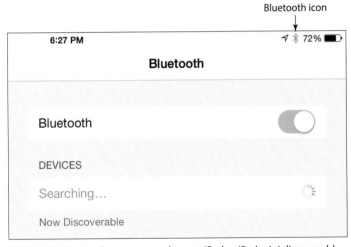

2.9 Use the Bluetooth screen to make your iPad or iPad mini discoverable.

Pairing or unpairing your tablet

Follow these general steps to pair your iPad or iPad mini with a Bluetooth device:

1. **On the Home screen, tap Settings.**
   The Settings screen appears.

2. **Tap Bluetooth.** The Bluetooth screen appears.

3. **If the device has a separate switch or button that makes it discoverable, switch it on or press it.** Wait until you see the device name appear in the Bluetooth screen, as shown in Figure 2.10.

2.10 The device name appears in the Bluetooth screen when it becomes discoverable.

4. **Tap the name of the Bluetooth device.** If your iPad or iPad mini can pair with the device automatically, you see Connected in the Bluetooth screen and you can skip the rest of these steps. Otherwise, your iPad or iPad mini displays a PIN that you must enter on the device.

5. **Type the device PIN.** Your iPad or iPad mini pairs with the device and returns you to the Bluetooth screen, where you now see Connected beside the device name.

6. **Tap Quit, and the device is ready to use.**

When you no longer plan to use a Bluetooth device for a long period of time, follow these steps to unpair it from your iPad or iPad mini:

1. **On the Home screen, tap Settings.** The Settings screen appears.

2. **Tap Bluetooth.** The Bluetooth screen appears.

3. **Tap the name of the Bluetooth device.**

4. **Tap Forget this Device.** Your iPad or iPad mini unpairs the device.

Making a paired headset the audio output device

After you pair a Bluetooth headset, your iPad or iPad Mini is usually smart enough to start blasting your tunes through the headset rather than the tablet's built-in speaker. If that doesn't happen, follow these steps to choose your Bluetooth headset as the output device:

1. **Swipe up from the bottom of the screen to open the Control Center.**

2. **Tap the Output button that appears to the right of the AirDrop section.** The AirPlay dialog appears, as shown in Figure 2.11.

3. **Tap the device you want to use for audio output.** Your tablet starts playing the song through the device.

2.11 Tap the Output button to see a list of audio output devices.

How Do I Configure My iPad or iPad mini?

If you've made your way through the first two chapters of this book, then you know your way around your iPad or iPad mini, and you're connected to a network. What else could anyone need? You'd be surprised. Although the iPad and iPad mini work like champs right out of the box, even champs can improve their game. You may find that the default settings make sense for the average user, but you're far from average — after all, you bought this book! This chapter shows you how to configure your tablet to work the way you do.

Creating a Custom Home Screen

When you first start your iPad or iPad mini (and each time you press the Home button), the Home screen appears. You use this screen as the launching pad (so to speak) for all your tablet adventures. Using the Home screen requires almost no training: just tap the app you want and it loads, lickety-split. It's perfection!

Oh, but things are never as perfect as they appear, are they? Consider the following:

- When you hold your iPad or iPad mini, the icons in the left and right columns are a bit easier to tap because they're easily reachable with your thumbs.

- If you have more than 20 icons, they extend to a second (or third, or fourth) Home screen. If the app you want isn't on the main Home screen, you must first flick to the screen that has the app icon (or tap the dot for the screen you want), and then tap the icon. Note, however, that even when your icons extend onto multiple Home screens, the four icons in the Dock area appear on every Home screen, so they're always available.

Therefore, you can make the Home screen more efficient (and that much closer to perfection) by doing three things: moving your four most-used icons to the Dock, moving eight other commonly used icons to the left and right columns of the main Home screen, and making sure any icon you tap frequently appears somewhere on the main Home screen.

You can do all of this by rearranging the Home screen icons as follows:

1. **Display the Home screen.**

2. **Tap and hold any Home screen icon.** When you see the icons wiggling, release your finger.

3. **Tap and drag the icons into the positions you prefer.** To move an icon to a different screen, tap and drag it to the left edge of the current screen if you want to move it to a previous screen, or to the right edge if you want to move it to a later screen. Next, wait for the new screen to appear and then drop the icon where you want it. You can also include a maximum of six icons on the Dock.

4. **Rearrange the existing Dock icons by dragging them left or right to change the order.**

5. **To replace a Dock icon, first tap and drag the icon off the Dock to create some space.** Then tap and drag any Home screen icon into the Dock.

6. **Press the Home button to save the new icon arrangement.**

Creating an app folder

The best way to make the main Home screen more manageable is to reduce the total number of icons with which you have to work. This isn't a problem when you're just starting out with your tablet because it comes with a limited number of apps. However, the addictive nature of the App Store almost always means that you end up with screen after screen of apps. The iPad or iPad mini lets you use a maximum of 11 screens. If you fill each screen to the brim — that's 20 apps per screen — you end up with 226 total icons (assuming you're using the maximum of six Dock icons). That's a lot of icons.

Now, when I tell you to reduce the number of icons on the Home screens, I don't mean that you should delete apps. Too drastic! Instead, you can take advantage of a feature called app folders. Just like a folder on your hard drive in which you can store multiple files, an app folder can store multiple app icons — up to 9 per page, in fact — and you can create multiple pages. This enables you to group related apps together under a single icon. This not only reduces your overall Home screen clutter, but also makes individual apps easier to find.

Here are the steps to follow to create and populate an app folder:

1. **Navigate to the Home screen that contains at least one of the apps you want to include in your folder.**

2. **Tap and hold any icon until you see all of the icons wiggling.**

3. **Tap and drag an icon that you want to include in the folder, and drop it on another icon that you want to include in the same folder.** Your iPad or iPad mini creates the folder and displays a text box so that you can type a name for the folder. The default name is the underlying category used by the apps, as shown in Figure 3.1. If the apps are in different categories, your iPad or iPad mini uses the category of the app you dragged and dropped.

4. **Tap inside the text box to edit the name if you want, and then tap Done.**

5. **Press the Home button to save your new icon arrangement.**

Use the following techniques to work with your app folders:

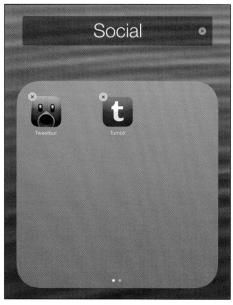

- **Add another app to the folder.** Tap and drag the app icon and drop it on the folder.

- **Launch an app.** Tap the folder to open it and then tap the app.

- **Rename a folder or rearrange apps within a folder.** Tap the folder to open it, and then tap and hold any app icon within the folder. You can then edit the folder name, and drag and drop the apps within the folder.

3.1 Drop one app icon on another to create an app folder.

- **Remove an app from a folder.** Tap the folder to open it, tap and hold any app icon within the folder, and then drag it out of the folder.

Adding a Safari web clip to the Home screen

Do you visit a certain web page all the time? You can set up a bookmark to that page in the Safari browser, but an even faster way to access it is to add it to the Home screen as a web clip icon. A *web clip* is a link to a page that preserves the page's scroll position and zoom level. For example, suppose a page has a form at the bottom. To use that form, you have to navigate to the page, scroll to the bottom, and then zoom in to see it better. However, you can perform all three actions — navigate, scroll, and zoom — automatically with a web clip.

Follow these steps to save a page as a web clip icon on the Home screen:

1. **Use the Safari browser to navigate to the page you want to save.**

2. **Scroll to the portion of the page you want to see.**

3. **Pinch and spread your fingers over the area on which you want to zoom in until you can comfortably read the text.**

4. **Tap the Actions button (the one with the arrow) at the top of the screen.** Safari displays a list of actions you can perform.

5. **Tap Add to Home Screen.** Safari prompts you to edit the web clip name.

6. **Edit the name as needed.** Names up to about 10–14 characters can be displayed on the Home screen without being broken. The fewer uppercase letters you use, the longer the name can be. For longer names, you see the first and last few characters (depending on the locations of spaces in the name), separated by an ellipsis (...). For example, if the name is My Home Page, it appears in the Home screen as My Ho...Page.

7. **Tap Add.** Safari adds the web clip to the Home screen and displays the Home screen. If your main Home screen is already filled to the brim with icons, Safari adds the web clip to the first screen that has space available.

Note

To delete a web clip from the Home screen, tap and hold any Home screen icon until the icon dance begins. Each web clip icon displays an X in the upper-left corner. Tap the X of the web clip you want to remove. When you see the confirmation message, tap Delete and then press the Home button to save the configuration.

Resetting the default Home screen layout

If you make a bit of a mess of your Home screen, or if someone else is going to be using your iPad or iPad mini, you can reset the Home screen icons to their default layout. Follow these steps:

1. **On the Home screen, tap Settings to open the Settings app.**

2. **Tap General.** The General screen appears.

3. **Tap Reset.** The Reset screen appears.

4. **Tap Reset Home Screen Layout.** Settings warns you that the Home screen will be reset to the factory default layout.

5. **Tap Reset.** Settings resets the Home screen to the default layout, but it doesn't delete the icons for any apps you've added.

Working with App Notifications

Lots of apps take advantage of an iOS feature called *notifications*, which enables them to send messages and other data to your iPad or iPad mini. For example, the Facebook app displays an alert when a friend sends you a message. Similarly, the Foursquare app, which lets you track where your friends are located, sends you a message when a friend checks in at a particular location.

If an app supports notifications, the first time that you start it, you usually see a message like the one shown in Figure 3.2, asking if you want to allow push notifications for the app. Tap OK if you're cool with that; tap Don't Allow if you're not.

> **"NYTimes" Would Like to Send You New Issues and Push Notifications**
>
> Notifications may include alerts, sounds and icon badges. These can be configured in Settings.
>
> | Don't Allow | OK |

3.2 You can allow or disallow push notifications for an app.

The following are the four kinds of push notifications:

- **Sound.** This is a sound effect that plays when some app-related event occurs.

- **Alert.** This is a message that pops up on your screen. You must then tap a button to dismiss the message before you can continue working with your current app.

- **Banner.** This is a message that appears at the top of the screen, as shown in Figure 3.3. Unlike an alert, a banner allows you to keep using your current app and disappears automatically after a few seconds. If you prefer to switch to the app to view the message, tap the banner.

- **Badge.** This is a small red icon that appears in the upper-right corner of an app icon. The icon usually displays a number, which might be the number of messages you have waiting for you on the server.

3.3 iOS can display alert notifications as banners that appear at the top of the screen.

44

Displaying the Notification Center

If you miss an alert or banner, or if you see a banner but ignore it, you can still eyeball your recent notification message by displaying the Notification Center, which combines all of your recent alerts and banners in one handy location. So, not only can you see the most recent alert (as you could in previous versions of iOS), but also you can see the last few so you don't miss anything.

Even better, displaying the Notification Center is a snap — just swipe down from the top of the screen. As you can see in Figure 3.4, the Notification Center displays a summary at the top, followed by your recent messages sorted by app. From here, you can either tap an item to switch to that app or swipe up from the bottom of the screen to hide the Notification Center.

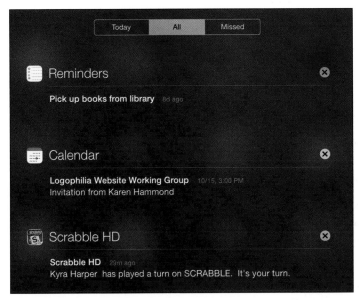

3.4 Swipe down from the top of the screen to display the Notification Center.

Customizing notifications

For each app, you can toggle individual notification types (sounds, alerts, and badges), switch between banner and alert messages, or even remove an app from the Notification Center altogether. You can also configure app notifications to appear in the Lock screen (that is, with the Lock screen displayed, swipe down from the top of the screen to see the Notification Center). This is handy because you can see your notifications without having to unlock your iPad or iPad mini.

Follow these steps to configure app notifications:

1. **On the Home screen, tap Settings.** The Settings app appears.

2. **Tap Notification Center.** The Notifications Center screen appears.

3. **Use the switches in the Access on Lock Screen section to configure what you want to see in the Lock screen version of the Notification Center.**

4. **Use the switches in the Today View section to configure the information that appears in the main part of the Notification Center.**

5. **Tap the app you want to customize.** The app notification settings appear. Figure 3.5 shows the settings for the Game Center app. Note that not all apps support all possible settings.

3.5 Use each app's notification settings to control notifications on your iPad or iPad mini.

6. **In the Alert Style section, tap the style you prefer for message notifications.** Tap None to turn off alerts, or tap the style you want: Banners or Alerts.

7. **If the app supports badges, use the Badge App Icon switch to toggle this type of notification on or off.**

8. **If the app supports sounds, use the Sounds switch to toggle this type of notification on or off.**

9. **To remove the app from the Notification Center, tap the Notification Center switch to Off.**

10. **To set the maximum number of app messages that appear on the Notification Center, tap Show, and then tap the number of messages.**

11. **Use the Show on Lock Screen switch to toggle whether the app notifications appear in the Lock screen.**

12. **If you prefer to see alerts only from people you know, tap Show Alerts from My Contacts.**

13. **Tap Notifications to return to the Notifications screen.**

14. **Repeat steps 5 to 12 to customize each app.**

Configuring Do Not Disturb settings

The Notification Center is a truly useful tool that helps you see what's going on in your world at a glance and gives you a heads-up about activities, incoming messages, app happenings, and more. The Notification Center is a great innovation, but it's also a distracting one with its banners, alerts, and sounds. If you're in a meeting, at a movie, or going to sleep, you certainly don't want your iPad or iPad mini disturbing the peace. Most people handle this by activating Airplane Mode, which turns off all the tablet's antennas. This ensures that you're distraction-free for a while. However, without any working antennas, your iPad or iPad mini can't communicate with the world, so it doesn't download messages or perform any other online activities. That might be what you want, but it's less than optimum if you're expecting something important.

iOS solves this conundrum by offering Do Not Disturb mode, which silences all distractions — including Notification Center alerts and incoming message sounds — but keeps your tablet online so that it can continue to receive data. That way, when you're ready to get back to the action, all of your new data is already on your iPad or iPad mini, and you can get back up to speed quickly.

Even better, you can configure Do Not Disturb to automatically start and stop at a scheduled time (say, when you usually go to sleep and wake up), so you never forget to set it.

To get more out of Do Not Disturb, follow these steps to configure it to suit the way that you work:

1. **Tap Settings to open the Settings app.**

2. **Tap Do Not Disturb.** The Do Not Disturb screen appears.

3. **To set a time to automatically activate and deactivate Do Not Disturb, tap the Scheduled switch to On, tap the From/To control, use From to set the start time, use To for setting the end time, and then tap Do Not Disturb.**

4. **If you want to allow certain FaceTime calls even when Do Not Disturb is activated, tap Allow Calls From, and then tap who you want to be able to get through: Everyone, No One, Favorites (that is, anyone in the FaceTime app's Favorites list), or a particular contact group.**

5. **If you want Do Not Disturb to allow a FaceTime call through when the same person calls twice within 3 minutes, leave the Repeated Calls switch in the On position.** If you don't want to allow this exception, tap the Repeated Calls switch to Off.

Note
To turn on Do Not Disturb, tap Settings, tap Do Not Disturb, and then tap the Manual switch to On.

More Useful Configuration Techniques

You've seen quite a few handy customization tricks so far, but you're not done yet — not by a long shot. The next few sections take you through a few more heartwarmingly useful customization techniques.

Changing the name of your tablet

When you first configure your iPad or iPad mini, one of the chores you perform is giving it a custom name. This might sound frivolous, but there's a good reason to give your tablet a unique name. First, as covered in Chapter 4, when you sync your iPad or iPad mini, iTunes automatically creates a backup of its data. Each backup is identified by the name of the device and the date the backup was performed. If you're in an environment where the same copy of iTunes is used to sync multiple devices, giving each one its own name enables you to differentiate between multiple backups.

Of course, you should feel free to give your tablet a cool, snappy name if the mood strikes. Follow these steps to rename your iPad or iPad mini:

1. **In the Home screen, tap Settings to open the Settings app.**

2. **Tap General.** The General settings appear.

3. **Tap About.** The About page appears.

4. **Tap Name.** The Settings app displays a text box with the current name of your tablet inside.

5. **Edit the name, as you see fit.**

Turning sounds on and off

Your iPad or iPad mini is often a noisy little thing that makes all manner of rings, beeps, and boops, seemingly at the slightest provocation. The following is a short list of the events that can give your tablet's lungs a workout:

- Incoming and outgoing e-mail and text messages

- Outgoing tweets and Facebook posts

- Calendar and reminder alerts

- Locking and unlocking the device

- Tapping the keys on the on-screen keyboard

What a racket! None of this may bother you when you're on your own. However, if you're in a meeting, a movie, or anywhere else where extraneous sounds are unwelcome, you may want to turn off some (or all) of these sound effects.

If you want to go the totally silent route, you can switch your tablet to silent mode, as described in Chapter 1, which means it doesn't play any alerts or sound effects. If silent mode is a bit too drastic, follow these steps to control exactly which sounds your iPad or iPad mini utters:

1. **On the Home screen, tap Settings to open the Settings app.**

2. **Tap Sounds.** The Sounds screen appears.

3. **In the Ringer and Alerts section, drag the volume slider to set the volume of the ringtone that plays when a FaceTime call or alert sounds.**

4. **To lock the ringer volume, tap the Change with Buttons switch to the Off position.** This means that pressing the volume buttons on the side of the device has no effect on the ringer volume.

5. **To set a different default ringtone, tap Ringtone to open the Ringtone screen.** Tap the ringtone you want to use (you hear a preview), and then tap Sounds to return to the Sounds screen.

6. **For each of the events on the list (from Text Tone to AirDrop), tap the event, and then tap the sound you want to hear.** You can also tap None to turn off the event sound.

7. **To turn off the sound that your tablet makes when you lock and unlock it, tap the Lock Sounds switch to Off.**

8. **To turn off the sound that your tablet makes each time you tap a key on the virtual keyboard, tap the Keyboard Clicks switch to Off.**

Configuring the Side switch

Back in Chapter 1 you learned about the control that Apple simply refers to as the Side switch. This switch doesn't have a name because you can configure it to perform one of two different tasks. By default, the Side switch is a mute control that toggles the volume on and off. However, you can also use the Side switch as a rotation lock control that, when activated, prevents your iPad or iPad mini from rotating when you change the orientation.

Follow these steps to configure the Side switch:

1. **On the Home screen, tap Settings to open the Settings app.**

2. **Tap General.** The General screen appears.

3. **In the Use Side Switch to section, tap either Mute or Lock Rotation.**

Customizing the keyboard

One of the nice innovations you get with the on-screen keyboard is a feature called Auto-Capitalization. If you type a punctuation mark that indicates the end of a sentence — for example, a period (.), a question mark (?), or an exclamation point (!) — or if you press Return to start a new paragraph, the keyboard automatically activates the Shift key because it assumes you're starting a new sentence.

On a related note, double-tapping the spacebar activates a keyboard shortcut. Instead of entering two spaces, the keyboard automatically enters a period (.) followed by a space. This is ever-so-slightly more efficient than tapping the period key and the spacebar separately.

Genius

Typing a number or punctuation mark normally requires three taps: tapping Number (.?123), tapping the number or symbol, and then tapping ABC. Here's a faster way: Tap and hold the Number key to open the numeric keyboard, slide the same finger to the number or punctuation symbol you want, and then release the key. This types the number or symbol and re-displays the regular keyboard all in one gesture.

For many people, one of the keys to quick on-screen typing is to clear the mind and just tap away without worrying about accuracy (I call this "Zen typing"). In many cases, you might be rather amazed at how accurate this willy-nilly approach can be. Why does it work? The secret is the Auto-Correction feature, which watches what you're typing and automatically corrects any errors. For example, if you tap *hte*, the keyboard automatically corrects this to *the*. You see the suggested correction before you complete the word (say, by tapping a space or a comma) and you can reject the suggestion by tapping it.

If you do end up with spelling errors (for example, by rejecting a proper correction), the screen lets you know by displaying the miscreant words underlined with red dots. Tap an underlined term to see a list of suggested corrections and then tap the one that works for you.

One thing the on-screen keyboard doesn't seem to have is a Caps Lock feature that enables you to type all uppercase letters. To do this, you need to tap and hold the Shift key, and then use a different finger to tap the uppercase letters. However, the keyboard actually *does* have a Caps Lock feature: double-tap Shift to turn Caps Lock on, then tap Shift to turn Caps Lock off.

Follow these steps to turn on any of these features:

1. **On the Home screen, tap Settings to launch the Settings app.**

2. **Tap General.** The General screen appears.

3. **Tap Keyboard.** The Keyboard screen appears.

51

4. **Use the Auto-Capitalization, Auto-Correction, Check Spelling, Enable Caps Lock, and "." Shortcut switches to toggle these features off and on.**

5. **To add an international keyboard layout, tap International Keyboards to open the Keyboards screen, and then set the keyboard layout you want to add to On.**

Note   When you're using two or more keyboard layouts, the keyboard sprouts a new key to the left of the spacebar (it looks like a stylized globe). Tap that key to run through the layouts, the names of which appear briefly in the spacebar.

Earlier in this chapter I mentioned that when you're holding your iPad or iPad mini, it's slightly easier to tap the Home screen icons in the left and right columns because they're within thumb distance. This also applies to the on-screen keyboard, where left-side keys (such as Q, A, and Z), as well as right-side keys (such as Delete and Return) are within easy reach of the thumbs. For this reason, most people prefer to put their iPad or iPad mini down on a flat surface so that they can type with multiple fingers rather than just the thumbs.

Typing while holding your tablet gets a whole lot easier if you split the on-screen keyboard into two halves — one that appears on the left side of the screen and one that appears on the right. Because both halves are within reaching distance of all but the shortest thumbs, you can type on and hold your tablet simultaneously.

Another on-screen keyboard conundrum is that, in many apps, the keyboard always appears docked at the bottom of the screen, but the text you are typing appears at (or near) the top of the screen. This relatively huge distance between keyboard and text makes it more difficult to type accurately and quickly. Once again, however, iOS rides to the rescue, enabling you to undock the keyboard and position it anywhere on the screen.

Splitting and undocking are controlled by a single setting, so you might want to first follow these steps to ensure this setting is turned on:

1. **On the Home screen, tap Settings to start the Settings app.**

2. **Tap General.** The General screen appears.

3. **Tap Keyboard.** The Keyboard screen appears.

4. **Tap the Split Keyboard switch to On.**

The next time the on-screen keyboard comes up, tap and hold the Hide Keyboard button, which appears in the lower-right corner of the keyboard. After a couple of seconds, you see the options shown in Figure 3.6.

Leave your finger on the screen and slide it up to one of the following:

- **Undock.** Tap this option to undock the keyboard and display it in the middle of the screen. To move the keyboard to the position you prefer, tap and drag the Hide Keyboard button.

- **Split.** Tap this option to undock the keyboard and split it in two halves, as shown in Figure 3.7. Again, you can move the split keyboard to a new position by tapping and dragging the Hide Keyboard button.

3.6 Tap and hold the Hide Keyboard button to see these options.

When you're ready to return to the normal keyboard layout, tap and hold the Hide Keyboard button, and then slide your finger up to Dock & Merge.

Genius

A slightly easier way to split or position the keyboard is to tap and hold the Hide Keyboard button for a couple of seconds, and then drag the button up or down.

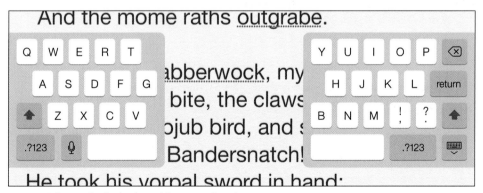

3.7 Tap Split to split the keyboard for easier thumb typing.

Creating text shortcuts

The Auto-Correction keyboard feature that I mentioned earlier can speed up your typing chores a tad because it displays suggestions whenever it recognizes the word you're currently typing. When the suggestion appears, tap a word-ending character, such as a space, comma, or period, and your iPad or iPad mini automatically fills in the rest of the word.

Still, this is only marginally useful for speeding up typing because Auto-Correction plays it safe and usually waits until you have only a character or two left before it displays the suggested word. If you really want to shift your typing into a higher gear, you need to take advantage of the text shortcuts feature.

If you've ever created a keyboard macro or used the AutoText feature in Microsoft Word, you'll know exactly what's happening here. A text shortcut is a short sequence of characters (usually just two or three) that represents a longer phrase. When you type the shortcut characters, you see the phrase (in much the same way that Auto-Correction does) and you then type a word-ending character to replace the shortcut characters with the entire phrase.

Note
When you see the longer phrase, you also see an X at the end, which you can tap to avoid entering the phrase. This is just like Auto-Correction but, remember, the two features aren't the same. If you turn off Auto-Correction, as I describe earlier in this chapter, you can still use text shortcuts.

These phrases can be dozens or even hundreds of characters long, so if you have phrases or boilerplate that you use all the time, your typing fingers will thank you for saving them a ton of wear and tear. Follow these steps to create a text shortcut:

1. **If you have the phrase you want to use somewhere on your tablet, copy it.** This saves you some time later when you create your shortcut.
2. **On the Home screen, tap Settings to launch the Settings app.**
3. **Tap General.** The General screen appears.
4. **Tap Keyboard.** The Keyboard screen appears.
5. **Tap Add New Shortcut.** The Shortcut screen appears.

6. **If you copied the phrase earlier, paste it into the Phrase text box.** Otherwise, type the phrase.

7. **Use the Shortcut text box to type the characters you want to use to represent the phrase.** The shortcut must be at least two characters long.

8. **Tap Save to save the text shortcut.**

Note

To remove a text shortcut, display the Keyboard screen, tap Edit, tap the red button to the left of the shortcut you want to remove, tap Delete, and then tap Done.

Configuring Siri

Controlling a computer with just voice commands has been a mainstream dream ever since the first *Star Trek* series. OS X and Windows come with speech-recognition features, but few people use them because they're difficult to configure and are more often than not frustrating to use. Third-party speech recognition programs are more powerful, but they tend to be expensive and still don't work all that well.

The dream of voice control remains unfulfilled on desktop machines, but on the iPad or iPad mini, voice control is a reality that comes in the form of the Siri app. Siri is one of the slickest iOS features because it goes well beyond this by also giving you voice control over web searching, your appointments, your contacts, your reminders, map navigation, text messages, notes, and more.

First, make sure that Siri is activated by tapping Settings in the Home screen, tapping General, tapping Siri, tapping the Siri switch to On, and then tapping Enable. While you're here, you should also tell Siri who you are, so that when you use references such as "home" and "work," Siri knows what you're talking about. In the Siri screen, tap My Info, and then tap your item in the Contacts list. You can also tap Voice Gender to switch Siri between a male and female voice.

You crank up Siri by using any of the following techniques:

- **Press and hold the Home button.**
- **Press and hold the Mic button on your Apple headphones.**
- **Press and hold the Mic equivalent on a Bluetooth headset.**

In each case, wait until you hear a two-tone beep and you see the Siri screen. Siri is often easier to use if you define relationships within Siri. So, for example, instead of saying "Call Sandy Evans," you can simply say, "Call Mom." You can define relationships in the following ways:

- **Within the Contacts app.** Open the Contacts app, tap your contact item, tap the Relationship field label (it's the one with the default label of "mother"), and then tap the relationship you want to use. Tap the blue Info button to open the All Contacts list and then tap the person you want to add to the field.

- **Within Siri.** Say "*Name* is my *relationship*," where *Name* is the person's name as given in your Contacts list, and *relationship* is the connection, such as *wife, husband, spouse, partner, brother, sister, mother,* or *father*. When Siri asks you to confirm, say "Yes."

Activating and using multitasking gestures

I introduced touchscreen gestures in Chapter 1, but I didn't cover all of them. The following extra gestures are actually quite useful:

- **When you're running an app, pinch four or five fingers to return to the Home screen.** This feels more natural than pressing an off-screen button to get back to the Home screen.

- **Swipe up with four or five fingers to reveal the multitasking bar.** Again, this feels more touch-friendly than having to double tap the Home button.

- **Swipe left or right with four or five fingers to switch between running apps.** This is often a better technique than using the multitasking bar to switch apps because you can see each app as you swipe.

These gestures are turned on by default, but you can follow these steps to make sure that's the case:

1. **On the Home screen, tap Settings to open the Settings app.**
2. **Tap General.** The General screen appears.
3. **Tap the Multitasking Gestures switch to On.**

Protecting your privacy

Third-party apps will occasionally request permission to use the data from another app. For example, an app might need access to your contacts, your calendars, your photos, or your Twitter and Facebook accounts. You can always deny these requests, of course, but if you've allowed access to an app in the past, you might later change your mind and decide you'd prefer to revoke that access. Fortunately, iOS offers a Privacy feature that enables you to control which apps have access to your data. Follow these steps to customize your privacy settings:

1. **On the Home screen, tap Settings to open the Settings app.**

2. **Tap Privacy.** The Privacy screen appears.

3. **Tap the app or feature for which you want to control access.** The Settings app displays a list of third-party apps that have requested access to the app or feature.

4. **To revoke a third-party app's access to the app or feature, tap its switch to Off.**

Resetting the iPad or iPad mini

If you've spent quite a bit of time in the Settings app, your device probably doesn't look much like it did fresh out of the box. That's okay, though, because your iPad or iPad mini should be as individual as you are. However, if you've gone a bit *too* far with your customizations, your tablet might feel a bit alien and uncomfortable. That's okay, too, because I know an easy solution to the problem: you can erase all of your customizations and revert to the default settings.

A similar problem comes up when you want to sell or give your iPad or iPad mini to someone else. Chances are good that you don't want the new owner to see your data — contacts, appointments, e-mail, favorite websites, music, and so on — and it's unlikely the other person wants to wade through all that stuff anyway (no offense). To solve this problem, you can erase not only your custom settings, but also all the content you stored on the tablet.

The Reset app handles these scenarios and a few more to boot. Follow these steps to reset or erase the content on your iPad or iPad mini:

1. **On the Home screen, tap Settings to open the Settings app.**

2. **Tap General.** The General screen appears.

3. **Tap Reset.** The Reset screen appears.

4. **Tap one of the following reset options:**

   - **Reset All Settings.** Tap this option to reset your custom settings to the factory default settings.

   - **Erase All Content and Settings.** Tap this option to reset your custom settings and remove any data you stored on your tablet.

Caution If you have any content on your iPad or iPad mini that isn't synced with iTunes — for example, iTunes music you've recently downloaded or an App Store program you've recently installed — you lose that content if you choose Erase All Content and Settings. First sync your tablet with your computer to save your content, and then run the reset.

● **Reset Network Settings.** Tap this option to delete your Wi-Fi network settings, which is often an effective way to solve Wi-Fi problems.

● **Reset Keyboard Dictionary.** Tap this option to reset your keyboard dictionary. This dictionary contains a list of the keyboard suggestions that you've rejected. Tap this option to clear the dictionary and start fresh.

● **Reset Home Screen Layout.** Tap this option to reset your Home screen icons to their default layout.

● **Reset Location & Privacy.** Tap this option to wipe out the location preferences for your apps. You see a location warning dialog when you start a GPS-aware app for the first time and your tablet asks if the app can use your current location. You tap either OK or Don't Allow, and these are the preferences you're resetting here.

5. **When you're asked to confirm, tap Reset.**

Note Remember that the keyboard dictionary contains rejected suggestions. For example, if you type *Viv*, iOS suggests *Big* instead. If you tap the *Big* suggestion to reject it and keep *Viv*, the word *Big* is added to the keyboard dictionary.

Configuring Your Tablet for Social Networking

Social networking needs no introduction because it has been a big part of our lives for a few years now. So it's all the more odd that iOS seems to have only recently discovered the phenomenon, with Twitter support only arriving in 2011 (in iOS 5) and Facebook support finally making the grade in 2012 (in iOS 6). Better late than never, I suppose, so let's see how you set up your iPad or iPad mini to do the social networking thing.

Signing in to your Facebook account

Much ink — both real and virtual — has been spilled in the past few years describing the technological juggernaut that is Facebook, with its hundreds of millions of users (probably more than a billion by the time you read this). While the world's pundits and talking heads can't seem to say enough about Facebook's impact on the world, the rest of us just use it day in and day out to stay in touch with friends, family, colleagues, and college buddies. On your iPad or iPad mini, this usually involves accessing the Facebook app. That's fine, but it has long seemed odd that all your Facebook friends and events have been separate from your other contacts and calendars, and that to perform simple social tasks, such as sharing a link or a photo, has required a few extra hoops to jump through.

That all changed with iOS 6, which came with Facebook support built right in to the system. You can integrate your Facebook friends with the Contacts app; see Facebook events in the Calendar app; easily post links, photos, and other content to your Facebook Timeline; and even send simple status updates without having to load the Facebook app.

Follow these steps to sign in to Facebook:

1. **On the Home screen, tap Settings to open the Settings app.**
2. **Tap Facebook.** The Facebook screen appears.
3. **Type your Facebook username or e-mail address in the User Name text box.**
4. **Type your account password in the Password text box.**
5. **Tap Sign In.** A screen appears with information about signing in to Facebook.
6. **Tap Sign In.** The Settings app connects to your Facebook account. It also prompts you to install the free Facebook app, so click Later or Install, as you prefer.
7. **If you don't want the Calendar app to display your Facebook events, tap the Calendar switch to Off.**
8. **If you don't want the Contacts app to display your Facebook friends, tap the Contacts switch to Off.**

Using Siri to update Facebook

With Siri activated and configured, and your iPad or iPad mini signed in to your Facebook account, it's time to combine these tools and use Siri to compose and send a Facebook status update.

Follow these steps to update your Facebook account with Siri:

1. **Press and hold the Home button to launch Siri.**

2. **Say "Post to Facebook."** Siri responds with "OK...what would you like to say?" (or something similar) and displays the Facebook dialog, as shown in Figure 3.8.

3. **Dictate your message.** Siri processes the speech, and then displays the text in the Facebook dialog.

4. **Say "Post."** Siri posts the status update to your Facebook account.

3.8 Siri is happy to pass along your status update to Facebook.

Signing in to your Twitter account

Twitter, that 140-characters-or-less phenomenon, started off by asking you the not-so-musical question, *What are you doing?* It's a question that seems crafted to elicit nothing but the most trivial of replies: I just woke up; I'm having toast for breakfast; I'm in a boring meeting; I just finished dinner; I'm going to bed.

But Twitter users took that original question and broadened it into a world of new questions: What are you reading? What great idea did you just come up with? What are you worried about? What interesting person did you just see or hear? What great information did you stumble upon on the web? What hilarious video would you like to share? Which is why, a couple of years ago, Twitter itself changed the original question from *What are you doing?* to *What's happening?*

Of course, what's most likely happening is that you're working or playing with your iPad or iPad mini, and you have something to share with your Twitter followers, such as a link, photo, or video. In the past, sharing such things required jumping through a few too many hoops. However, iOS gets rid of those hoops by baking Twitter right into the system. Once you sign in to your Twitter account using the Settings app, you can tweet stuff directly from apps such as Safari and Photos.

Follow these steps to sign in to Twitter:

1. **On the Home screen, tap Settings.** The Settings screen appears.

2. **Tap Twitter.** The Twitter screen appears.

3. **Type your Twitter account name in the User Name text box.**

4. **Type your account password in the Password text box.**

5. **Tap Sign In.** Your iPad or iPad mini connects to your Twitter account. It also prompts you to install the free Twitter app. Click Later or Install, as you prefer.

Genius If you have multiple Twitter accounts, you can add more by displaying the Twitter screen, tapping Add Account, typing the account username and password, and then tapping Sign In.

Using Siri to send a tweet

Earlier I showed you how to use Siri to post a Facebook status update, so it will come as absolutely no surprise that you can also use Siri to tweet. Follow these steps to Tweet using Siri:

1. **Press and hold the Home button to launch Siri.**

2. **Say "tweet."** Siri responds with "OK...what would you like to say?" (or something similar) and displays the Twitter dialog.

3. **Dictate your message.** Siri processes the speech, and then displays the text in the Twitter dialog.

4. **Say "Send."** Siri posts the tweet to your Twitter account.

How Do I Keep My iPad or iPad mini in Sync?

The iPad weighs a mere pound and a half and the iPad mini is less than half that, so they're as portable as computers can get. This means you often have your tablet with you when you venture out, but hello? Aren't you forgetting something? You were just about to waltz outside without any of your *data*. Your contacts, calendars, bookmarks, music, videos, and other media are on your main computer. Why not take them with you? You can if you sync that data with your tablet. I show you how to do so in this chapter.

Connecting Your Tablet to Your Computer

When the iPad was first released, it looked as though we might have finally arrived at that glorious day when computers and devices could just sort of *sense* each other's presence and begin a digital conversation without requiring something as inelegant as a *physical* connection. Ugh. However, despite the fact that the fancy-schmancy iPad supported *two* wireless connection technologies — Wi-Fi and Bluetooth (I cover both in Chapter 2) — exchanging data between it and a Mac or PC required a wired connection.

Well, I'm happy to report that those days are behind us. Sort of. Yes, you can still use a cable to connect your iPad or iPad mini and your computer, but iOS now also supports *wireless* connections via Wi-Fi. The next couple of sections provide the details.

Connecting via USB

Although iOS supports Wi-Fi syncing, USB connections are still important for those times when you want to use iTunes to change your sync settings. To make an old-fashioned USB-style connection, you can proceed in one of the following ways:

- **USB cable.** Use the cable that comes with your iPad or iPad mini to attach the USB connector to a free USB port on your Mac or PC. Next, attach the other end of the cable to your tablet in one of the following ways:
  - **Fourth-generation iPad or later, or iPad mini.** Attach the cable to the 8-pin Lightning port on the bottom of the tablet.
  - **Third-generation iPad or earlier.** Attach the cable to the 30-pin connector port on the bottom of the tablet.
- **Dock.** Using a 30-pin to USB cable, attach the USB connector to a free USB port on your Mac or PC, and then attach the other end of the cable to the 30-pin connector port on the back of the dock. Now, connect your tablet in one of the following ways:
  - **Fourth-generation iPad or later, or iPad mini.** Insert a Lightning to 30-Pin Adapter into the dock cradle and connect your tablet to the adapter.
  - **Third-generation iPad or earlier.** Insert the iPad into the dock cradle.

Note The dock connection for the fourth-generation iPad or later and the iPad mini would be much less convoluted if you could use a Lightning-friendly dock. However, Apple claims it won't be making such a dock, so we're out of luck.

The first time you connect your tablet to your computer, iTunes displays a dialog telling you that you haven't elected to have your tablet trust this computer. Meanwhile, on your tablet, you see a Trust This Computer? dialog, as shown in Figure 4.1. Tap Trust to proceed, and in iTunes, click Continue.

Connecting via Wi-Fi

As long as your iPad or iPad mini and your computer are connected to the same Wi-Fi network, the Wi-Fi connection happens automatically, but only if you prepare your tablet. Specifically, you need to follow these steps:

1. **Connect your iPad or iPad mini to your computer.**

2. **In iTunes, when your tablet appears in the Devices list, click it.** In iTunes 11, the Devices list appears just to the left of the iTunes Store button.

Trust This Computer?

Your settings and data will be accessible from this computer when connected via USB or Wi-Fi.

| Trust | Don't Trust |

4.1 The first time you connect your iPad or iPad mini to your computer, you have to tell your tablet to trust the computer.

3. **In the Summary tab, select the Sync with this iPad over Wi-Fi check box.**

4. **Click Apply.** iTunes configures your tablet to sync over Wi-Fi.

5. **Click Done.**

6. **Disconnect your iPad or iPad mini.** Your tablet remains in the iTunes Devices list without being physically connected to your computer.

After you do all of that, you're ready to sync over Wi-Fi, as I describe how to do a bit later in this chapter.

Syncing Your Tablet Automatically

Depending on the storage capacity of your iPad or iPad mini — 16GB, 32GB, or 64GB — you may be able to cram all of your computer's tablet-friendly digital content onto the device's hard drive. If that sounds like the way you want to go, then you can take advantage of the easiest of the syncing scenarios, in which case you don't have to pay any attention in the least: automatic syncing. (If that does *not* sound like the way you want to go, no worries: see the section on syncing your iPad or iPad mini manually a bit later in this chapter.)

Because you know all of the tablet-able content on your Mac or PC is going to fit, all you have to do is turn on your iPad or iPad mini, and connect it to your computer.

Yep, that's all there is to it! iTunes opens automatically, connects to your tablet, and begins syncing. Your iPad or iPad mini displays the Sync icon in the menu bar while the sync runs, as shown in Figure 4.2. As an added bonus, the USB port also begins charging the tablet battery. Note, too, that iOS offers another welcome little perk: you can use your iPad or iPad mini while the sync is running.

Sync icon

4.2 While your iPad or iPad mini is in mid-sync, you see the Sync icon in the menu bar.

When the sync is done, do the following two things:

- **In iTunes, click the Eject icon beside your tablet's name.**
- **Remove the cable from the tablet's connector port.**

Bypassing the automatic sync

Sometimes, you may want to connect your iPad or iPad mini to your computer, but you don't want it to sync automatically. I'm not talking about switching to manual syncing full time; I get to that in a second. Instead, I'm talking about bypassing the sync one time only. For example, you may want to connect your tablet to your computer just to charge it (assuming you either don't have the optional dock or you don't have it with you), use iTunes to see how much free space is left on your tablet, or check for updates to the iOS software.

Whatever the reason, you can tell iTunes to hold off on the syncing by using one of the following techniques:

- **Mac.** Connect the tablet to the Mac, and then quickly press and hold the Option and ⌘ keys.

- **PC.** Connect the tablet to the Windows PC, and then quickly press and hold the Ctrl and Shift keys.

When you see your tablet in the iTunes Devices list, you can release the keys. Note, however, that you don't need to use iTunes to see how much free space is left on your device. On the Home screen, tap Settings, tap General, and then tap About. In the About screen that slides in, the Available value tells you how many gigabytes (or megabytes) of free space you have left.

Troubleshooting automatic syncing

Okay, so you connect your iPad or iPad mini to your computer and then nothing. If iTunes isn't already running, it refuses to wake up from its digital slumbers. What's up with that?

A couple of things could be the problem. First, connect your iPad or iPad mini, switch to iTunes on your computer, and then click your tablet in the Devices list. On the Summary tab, make sure that the Open iTunes when this iPad is connected check box is selected.

If that check box is already selected, you need to follow these steps and delve a bit deeper to solve the mystery:

1. **Open the iTunes preferences in one of the following ways:**
   - **Mac.** Choose iTunes ⇨ Preferences, or press +. (period).
   - **Windows.** Choose Edit ⇨ Preferences (if you don't see the menu bar, press Alt), or press Ctrl+. (period).
2. **Click the Devices tab.**
3. **Deselect the Prevent iPods, iPhones, and iPads from syncing automatically check box.**
4. **Click OK to put the new setting into effect and enable automatic syncing again.**

Syncing Your Tablet Manually

When you first connected your iPad or iPad mini to iTunes, the brief setup routine included a screen that asked if you wanted to automatically sync certain content, such as music and photos. If you selected a check box for a particular type of content, iTunes configured the tablet to sync *all* of that content. That's fine, but depending on how much content you have, you might end up throwing a lot of stuff at your iPad or iPad mini.

One fine day, you'll be minding your own business, performing what you believe to be a routine sync operation, when a dialog like the one shown in Figure 4.3 rears its nasty head.

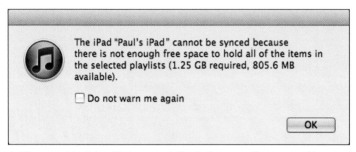

The iPad "Paul's iPad" cannot be synced because there is not enough free space to hold all of the items in the selected playlists (1.25 GB required, 805.6 MB available).

☐ Do not warn me again

OK

4.3 You see this dialog if iTunes can't fit all of your stuff on your tablet.

Groan! This most unwelcome dialog means just what it says: You don't have enough free space on your iPad or iPad mini to sync all of the content from your computer. You can handle this in one of the following ways:

- **Remove some of the content from your computer.** This is a good way to go if your tablet is really close to having enough space, such as if the dialog says your computer wants to send 100MB of data, but your tablet has only 98MB of free space. Get rid of a few megabytes of stuff on your computer, and you're back in the sync business.

- **Synchronize your tablet manually.** This means that you no longer sync everything on your computer. Instead, you handpick which playlists, podcasts, audiobooks, and so on are sent to your iPad or iPad mini. It's a bit more work, but it's the way to go if there's a big difference between the amount of content on your computer and the amount of space left on your tablet.

Syncing manually means that you handle the syncing yourself for the various content types: Contacts, calendars, e-mail, bookmarks, music, podcasts, audiobooks, e-books, photos, videos, and apps. You do this using the other tabs in the iTunes window: Info, Music, Photos, and so on. To learn the specifics for each type of data, see the following chapters:

- **Safari bookmarks.** See Chapter 5.

- **E-mail account info.** See Chapter 6.

- **E-books.** See Chapter 7.

- **Photos.** See Chapter 8.

- **Music, podcasts, and audiobooks.** See Chapter 9.

- **Movies and TV shows.** See Chapter 10.

- **Contacts.** See Chapter 11.

- **Calendars.** See Chapter 12.

When your sync settings are ready to go, click Sync to perform the synchronization.

Syncing Your Tablet via Wi-Fi

The ability to sync your iPad or iPad mini with your computer without a wire in sight is one of the nicest iOS features. If you're sitting in your easy chair or relaxing on the front porch, who wants to get up, go to the computer, connect your tablet, and then run a sync just to get, say, the latest podcasts? As long as your device is on AC and connected to the same Wi-Fi network as your computer, you can run the sync by barely moving a muscle.

Follow these steps to sync with iTunes right where you are by using Wi-Fi:

1. **Make sure your computer is running and connected to the same Wi-Fi network as your iPad or iPad mini.**
2. **On the Home screen, tap Settings to launch the Settings app.**
3. **Tap General.**
4. **Tap iTunes Wi-Fi Sync.**
5. **Tap Sync Now.** The Settings app syncs with iTunes on your computer.

Taking Syncing to a Higher Level

Syncing data between your tablet and your Mac or PC isn't complicated. Most of the time it's a straight connect-and-sync task (or, in the Wi-Fi case, it's a straight sync task). I'm loath to add complexity to such an admirably simple procedure, but you need to know how to handle the main sync challenges that might come your way. The next few sections cover how to handle sync conflicts, deal with large sync changes, replace and refresh tablet data, and merge and sync data from two (or more) computers.

Handling sync conflicts

When you sync information between your tablet and a computer, you might think it's exclusively new data that's being transferred, such as new songs, new contacts, new calendar appointments, and so on. However, the sync also includes edited or changed data. For example, if you change someone's e-mail address on your iPad or iPad mini, the next time that you sync, iTunes updates the e-mail address on the computer, which is exactly what you want.

However, what if you already changed that person's address on the computer? If you made the same edit, it's no big deal because there's nothing to sync. But what if you made a different edit? Ah, that's a problem, because now iTunes doesn't know which version has the correct information. In that case, it shrugs its digital shoulders and passes off the problem to a program called Conflict Resolver, which displays the dialog shown in Figure 4.4.

4.4 If you make different edits to the same bit of information on your tablet and your computer, the Conflict Resolver springs into action.

If you want to deal with the problem now, click Review Now. Conflict Resolver offers you the details of the conflict. For example, in Figure 4.5, you can see that a contact's work e-mail address is different in Contacts and on the tablet. To settle the issue once and for all (you hope), click the correct version of the information, and then click Done. When Conflict Resolver tells you it will fix the problem during the next sync, click Sync Now to make it happen right away.

4.5 Conflict Resolver shows you the details of any conflicts.

Handling large tablet-to-computer sync changes

Syncing works both ways: Not only does your tablet receive content from your computer, but your computer also receives content from your tablet. For example, if you create any bookmarks, contacts, or appointments on your iPad or iPad mini, those items are sent to your computer during the sync.

However, it's implied that the bulk of the content flows from your computer to your tablet, which makes sense because, for most things, it's a bit easier to add, edit, and delete stuff on the computer. That's why, if you make a lot of changes to your iPad or iPad mini content, iTunes displays a warning that the sync is going to make lots of changes to your computer content. The threshold is 5 percent, which means that if the sync changes more than 5 percent of a particular type of content on your computer — such as bookmarks or calendars — the warning appears. For example, Figure 4.6 shows the Sync Alert dialog you see if the sync will change more than 5 percent of your contacts or groups.

○ ○ ○	Sync Alert				
	Syncing with Paul's iPad will change more than 5% of your Contacts on this computer.				
Information			Add	Modify	Delete
	Contacts		0	8	0
? Show Details			Cancel	Sync Contacts	

4.6 iTunes warns you if a sync will mess with more than 5 percent of the content.

If you're expecting this (because you did change a lot of stuff on your iPad or iPad mini), click the Sync *Whatever* button, where *Whatever* is the type of data: Bookmarks, Contacts, and so on. If you're not sure, click Show Details to see what the changes are. If you're still scratching your head, click Cancel to skip that part of the sync.

If you're running iTunes for Windows, you can follow these steps to either turn off this warning or adjust the threshold (For some unfathomable reason, iTunes for Mac doesn't offer this handy option.):

1. **Choose Edit ⇨ Preferences, or press Ctrl+, (comma).** The iTunes dialog appears.

2. **Click the Devices tab.**

3. **If you want to disable the sync alerts altogether, deselect the Warn When check box.** Otherwise, leave that check box selected and move to step 4.

4. **Use the Warn When *Percent* of the Data on the Computer will be Changed list to set the alert threshold, where *Percent* is one of the following:**

   - **any.** Select this option to see the sync alert whenever syncing with the tablet will change data on your computer. iPad or iPad mini synchronizations routinely modify data on the computer, so be prepared to see the alerts every time you sync. (Of course, that may be exactly what you want.)

   - **more than *X*%.** Select one of these options — 5% (the default), 25%, or 50% — to see the alert only when the sync will change more than *X* percent of some data type on the computer.

5. **Click OK to put the new settings into effect.**

Removing and replacing tablet data

After you know what you're doing, syncing contacts, calendars, e-mail accounts, and bookmarks to your iPad or iPad mini is a relatively bulletproof procedure that should happen without a hitch each time. Of course, this is technology you're dealing with, so hitches do happen every now and then. As a result, you might end up with corrupt or repeated information on your tablet.

Perhaps you've been syncing your tablet with a couple of different computers (see the section on syncing media with two or more computers later in this chapter) and you decide to cut one of them out of the loop, and use a single machine for all of your syncs.

In both of these scenarios, you need to replace the existing information on your iPad or iPad mini with a freshly baked batch of data. Fortunately, iTunes has a feature that lets you do exactly that. Follow these steps to replace data on your tablet:

1. **Connect your tablet to your computer.**

2. **In the iTunes Devices list, click the iPad or iPad mini.**

3. **Click the Info tab.**

4. **Select the Sync check boxes for each type of information with which you want to work (contacts, calendars, e-mail accounts, bookmarks, or notes).** If you don't select a check box, iTunes won't replace that information on your tablet. For example, if you like your bookmarks just the way they are, don't select the Sync Safari Bookmarks check box.

5. **In the Advanced section, select the check box beside each type of information you want to replace.** Figure 4.7 shows five check boxes: Contacts, Calendars, Mail Accounts, Bookmarks, and Notes.

6. **Click Apply.** iTunes replaces the selected information on your tablet.

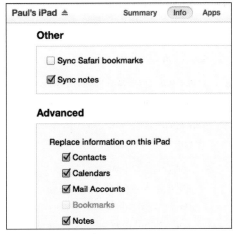

4.7 Use the check boxes in the Advanced section to decide which information to replace on your iPad or iPad mini.

Note

If a check box in the Advanced section is disabled, it's because you didn't select the corresponding Sync check box. For example, if the Sync Safari bookmarks check box is deselected, as shown in Figure 4.7, the Bookmarks check box is disabled in the Advanced section.

Merging data from two or more computers

Long gone are the days when your information resided on a single computer. Now, it's common to have a desktop computer (or two) at home, a work computer, a smartphone (such as an iPhone), and, of course, your iPad or iPad mini. It's nice to have all that digital firepower, but it creates a big problem: you end up with contacts, calendars, and other information scattered over several devices. How are you supposed to keep track of it all?

The latest solution from Apple is iCloud (I cover it later in this chapter), which provides seamless information integration across multiple computers, including Macs and Windows PCs. If you don't have an iCloud account, you can still achieve a bit of data harmony. That's because iTunes offers the welcome ability to *merge* information from two or more computers on the iPad or iPad mini. For example, if you have contacts on your home computer, you can sync them with your tablet. If you have a separate collection of contacts on your notebook, you can also sync them with your tablet, but iTunes gives you the following two choices:

- **Merge Info.** With this option, your tablet keeps the information synced from the first computer and merges it with the information synced from the second computer.

- **Replace Info.** With this option, your tablet deletes the information synced from the first computer and replaces it with the information synced from the second computer.

Follow these general steps to set up your merged information:

1. **Sync your tablet with information from one computer.** This technique works with contacts, calendars, e-mail accounts, and bookmarks.

2. **Connect your iPad or iPad mini to the second computer.**

3. **In iTunes, click your tablet in the Devices list.**

4. **Click the Info tab.**

5. **Select the Sync check boxes that correspond with information already synced on the first computer.** For example, if you synced contacts on the first computer, select the Sync Contacts check box.

6. **Click Apply.** iTunes displays a dialog like the one shown in Figure 4.8.

7. **Click Merge Info.** iTunes syncs your iPad or iPad mini and merges the computer's information with that from the first computer.

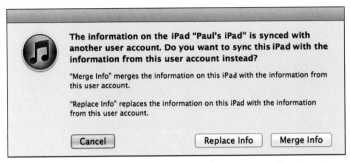

The information on the iPad "Paul's iPad" is synced with another user account. Do you want to sync this iPad with the information from this user account instead?

"Merge Info" merges the information on this iPad with the information from this user account.

"Replace Info" replaces the information on this iPad with the information from this user account.

Cancel   Replace Info   Merge Info

4.8 You can merge contacts, calendars, e-mail accounts, and bookmarks from two or more computers.

Syncing media with two or more computers

It's a major drag, but you can't sync the same type of content to your tablet from more than one computer. For example, suppose you're syncing photos from your desktop computer. If you then connect your tablet to another computer (your notebook, for example), crank up iTunes, and select the Sync Photos from check box, iTunes coughs up the dialog shown in Figure 4.9. As you can see, iTunes tells you that if you go ahead with the photo sync on this computer, it will blow away all of your existing iPad or iPad mini data!

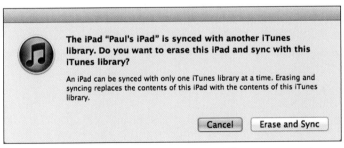

The iPad "Paul's iPad" is synced with another iTunes library. Do you want to erase this iPad and sync with this iTunes library?

An iPad can be synced with only one iTunes library at a time. Erasing and syncing replaces the contents of this iPad with the contents of this iTunes library.

Cancel   Erase and Sync

4.9 Syncing the same type of content from two different computers is a no-no in the iTunes world.

The deal here is that if iTunes sees that you don't have any examples of a particular type of content (such as movies) on your iPad or iPad mini, it lets you sync that type of content, no questions asked.

In other words, you *can* sync your tablet with multiple computers, albeit in a roundabout kind of way. The secret is to have no overlapping content types on the various computers you use for the syncing. For example, let's say you have a home desktop computer, a notebook computer, and a work desktop computer. The following is a sample scenario for syncing your iPad or iPad mini with all three machines:

- **Home desktop (music and video only).** Select the Sync music check box in the Music tab, and select all of the Sync check boxes in the Movies tab. Deselect the Sync check boxes on the Photos and Podcasts tabs.

- **Notebook (photos only).** Select the Sync photos from check box on the Photos tab. Deselect all of the Sync check boxes in the Music, Podcasts, and Movies tabs.

- **Work desktop (podcasts only).** Select the Sync box in the Podcasts tab. Deselect the Sync check boxes in the Music, Photos, and Movies tabs.

Syncing Your Tablet with iCloud

When you go online, you take your life along with you, of course, so your online world becomes a natural extension of your real world. However, just because it's online doesn't mean the digital version of your life is any less busy, chaotic, or complex than the rest of your life. The Apple iCloud service is designed to ease some of that chaos and complexity by automatically syncing your most important data — your e-mail, contacts, calendars, and bookmarks. Although the syncing itself may be automatic, setting it up is not, unfortunately. The rest of this chapter shows you what to do.

iCloud works particularly well with the iPad or iPad mini, because when you're on the town or on the road, you need data pushed to you. To ensure that your tablet works seamlessly with your iCloud data, you need to add your iCloud account and configure the iCloud sync settings.

Setting up your iCloud account on your tablet

Follow these steps to set up your iCloud account on your iPad or iPad mini:

1. **On the Home screen, tap Settings to open the Settings app.**

2. **Tap Mail, Contacts, Calendars.** The Mail, Contacts, Calendars screen appears.

3. **Tap Add Account.** The Add Account screen appears.

4. **Tap the iCloud logo.** The Settings app displays the iCloud dialog, as shown in Figure 4.10.

Cancel	iCloud	Next

Apple ID	example@icloud.com
Password	Required

Forgot Apple ID or Password?

Get a Free Apple ID >

Learn More about iCloud

4.10 Use the iCloud dialog to configure your iCloud account on your iPad or iPad mini.

5. **Tap the Apple ID text box and type your iCloud e-mail address.**

6. **Tap the Password text box and type your iCloud password.**

7. **Tap Next.** The Settings app verifies the account information and then displays the iCloud screen, as shown in Figure 4.11.

8. **For each type of data you do not want pushed to your tablet, tap the corresponding switch to set it to Off.**

9. **Tap Save.**

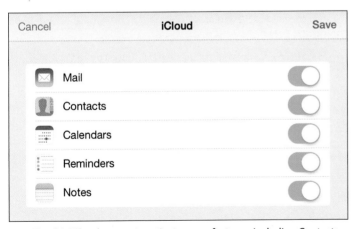

Cancel	iCloud	Save

Mail

Contacts

Calendars

Reminders

Notes

4.11 Use this iCloud screen to activate many features, including Contacts, Calendars, and Reminders.

Setting up iCloud synchronization on your tablet

The *cloud* part of iCloud means that no matter where you are, your e-mail messages, contacts, and calendars get pushed to your iPad or iPad mini, and remain fully synced with all of your other devices. iOS comes with the push feature turned on, but if you want to double-check this or turn it off, you can follow these steps to configure the setting:

1. **In the Home screen, tap Settings.** The Settings app appears.

2. **Tap Mail, Contacts, Calendars.** The Mail, Contacts, Calendars screen appears.

3. **Tap Fetch New Data.** The Settings app displays the Fetch New Data screen.

4. **Tap your iCloud account.** Settings displays the iCloud screen shown in Figure 4.12.

5. **If you want iCloud data sent to you automatically, tap Push.** Otherwise, tap Fetch to use the Fetch schedule (see step 8) or Manual to disable automatic syncing.

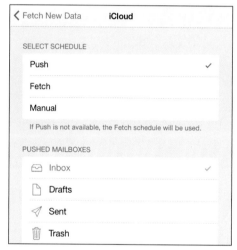

4.12 Use this iCloud screen to configure iCloud synchronization on your iPad or iPad mini.

6. **If you selected Push in step 5, use the Pushed Mailboxes section to tap each mailbox that you want pushed to your tablet.**

7. **Tap Fetch New Data to return to the Fetch New Data screen.**

8. **If you selected Fetch in step 5, use the Fetch section options to tap the frequency with which your device should fetch new data: Every 15 Minutes, Every 30 Minutes, or Hourly.** You can also tap Manually to sync by hand.

Setting up iCloud synchronization on your Mac

If you want to keep your iPad or iPad mini and your Mac in sync with the iCloud push services, you need to add your iCloud account to the Mail application and configure your Mac's iCloud synchronization feature.

Follow these steps to get your iCloud account into the Mail application:

1. **In the Dock, click the Mail icon.** The Mail application appears.

2. **Choose Mail ⇨ Preferences to open the Mail preferences.**

3. **Click the Accounts tab.**

4. **Click Add (+).** Mail displays the Add Account dialog.

5. **Select the iCloud option and click Continue.**

6. **Type your iCloud e-mail address in the Apple ID text box.**

7. **Type your iCloud password in the Password text box.**

8. **Click Sign In.** Mail verifies the account info and displays the iCloud dialog.

9. **Select the check box beside each type of data you want to set up.**

10. **Click Add Account.** Mail returns you to the Accounts tab with the iCloud account added to the Accounts list.

Macs were made to sync with iCloud, so doing so should be a no-brainer. To ensure that's the case, you need to configure your Mac to make sure iCloud sync is activated, and that your e-mail accounts, contacts, and calendars are part of the sync process. Follow these steps to set your preferences:

1. **Click the System Preferences icon in the Dock.** Your Mac opens the System Preferences window.

2. **In the Internet & Wireless section, click the iCloud icon.** The iCloud preferences appear.

3. **Select the check box beside each data item you want to sync with your iCloud account, as shown in Figure 4.13.**

4.13 Open the iCloud preferences, and then select the items that you want to sync.

Setting up iCloud Keychain

A *keychain* is a master list of usernames and passwords that a system stores for easy access by an authorized user. iCloud Keychain is a special type of keychain that stores website passwords auto-generated by Safari. This means that you don't have to remember these passwords because Safari can automatically retrieve them from your iCloud account. Even better, any other iOS device or Mac that uses the same iCloud account has access to the same keychain, so your website passwords also work on those devices.

Follow these steps to set up your iCloud Keychain on your iPad or iPad mini:

1. **In the Home Screen tap Settings.** The Settings app appears.
2. **Tap iCloud to open the iCloud settings.**
3. **Tap Keychain.**

4. **Tap the iCloud Keychain switch to On.** Settings prompts you to enter your iCloud password.

5. **Type the password and then tap OK.** iCloud sets up keychain access, which usually takes a few moments.

6. **Allow your iPad or iPad mini to use your iCloud Keychain:**

   - **If you're already using iCloud keychain on another device,** that device prompts you to allow your tablet to access the iCloud keychain. In this case, type your iCloud password and then click Allow.

   - **If you're not using iCloud Keychain on any other device,** tap Reset iCloud Keychain.

Configuring iCloud on a Windows PC

iCloud is happy to push data to your iPad or iPad mini and PC. However, unlike with a Mac, your Windows machine wouldn't know iCloud if it tripped over it. To get Windows hip to the iCloud thing, you need to do the following two things:

- **Download and install the latest version of iTunes.**

- **Download and install the iCloud Control Panel for Windows, which you can find at: http://support.apple.com/kb/DL1455.**

After you do this, you can configure iCloud to work with your PC by following these steps:

1. **On the PC that you want to configure to work with iCloud, open the Control Panel in one of the following ways:**

   - **Windows 8 or 8.1.** Press Windows Logo+X, and then click Control Panel.

   - **Earlier versions of Windows.** Choose Start ⇨ Control Panel.

2. **Double-click the iCloud icon.** If you don't see this icon, first open the Network and Internet category. The iCloud Preferences window appears.

3. **Use the Apple ID text box to type your iCloud address.**

4. **Use the Password text box to type your iCloud password.**

5. **Click Sign In.** Windows signs in to your account, and then displays the iCloud control panel, as shown in Figure 4.14.

4.14 Use the iCloud control panel to set up your PC to work with iCloud.

6. **Select the check box beside each type of data you want to sync.**

7. **Click Apply.**

How Can I Get More Out of Web Surfing?

One of the most popular modern pastimes is web surfing. Now, you can surf even when you're out and about thanks to the large screen on your iPad or iPad mini, and support for speedy networks, such as LTE and Wi-Fi. You perform these surfin' safaris using (appropriately enough) the easy-to-use Safari web browser app. The Safari app has many options and features, some of which are hidden in obscure nooks and crannies of the iOS interface. If you think your surfing activities could be faster, more efficient, more productive, or more secure, this chapter can help.

Touchscreen Tips for Surfing

The case in favor of crowning the iPad and iPad mini the best web surfing appliances ever isn't hard to make: they're blazingly fast, render most sites perfectly, and the large screens mean that you almost always see a complete (horizontally, at least) view of the regular version of each page, rather than a partial view, or an ugly, dumbed-down mobile version.

But what really sets iPad and iPad mini web surfing apart, not only from other tablets, but also from desktop, notebook, and netbook computers, is the touchscreen. With other devices, although you can click links and fill in forms, the page is really a static entity that just sits there. However, with the iPad and iPad mini (as well as their smaller touchscreen cousins, the iPhone and iPod touch), you can zoom in and out of the page by spreading and pinching your fingers. You can also pan the page by flicking a finger in the direction that you want to go. You really feel as though you're not just interacting with the web page, but *manipulating* it with your bare hands!

The touchscreen is the key to efficient and fun web surfing on your tablet, so the following is a little collection of touchscreen tips that ought to make your web excursions even easier and more pleasurable:

- **Double-tap.** A quick way to zoom in on a page that has various sections is to double-tap the specific section — be it an image, a paragraph, a table, or a column of text — that you want magnified. Safari enlarges the section to fill the width of the screen; double-tap again to return the page to the regular view.

Note The double-tap-to-zoom trick works only on pages that have identifiable sections. If a page is just a wall of text, you can double-tap until the cows come home (that's a long time) and nothing much happens.

- **Precision zooming.** Zooming on the iPad or iPad mini is straightforward. To zoom in, spread two fingers apart, and to zoom out, pinch two fingers together. However, when you zoom in on a web page, it's almost always because you want to zoom in on something. It may be an image, a link, a text box, or just a section of text. To ensure that your target ends up in the middle of the zoomed page, place your thumb and forefinger together on the section of the screen you want to zoom, and then spread your thumb and forefinger apart to zoom in.

The old pan-and-zoom. Another useful technique for getting a target in the middle of a zoomed page is to zoom and pan at the same time. That is, as you spread (or pinch) your fingers, you also move them up, down, left, or right to pan the page at the same time. This takes a bit of practice, and often you can pan either horizontally or vertically (not both), but it's still a useful trick.

One tap to the top. If you're reading a particularly long-winded web page and are near the bottom, you may have quite a long way to scroll if you need to head back to the top of the page. Save the wear and tear on your flicking finger! Instead, tap the page title, which appears just above the address/search box, and Safari immediately transports you to the top of the page.

Tap and hold to see where a link takes you. You click a link in a web page by tapping it with your finger. In a regular web browser, you can see where a link takes you by hovering the mouse pointer over it and checking the URL in the status bar. That doesn't work on your tablet, but you can still find the URL of a link before tapping it. Hold your finger on the link for a few seconds and Safari displays a pop-up screen that shows the link address, as shown in Figure 5.1. If the link looks legit, either tap Open to surf there in the current browser page, or tap Open in New Tab to start a fresh page (browser pages are covered later in this chapter). If you decide not to go there, tap anywhere outside of the pop-up screen.

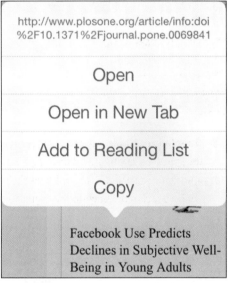

5.1 Hold your finger on a link to see the URL and several options.

Tap and hold to make a copy of a link address. If you want to include a link address in another app, such as a note or an e-mail message, you can copy it. Tap and hold your finger on the link for a few seconds, and Safari displays the pop-up screen (see Figure 5.1). Tap Copy to place the link address into memory, switch to the other app, tap the cursor, and then tap Paste.

- **Use the portrait view to navigate a long page.** When you rotate your iPad or iPad mini 90 degrees, the touchscreen switches to landscape view, which gives you a wider view of the page. Return the tablet to its upright position, and you return to portrait view. If you have a long way to scroll in a page, use the portrait view to scroll down, and then switch to landscape view to increase the text size. Scrolling in the portrait view goes much faster than in landscape.

- **Two-fingered frame scrolling.** Some websites are organized using a technique called *frames*. In this format, the overall site takes up the browser window, but some of the site pages appear in a separate rectangular area — called a frame — usually with its own scroll bar. In such sites, you may find that the usual one-fingered scroll technique scrolls only the entire browser window, not the content within the frame. To scroll the frame stuff, you must use two fingers. Weird!

- **Get a larger keyboard.** The on-screen keyboard appears when you tap into a box that allows typing. I've noticed, however, that the keyboard you get in landscape view uses noticeably larger keys than the one you see in portrait view. For the fumble-fingered among us, larger keys are a must, so always rotate the tablet into landscape mode to type text.

Note

Remember that rotating the iPad or iPad mini changes the view only if your device is upright. The tablet uses gravity to sense the change in orientation, so if it's lying flat on a table, rotating it won't do anything — rotate it before you put it on the table.

- **Quick access to common top-level domains.** A top-level domain (TLD) is the part of the domain name that comes after the last dot. For example, in wiley.com, the *.com* part is the TLD. You might think you have to type them the old-fashioned way. Nope! Tap and hold the period (.) key, and a pop-up appears with keys for .us, .org, .edu, .com, and .net. Just slide your finger over the one you want (or release to choose the default, which is .com).

Browsing Tips for Faster Surfing

If you're like me, the biggest problem you have with the web is that it's just so darned huge. We spend great big chunks of our day visiting sites and still never seem to get to everything on that day's To Surf list. The iPad or iPad mini helps lessen (but, alas, not eliminate) this problem by allowing you to surf wherever Wi-Fi can be found (or just wherever if you have a cellular version of the tablet). Even so, the faster and more efficient your surfing sessions are, the more sites you see. The touchscreen tips I covered earlier can help and in this section I take you through a few more useful tips for speedier surfing.

Browsing with tabs

These days, it's a rare web surfer who marches sequentially through a series of web pages. In your own surfing sessions, you probably leave a few web pages open full time (for things like Google searches and RSS feed monitoring). It's also likely that you'll come across a lot of links that you want to check out while leaving the original page open in the browser. In your computer's web browser, you probably handle these and similar surfing situations by launching a tab for each page you want to leave open in the browser window. It's an essential web-browsing technique, but can it be done with the Safari browser?

Yes, indeed, and the even better news is that Safari supports tabbed browsing instead of the slightly clunky pages it used in older versions. And you're not restricted to a meager two tabs — no ma'am. In iOS 7, your iPad or iPad mini lets you open up to 24 — count 'em, 24 — tabs, so you can throw some wild web page parties.

Caution Be careful if you have the full complement of 24 browser tabs opened. If you click a link that automatically opens in a new browser tab, Safari automatically shuts down one of your existing browser tabs to make way for the new tab. This could be a problem if you had some important info in that window. To avoid this, consider opening a maximum of 23 Safari tabs so you always have an extra one available if you need it.

You can use either of the following methods to open a page in a new tab:

- **In Safari, tap the New Tab button (+) shown in Figure 5.2.** Safari creates the new tab. You can then select a page from your bookmarks, type the page address, or run a search to find the page you want.

Note Some web-based apps and web page links are configured to automatically open the tab in a new window, so you may see a new tab being created when you tap a link. Also, if you add a web clip to your Home screen (as I describe in Chapter 3), tapping the button opens the web clip in a new Safari tab.

- **On a web page, tap and hold a link to display the link options (see Figure 5.2), and then tap Open in New Tab.**

Once you have multiple tabs on the go, you navigate them by tapping the tab you want to view. To close a tab that you no longer need, tap it and then tap the X that appears on the left side of the tab.

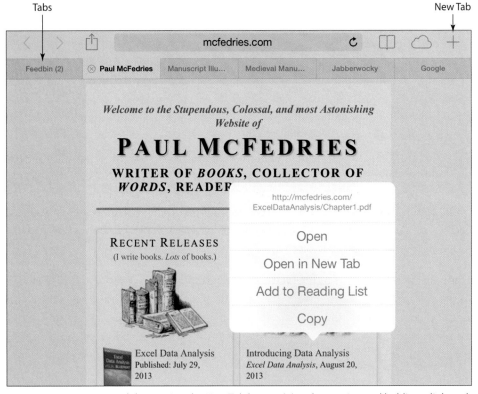

5.2 You can open a new tab by tapping the New Tab button (+), or by tapping and holding a link, and then tapping Open in New Tab.

When you tap and hold a link, and then tap Open in New Tab, Safari keeps the current page active and loads the new one in the background. That's often the behavior you want because it lets the new page take its sweet time loading while you continue to read the current one. However, you might find that most of the time you open the new tab and then switch to it immediately. Performing that extra tap to select the new tab gets old in a hurry.

The solution is to follow these steps and configure Safari to always open new tabs in the foreground:

1. **On the Home screen, tap Settings to open the Settings app.**

2. **Tap Safari.** The Settings app displays the Safari screen.

3. **Tap the Open New Tabs in Background switch to Off.**

Working with iCloud tabs

Safari tabs in iOS, OS X, or Windows are handy browsing tools because they let you keep multiple websites open and available while you surf other sites. That's fine as long as you use a single device to surf the web, but how realistic is that? It's much more likely that you do some web surfing, not only on your iPad or iPad mini, but also on your Mac or PC, your iPhone, or perhaps even your iPod touch. So, what do you do if you're using your tablet to surf and you remember a site that's open in a tab on one of your other devices?

In the past, you either had to wait until you could use the other device again, or you could try to find the site on your tablet. Neither is a satisfying solution, so Safari offers a much better idea: iCloud tabs. If you have an iCloud account, you can use it to sync your open Safari tabs with multiple devices, and then access those tabs on your iPad or iPad mini. For this to work, you must be using Safari 6 or later on iOS, OS X, or Windows and you must configure iCloud on each device to sync Safari data.

When that's done, open Safari on your tablet, and then tap iCloud Tabs (pointed out in Figure 5.3). Safari opens the iCloud Tabs list, which displays the open tabs on your other devices, as shown in Figure 5.3.

iCloud Tabs

Viewing a page without distractions

It seems like only a few years ago that purse-lipped pundits and furrow-browed futurologists were lamenting that the Internet signaled the imminent demise of reading. With pursuits such as viral videos and online gaming a mere click or two away, who would ever sit down and actually *read* things? Well, a funny thing happened on the way to the future: people read more now than they ever have. Sure, there's some concern that we're no longer reading long articles and challenging books, but most of us spend much of the day reading online.

5.3 Tap iCloud Tabs to see a list of the Safari tabs that you have open on your other devices.

On the one hand, this isn't all that surprising because there's just so much text out there, most of it available for free, and much of it professionally written and edited. On the other hand, this is actually quite surprising, because reading an article or essay online is no picnic. The problem is the sheer amount of distractions on almost any page: Background colors or images that clash with the text; ads above, to the side of, and within the text; site features such as search boxes, feed links, and content lists; and those ubiquitous icons for sharing the article with your friends on Facebook, Twitter, Google+, and on and on. Figure 5.4 shows a typical example.

Fortunately, Safari helps solve this problem by offering the Reader feature. Reader removes all of those extraneous page distractions that get in the way of your reading pleasure. So, instead of a cacophony of text, icons, and images, you see pure, simple, large-enough-to-be-easily-read text. How do you arrive at this blissful state? By tapping the Reader icon, which appears on the left side of the address bar (see Figure 5.4). Safari instantly transforms the page, and you see something similar to what is shown in Figure 5.5, which is the Reader version of the page shown in Figure 5.4.

Reader icon

5.4 Today's web pages are all too often festooned with ads, icons, and other bric-a-brac.

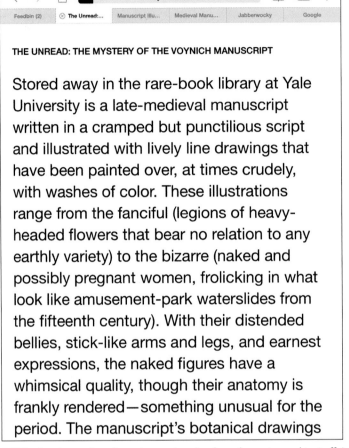

5.5 The Reader version of a web page is a simple and easy-to-read text affair.

Working with bookmarks

The web era is into its third decade now, so you certainly don't need me to tell you that the web is a manifestly awesome resource that redefines the phrase *treasure trove*. No, at this stage of your web career you're probably most concerned with finding great web treasures and returning to the best or most useful of them in subsequent surfing sessions. The Safari History list can help here (I talk about it later in this chapter), but the best way to ensure that you can easily return to a site a week, a month, or even a year from now is to save it as a bookmark.

Syncing bookmarks

By far, the easiest way to get bookmarks for your favorite sites into your iPad or iPad mini is to take advantage of your best bookmark resource: the Safari browser on your Mac (or PC), or the Internet Explorer browser on your PC (which calls them *favorites*). You've probably used those browsers for a while and have all kinds of useful and fun bookmarked sites at your fingertips.

Genius

Having used Safari or Internet Explorer for a while means having lots of great sites bookmarked, but it likely also means that you have lots of digital dreck — that is, sites you no longer visit or that have gone belly-up. Before synchronizing your bookmarks with the iPad or iPad mini, consider taking some time to clean up your existing bookmarks. You'll thank yourself in the end.

To get those bookmarks at your literal fingertips — that is, on your tablet — you have two choices:

- **iCloud.** If you have an iCloud account and you've configured your iPad or iPad mini to sync Safari data, and you've also set up your Mac or PC to sync bookmarks (I discuss all this in Chapter 4), then your Mac or PC bookmarks will flow automatically to your tablet via iCloud.

- **iTunes.** If you don't have an iCloud account, or if you've turned off Safari data syncing on your tablet and on your Mac or PC, then you need to include bookmarks as part of the synchronization process between the tablet and iTunes (which I talk about in general terms in Chapter 4).

iTunes bookmark syncing is turned on by default, but you should follow these steps to make sure:

1. **Connect your tablet to your computer.**
2. **In the iTunes Devices list, click the iPad or iPad mini.**
3. **Click the Info tab.**
4. **Scroll down to the Web Browser section and use one of the following techniques:**
   - **Mac.** Select the Sync Safari bookmarks check box.
   - **PC.** Select the Sync Bookmarks With check box, and then select your web browser from the drop-down list.
5. **Click Apply.** iTunes begins syncing the bookmarks from your computer to your tablet.

Genius

What's that? You've already synced your bookmarks to your iPad or iPad mini, and you now have a bunch of useless sites clogging up the Safari bookmark arteries? Not a problem! Return to your desktop Safari (or Internet Explorer), purge the bogus bookmarks, and then resync your tablet. Any bookmarks that you blew away also get trashed from your device.

Adding bookmarks

Even if you get your tablet bookmarks off to a flying start by copying a bunch of them from your Mac or PC, and now have a large collection at your beck and call, that doesn't mean your bookmark collection is complete. After all, you might (heck, you *will*) find some interesting sites while you're surfing with the iPad or iPad mini. If you think you might want to pay a site another visit down the road, you can follow these steps to create a new bookmark right on the tablet:

1. **Use Safari to navigate to the site that you want to save.**

2. **Tap the Actions button shown in Figure 5.6.**

3. **Tap Bookmark.** This opens the Add Bookmark screen shown in Figure 5.6.

4. **Tap in the top box, and type a name for the site that helps you remember it.** This name is what you see when you scroll through your bookmarks.

5. **Tap Location.** This displays a list of your bookmark folders.

6. **Tap the folder you want to use to store the bookmark.** Safari returns you to the Add Bookmark screen.

7. **Tap Save.** Safari saves the bookmark.

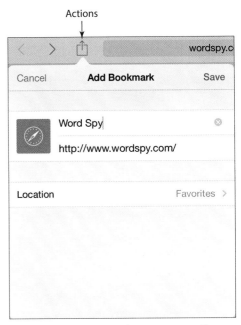

Actions

5.6 Use the Add Bookmark screen to specify a bookmark's name and location.

Managing bookmarks

After you have a few bookmarks stashed away in the bookmarks list, you may need to perform a few housekeeping chores from time to time, including changing a name, address, or folder of a bookmark; reordering bookmarks or folders; or getting rid of bookmarks that have worn out their welcome.

Before you can do any of this, though, follow these steps to get the Bookmarks list into Edit mode:

1. **In Safari, tap the Bookmarks button (see Figure 5.7).** Safari opens the Bookmarks dialog.

2. **Tap the Bookmarks tab.**

3. **If the bookmark you want to mess with is located in a particular folder, tap to open it.** For example, if you've synced with Safari, you should have a folder named Bookmarks Bar that includes all of the bookmarks and folders you've added to the Bookmarks Bar in your desktop version of Safari.

4. **Tap Edit.** Safari switches the Bookmarks list to Edit mode, and you're now free to toil away at your bookmarks. Here, you can master the following techniques:

   - **Edit bookmark info.** Tap the bookmark to fire up the Edit Bookmark screen. From here, you can edit the bookmark name, or change its address or folder. When you finish, tap the name of the current bookmark folder in the top-left corner of the screen.

   - **Change the bookmark order.** Use the drag button (the three horizontal bars) on the right to tap and drag a bookmark to a new position in the list. Ideally, you should move your favorite bookmarks near the top of the list for easiest access.

   - **Add a bookmark folder.** Tap New Folder to launch the Edit Folder screen, and then tap a folder title and select a location. Feel free to use bookmark folders at will because they're a great way to keep your bookmarks neat and tidy (if you're into that kind of thing).

   - **Delete a bookmark.** Tap the Delete button to the left of the bookmark, and then tap the Delete button that appears.

When the dust settles and your bookmark chores are finished, tap Done to get out of Edit mode.

Surfing links from your Twitter feed

If you've used your iPad or iPad mini to connect to your Twitter account, as I describe in Chapter 3, Safari offers a bonus: the Shared Links list, which displays the recent links that have been shared by the people you follow on Twitter. To get there from here, tap the Bookmarks button in the menu bar to open the Bookmarks dialog, and then tap the Shared Links tab (the @ sign). Safari displays your Twitter feed's most recent links, as shown in Figure 5.7.

Adding pages to your Reading List

In your web travels, you'll often come upon a page with fascinating content that you can't wait to read. Unfortunately, a quick look at the length of the article tells you that you're going to need more time than what you currently have available. So what's a body to do? Quickly scan the article and move on with your life? No, when you come across good web content, you need to savor it. So, should you bookmark the article for future reference? That's not bad, but bookmarks are really for things you want to revisit often, not for pages that you might only read once.

The best solution is the Safari feature called the Reading List. As the name implies, this is a simple list of things to read. When you don't have time to read something immediately, add it to your Reading List and you can read it at your leisure.

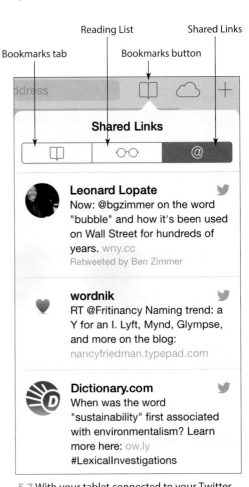

5.7 With your tablet connected to your Twitter account, the Safari Shared Links list offers up recent links from the folks you follow.

You can use either of the following techniques to add a page to your Reading List:

- **Use Safari to navigate to the page that you want to read later, tap the Actions button, and then tap Add to Reading List.**

- **Tap and hold a link for the page that you want to read later, and then tap Add to Reading List.**

When you're settled into your favorite easy chair and have the time (finally!) to read, open Safari, tap the Bookmarks button, and then tap the Reading List tab (which looks like a pair of glasses; see Figure 5.7). Safari displays all the items you've added to the list and you just tap the article you want to read. To make the list a bit easier to manage, tap Show Unread to see just the pages you haven't yet perused.

Note

If you have a cellular-friendly iPad or iPad mini, Safari uses the cellular network to access your reading list when there's no Wi-Fi in sight. To prevent this (for example, if you're nearing your plan's data cap), tap Settings, tap Safari, and then, in the Reading List section, tap the Use Cellular Data switch to Off.

Retracing your steps with the History list

Bookmarking a website (as I described earlier in this chapter) is a good idea if that site contains interesting or fun content that you want to revisit. Sometimes, however, you may not realize that a site had useful data until a day or two later. Similarly, you may like a site's stuff but decide against bookmarking it, only to regret that decision down the road. You could waste a big chunk of your day trying to track down the site, or you may run into Murphy's Web Browsing Law: a cool site that you forget to bookmark is never found again.

Fortunately, your tablet has your back. As you navigate the nooks and crannies of the web, Safari keeps track of where you go, and stores the name and address of each page in the History list. The limited iPad or iPad mini memory means that it can't store tons of sites, but it might have saved the one that you want. Follow these steps to use the History list:

1. **In Safari, tap the Bookmarks button in the status bar.** Safari opens the Bookmarks list.
2. **Tap the Bookmarks tab.**

3. **Tap History.** Safari opens the History screen. This shows the sites you've visited today at the top, followed by a list of previous surfing dates.

4. **Tap the site you want to revisit.** Safari loads the site.

Filling in Online Forms

Many web pages include forms where you fill in some data and then submit the form, which sends the data off to some server for processing. Doing this in the Safari browser is pretty straightforward. Use the following techniques to fill in online forms on your iPad mini:

- **Text box.** Tap inside the box to display the touchscreen keyboard, type your text, and tap Done.

- **Text area.** Tap inside the text area, and then use the keyboard to type your text. Most text areas allow multiline entries, so you can tap Return to start a new line. When you finish, tap Done.

- **Check box.** Tap the check box to toggle the check mark on and off.

- **Radio button.** Tap a radio button to activate it.

- **Command button.** Tap the button to make it do its thing (usually, submit the form).

Many online forms consist of a bunch of text boxes or text areas. If the idea of performing the tap-type-Done cycle over and over isn't appealing to you, fear not. The Safari browser offers the following easier method:

1. **Tap inside the first text box or text area.** The keyboard appears.

2. **Type the text you want to enter.** Above the keyboard, notice the Previous and Next buttons, as shown in Figure 5.8.

3. **Tap Next to move to the next text box or text area.** If you need to return to a text box, tap Previous.

4. **Repeat steps 2 and 3 to fill in the text boxes.**

5. **Tap Done.** Safari returns you to the page.

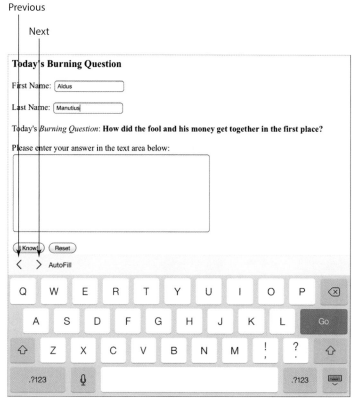

5.8 If the form contains multiple text boxes or text areas, you can use the Previous and Next buttons to navigate them.

I haven't yet talked about selection lists, and that's because the Safari browser handles them in an interesting way. When you tap a list, Safari displays the list items in a separate box, as shown in Figure 5.9. In the list of items, the currently selected one appears with a check mark next to it. Tap the item that you want to select.

Putting On Hairs: Reader Survey

Select your hair color:

Something neon ▼

Select your hair style:

Straight ▼

Bouffant	
Mohawk	year:
Page Boy	
Permed	
Shag	
Straight	✓
Style? What style?	

5.9 Tap a list to see its items in a separate box for easier selection.

Turning on AutoFill

The Safari browser makes it relatively easy to fill in online forms, but it can still be slow going, particularly if you have lots of text boxes or text areas. To help make forms less of a chore, Safari supports a welcome feature called AutoFill. Just as with the desktop version of Safari (or just about any other mainstream browser), AutoFill remembers the data you type into forms and then enables you to fill in similar forms with the simple tap of a button. You can also configure AutoFill to remember usernames and passwords.

To take advantage of this nifty new feature, you first have to turn it on by following these steps:

1. **On the Home screen, tap Settings to open the Settings app.**

2. **Tap Safari.** The Safari screen appears.

3. **Tap Passwords & AutoFill to open the Passwords & AutoFill screen.**

4. **Tap the Use Contact Info switch to the On position.** This tells Safari to use your item in the Contacts app to grab data for a form. For example, if a form requires your name, Safari uses your contact name.

5. **The My Info field should show your name; if it doesn't, tap the field, and then tap your item in the All Contacts list.**

6. **If you want Safari to remember the usernames and passwords you use to log in to websites, tap the Names & Passwords switch to the On position.**

7. **If you want Safari to remember the credit card data you enter when making online purchases, tap the Credit Cards switch to On.**

Now when you visit an online form and access any text field in the form, the AutoFill button becomes enabled. Tap AutoFill to fill in those portions of the form that correspond with your contact data, as shown in Figure 5.10. Notice that the fields Safari is able to automatically fill in display with a yellow background.

Saving website login passwords

If you enabled the Names & Passwords option in the AutoFill screen, each time that you fill in a username and password to log in to a website, Safari displays the dialog shown in Figure 5.11.

Please tell me about yourself:

First Name: [Paul]

Last Name: [McFedries]

Nickname: [   ]

(Just Do It!) (Just Reset It!)

⟨ ⟩ AutoFill

5.10 Tap AutoFill to fill in form fields with your contact data.

The dialog gives you the following three choices:

- **Save Password.** Tap this button to have Safari remember your username and password.

- **Never for This Website.** Tap this button to tell Safari not to remember the username and password, and to never again prompt you to save the login data.

- **Not Now.** Tap this button to tell Safari not to remember the username and password this time, but to prompt you again next time you log in to this site.

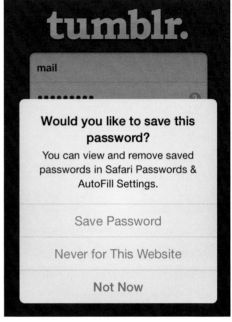

5.11 If you configure Safari to remember usernames and passwords, you see this dialog when you log in to a site.

Note

Your iPad or iPad mini is a cautious beast — it doesn't offer to save all of the passwords you enter. If the login form is part of a secure site, then Safari doesn't ask if you want to save the password. This means you won't be tempted to store the password for your online bank, corporate website, or any site where you saved your credit card data (such as Amazon and similar online shopping sites).

Genius

If you save a site's password, but then change your mind, you can remove the saved password from your tablet. Tap Settings, tap Safari, tap AutoFill, and then tap Saved Passwords to see a list of the sites with saved passwords. Tap Edit, tap the select button to the left of the password you want to remove, and then tap Delete. When Settings asks you to confirm, tap Delete.

Getting Even More Out of Safari

You've seen lots of great Safari tips and techniques so far in this chapter, but I hope you're up for even more. The rest of this chapter covers useful techniques, such as deleting the History list, changing the default search engine, and searching the web with Siri voice commands.

Deleting the History list

The Safari History list of sites you've recently surfed is a great feature when you need it and an innocuous one when you don't. However, at times the History list is just plain uncool. For example, suppose you shop online to get a nice gift for your spouse's birthday. If your significant other also uses your iPad or iPad mini, your surprise might be ruined if the purchase page accidentally shows up in the History list.

Similarly, if you visit a private corporate site, a financial site, or any other site you wouldn't want others to see, the History list might betray you.

And sometimes unsavory sites can end up in your History list by accident. For example, you might tap a legitimate-looking link in a web page or e-mail message, only to end up in some dark, dank Net neighborhood. Of course, you high-tail it out of there right away with a quick tap of the Back button, but that nasty site is now lurking in your History.

Whether you have sites on the History list that you wouldn't want anyone to see, or if you just find the idea of your tablet tracking your web movements to be a bit sinister, follow these steps to wipe out the History list:

1. **In Safari, tap the Bookmarks button.** Safari opens the Bookmarks dialog.
2. **Tap the Bookmarks tab.**
3. **Tap History.** Safari opens the History screen.
4. **Tap Clear.** Safari prompts you to confirm the deletion.
5. **Tap Clear History.** Safari deletes every site from the History list.

Genius

There's another way to clear the History and it may be faster if you're not currently working in Safari. In the Home screen, tap Settings, tap Safari, and then tap Clear History. When Settings ask you to confirm, tap Clear.

Deleting website data

As you wander around the web, Safari gathers and saves bits of information for each site. For example, it stores some site text and images so that it can display the page faster if you revisit the site in the near future. Similarly, if you activated AutoFill for names and passwords, Safari stores that data on your tablet. Finally, most major sites store small text files called cookies on your iPad or iPad mini. Cookies save information for things like site preferences and shopping carts.

Storing all of this data is generally a good thing because it can speed up your surfing. However, it's not always a safe or private thing. For example, if you elect to have Safari save a site password, you might change your mind later on, particularly if you share your tablet with other people. Similarly, cookies can sometimes be used to track your activities online, so they're not always benign.

Prior to iOS 6, you could use the Settings app to clear all of your stored cookies, saved passwords, or stored web page text and images (this is called the *cache*). However, those were awfully blunt instruments, particularly if you were only concerned about a site or two. Fortunately, iOS 6 and 7 offer a more finely-honed tool that enables you to delete the data for an individual website — follow these steps to use it:

1. **On the Home screen, tap Settings.** Your tablet opens the Settings app.
2. **Tap Safari.** The Safari screen appears.
3. **Tap Advanced to open the Advanced screen.**
4. **Tap Website Data.** Safari displays a list of the recent sites for which it has stored data, as well as the size of that data.
5. **If you don't see the site you want to remove, tap Show All Sites at the bottom of the list.**
6. **Tap Edit.**
7. **Tap the red Delete button to the left of the site you want to clear.**
8. **Tap the Delete button that appears to the right of the site's data size value.** Safari removes the site's data.

Browsing privately

If you find yourself constantly deleting your browsing history or website data, you can save yourself a bit of time by configuring Safari to do this automatically. This is called *private browsing* and it means that Safari doesn't save any data as you browse. Private browsing works in the following ways:

- Sites aren't added to the history (although the Back and Forward buttons still work for navigating sites that you've visited in the current session).
- Web page text and images aren't saved.
- Search text isn't saved with the search box.
- AutoFill passwords aren't saved.

To activate private browsing in Safari, tap the New Tab button (+), shown earlier in Figure 5.2, and then tap **Private in the lower-left corner of the screen.** When Safari asks if you want to close your existing Safari tabs, tap **Close All or, if** you prefer to keep the tabs open, tap Keep All.

Tweeting a web page

If you have a Twitter account, there's a good chance that one of your favorite 140-characters-or-less pastimes is sharing interesting, useful, or funny websites with your followers. Using a client, such as the official Twitter app or TweetBot is fine for this, but it means that you have to copy the site address, switch to the app, and then paste the address. For quick tweets, it's easier and faster just to stay in Safari. Follow these steps to send a tweet directly from a web page:

1. **Use Safari to navigate to the page that you want to tweet.**

2. **Tap the Actions button.**

3. **Tap Twitter.** Safari displays the Tweet dialog.

4. **Type your tweet text in the large text box.** As you can see in Figure 5.12, the Tweet dialog displays a number in the lower-left corner telling you how many characters you have left.

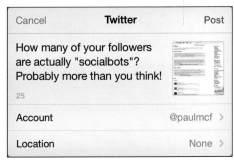

5.12 iOS lets you tweet about a website directly from Safari.

107

5. **If you added more than one account to the Twitter settings, tap the username in the Account section, and then tap the name of the account you want to use to send the tweet.**

6. **If you want to include your present whereabouts as part of the tweet, tap Location.** The first time you do this, iOS asks if Twitter can use your current location, so be sure to tap OK.

7. **Tap Post.** Safari posts the tweet.

Sharing a link on Facebook

As covered in Chapter 3, if you've signed in to your Facebook account on your iPad or iPad mini, you can use Siri to update your Facebook status. A timely, pithy, or funny status update is a time-honored (relatively speaking) Facebook tradition, but your friends would probably appreciate at least the occasional tidbit of non-narcissistic content. I speak, in this case, of sharing links to useful, interesting, funny, or even downright weird web pages.

Happily, link-sharing with your Facebook pals is now built directly in to Safari, so there's no need to surf to the Facebook site or fire up the Facebook app to get the job done. Follow these steps to share a link on Facebook:

1. **Use Safari to display the web page you want to share.**

2. **Tap the Actions button.**

3. **Tap Facebook.** Safari displays the Facebook dialog.

4. **Type your descriptive text in the large text box, as shown in Figure 5.13.**

5. **If you want to include your current location as part of the post, tap Location.** If iOS asks whether Facebook can use your current location, tap OK.

5.13 You can post a link to your Facebook posse right from Safari.

6. **To select who will see the link, tap Audience, and then tap a group in the Audience list that appears.**

7. **Tap Post.** Safari posts the link to your Facebook timeline.

Changing the default search engine

When you use the Search box at the top of the Safari screen to run a web search, Safari passes your search text to the Google search engine by default. If you have something against Google, you can follow these steps to switch to your search engine of choice:

1. **In the Home screen, tap Settings to launch the Settings app.**
2. **Tap Safari.** The Safari screen appears.
3. **Tap Search Engine.** The Settings app opens the Search Engine screen.
4. **Tap Bing or Yahoo!.** Safari now uses your choice as the default search engine.

Searching web page text

When you're perusing a page on the web, it's not unusual to be looking for specific information. In those situations, rather than reading through the entire page to find the info you seek, it would be a lot easier to search for the data. You can easily do this in the desktop version of Safari or any other computer browser, but, at first glance, the Safari app doesn't seem to have a Find feature anywhere. It's there all right, but you need to know where to look. Follow these steps to locate Find:

1. **Use the Safari app to navigate to the web page that contains the information you seek.**
2. **Use the address/search box to type the search text you want to use.** Safari displays the usual web page matches, but it also displays an On This Page section that tells you the number of times your searched text appears on the web page.
3. **Tap Find search (where search is the search text you entered).** Safari highlights the first instance of the search term, as shown in Figure 5.14.
4. **Tap the right-pointing arrow to cycle through the instances of the search term that appear on the page.** Note that you can also cycle backward through the results by tapping the left-pointing arrow. Also, when you tap the right-pointing arrow after the last result appears, Safari returns you to the first result.
5. **When you're finished with the search, tap Done.**

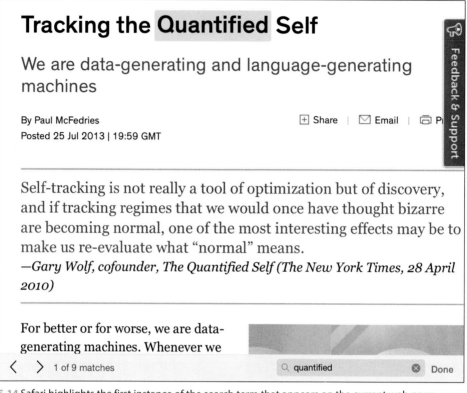

Tracking the Quantified Self

We are data-generating and language-generating machines

By Paul McFedries
Posted 25 Jul 2013 | 19:59 GMT

⊞ Share | ✉ Email | 🖶 Pr

Self-tracking is not really a tool of optimization but of discovery, and if tracking regimes that we would once have thought bizarre are becoming normal, one of the most interesting effects may be to make us re-evaluate what "normal" means.
—*Gary Wolf, cofounder, The Quantified Self (The New York Times, 28 April 2010)*

For better or for worse, we are data-generating machines. Whenever we

< > 1 of 9 matches   🔍 quantified   ⊗ Done

5.14 Safari highlights the first instance of the search term that appears on the current web page.

Searching the web with Siri voice commands

You can use Safari to type search queries either directly into the Search box or by navigating to a search engine site. However, with your iPad or iPad mini typing suddenly seems like such a quaint pastime thanks to the voice recognition prowess of the Siri app. So why type a search query when you can just tell Siri what you're looking for?

Launch Siri by tapping and holding the Home button (or pressing and holding the Mic button on a pair of Apple headphones, or the equivalent button on a Bluetooth headset). The following are some general tips for web searching with Siri:

- **Searching the entire web.** Say "Search the web for *topic*," where *topic* is your search criteria.

- **Searching Wikipedia.** Say "Search Wikipedia for *topic*," where topic is the subject you want to look up.

- **Searching with a particular search engine.** In this case, say "*Engine topic*," where *Engine* is the name of the search engine, such as Google or Bing, and *topic* is your search criteria.

Siri also understands commands related to searching for businesses and restaurants through its partnership with Yelp. To look for businesses and restaurants using Siri, the general syntax to use is the following (although, as usual with Siri, you don't have to be too rigid about this): Find (or Look for) *something somewhere.*

Here, the *something* part can be the name of a business (such as "Starbucks"), a type of business (such as "gas station"), a type of restaurant (such as "Thai restaurants"), or a generic product (such as "coffee"). The *somewhere* part can be something relative to your current location (such as "around here" or "near me" or "within walking distance") or a specific location (such as "in Indianapolis" or "in Broad Ripple"). Review the following examples:

- "Find a gas station within walking distance."
- "Look for pizza restaurants in Indianapolis."
- "Find coffee around here."
- "Look for a grocery store near me."

Note, too, that if you add a qualifier such as "good" or "best" before the *what* portion of the command, Siri returns the results organized by their Yelp rating. Siri also partners with Wolfram Alpha, the "computational knowledge engine," so you can search for specific tidbits of information, such as "What was the Best Picture of 1959?" or "What is the population of Scotland?"

Note   Wolfram Alpha is a massive knowledge base that allows you to query information on dozens of topics. To learn the kinds of data it can provide (and, therefore, the kinds of questions you can ask Siri), see the Examples by Topic page at www.wolframalpha.com/examples/.

Sharing a link via AirDrop

Here's an all-too-common scenario in this digital, mobile age: You're out with friends or colleagues, you look up something on your iPad or iPad mini, and you find a page that one of your peeps wants to check out. How do you get the page address from your tablet to her device? In the past you had to give the address verbally or send it in an e-mail or text message. Now, however, iOS 7 introduces AirDrop, a Bluetooth service that lets two nearby devices — specifically, a fourth-generation iPad or later; an iPad mini; an iPhone 5s, 5c or 5; or a fifth-generation iPod touch or later — to exchange a link wirelessly. Here's how it works:

1. **Use Safari to navigate to the web page you want to share.**

2. **Tap the Actions icon.** The AirDrop section shows an icon for each nearby device, as shown in Figure 5.15.

3. **Tap the icon for the person with whom you want to share the link.** The other person sees a dialog similar to the one shown in Figure 5.16. When she taps Accept, her version of Safari loads and displays the page. Pie-easy!

5.15 When you tap Actions, the AirDrop section shows an icon for each nearby AirDrop-friendly device.

5.16 When you share a link via AirDrop, the other person taps Accept to load the page into the browser.

Note

If you don't see an icon for the other person's device in the AirDrop section, it's probably because AirDrop is set to Contacts Only, which means it connects only with people in your Contacts list. Swipe up from the bottom of the screen to display the Control Center, tap AirDrop, and then tap Everyone.

How Do I Make the Most of E-mail?

As more people start texting, tweeting, and Skyping, the more old-fashioned e-mail seems. Yes, reading and composing e-mail is dishwater dull, but do you know what else it is? It's *universal*. Almost everyone who's online has an e-mail account, and it remains the best way to get in touch and exchange information (at least digitally). Your iPad or iPad mini comes with a decent e-mail app that's easy to use, but there are still plenty of tricks and techniques you should know to help you get the most out of Mail on your tablet.

Managing Your E-mail Accounts

The Mail app is a nice e-mail program that makes the most of the two iPad or iPad mini orientations. In portrait mode, you see a big version of the current message, complete with embedded photos and other media. In landscape mode, you get a two-pane view with your Inbox messages in one pane and the current message in the other. Landscape mode is great for composing messages because you get the larger keyboard and a nice, big compose window.

The Mail app also has a few features and settings that make it ideal for doing e-mail away from your desk. First, however, you have to set up your tablet with one or more e-mail accounts.

Syncing your e-mail accounts

The Mail app is most useful when it's set up to use an e-mail account that you also use on your computer. That way, when you're on the road or out on the town, you can check your messages and rest assured that you won't miss anything important (or even anything unimportant, for that matter). The easiest way to do this is to sync an existing e-mail account between your computer and your tablet. If you already have an existing account up and running — whether it's a Mail account on your Mac, or an Outlook or Windows Mail account on your PC (not, however, the Windows 8 Mail app or Windows Live Mail, which aren't supported by iTunes) — you can convince iTunes to gather all of the account details and pass them along to your tablet.

Note

The version of iTunes that comes with OS X Mavericks does *not* support syncing e-mail accounts directly between iTunes and an iPad or iPad mini. Instead, you must configure your Mac to sync this data to your iCloud account, and then configure your tablet to have this data synced from your iCloud account. See Chapter 4 for the details.

Follow these steps to sync e-mail accounts:

1. **Connect your tablet to your computer.**

2. **In the iTunes Devices list, click the iPad or iPad mini.**

3. **Click the Info tab.** Remember that you won't see the Info tab if you're running OS X Mavericks.

4. **In the Mail Accounts section, use one of the following techniques:**

• **Mac.** Select the Sync Mail Accounts check box, and then select the check box beside each account that you want to add to the tablet, as shown in Figure 6.1.

• **PC.** Select the Sync Mail Accounts From check box, select your e-mail program from the drop-down list, and select the check box beside each account that you want to add to your tablet.

Caution For some accounts, you need to be careful that your tablet doesn't delete incoming messages from the server before you have a chance to download them to your computer. I show you how to set that up later in this chapter.

Paul's iPad ⏏   Summary   Info   Apps

☑ **Sync Mail Accounts**

Selected Mail accounts
☑ iCloud
☑ POP

6.1 Make sure that you select the Sync Mail Accounts check box and at least one account in the list.

5. **Click Apply.** You may see a message asking if AppleMobileSync can be allowed access to your keychain (your Mac's master password list).

6. **If you see that message, click Allow.** iTunes begins syncing the selected e-mail account settings from your computer to your tablet.

Note Remember that your iPad or iPad mini syncs only your e-mail account *settings* (username, password, mail servers, and so on), not your e-mail account *messages*.

Adding an account manually

Syncing e-mail accounts as I describe in the previous section is useful when you want to do the e-mail thing on multiple devices. However, you may also prefer to have an e-mail account that's tablet-only. For example, if you join an iPad or iPad mini mailing list, you may prefer to have those messages sent only to your device. That's a darn good idea, but it means that you have to set up the account on the iPad or iPad mini itself, which requires a fair amount of tapping.

Note
You may think you can avoid the often excessive tapping required to enter a new e-mail account into your iPad or iPad mini by creating the account in your computer's e-mail program and then syncing with your tablet. That works, but there's a hitch: you *must* leave the new account in your e-mail program. If you delete or disable it, iTunes deletes the account from the iPad or iPad mini.

How you create an account on your tablet with the sweat of your own brow depends on the type of account that you have. iOS recognizes the following six e-mail services:

- **iCloud.** This is the Apple web-based e-mail service (that also comes with applications for calendars, contacts, storage, and more).

- **Microsoft Exchange.** This is an account on an Exchange server, which is common in large organizations. Exchange uses a central server to store messages, and you usually work with your messages on the server, not your tablet. However, one of the great features in iOS is support for Exchange ActiveSync, which automatically keeps your tablet and your account on the server synchronized. I discuss the ActiveSync settings later in this chapter.

- **Google Gmail.** This is a web-based e-mail service run by Google.

- **Yahoo!.** This is a web-based e-mail service run by Yahoo!.

- **AOL.** This is a web-based e-mail service run by AOL.

- **Outlook.com.** This is a web-based e-mail service run by Microsoft.

iOS knows how to connect to these services, so to set up any of these e-mail accounts, you only need to know the address and the account password. Otherwise, the Mail app supports the following e-mail account types:

- **POP (Post Office Protocol).** This is the most popular type of account. Its main characteristic for your purposes is that incoming messages are stored only temporarily on the provider's mail server. When you connect to the server, the messages are downloaded to your tablet and removed from the server. In other words, your messages (including copies of messages you send) are stored locally on your iPad or iPad mini. The advantage here is that you don't need to be online to read your e-mail — after it's downloaded to your tablet, you can read it (or delete it) at your leisure.

- **IMAP (Internet Message Access Protocol).** This type of account is most often used with web-based e-mail services. It's the opposite of POP (sort of) because all of your incoming messages, as well as copies of messages you send, remain on the server. In this case, when Mail works with an IMAP account, it connects to the server and works with the messages on the server itself, not on your tablet (although it *looks* like you're working with the messages locally). The advantage here is that you can access the messages from multiple devices and multiple locations, but you must be connected to the Internet to work with your messages.

Your network administrator or your e-mail service provider can let you know what type of e-mail account you have. Your administrator or provider can also give you the information you need to set up the account. This includes your e-mail address, the username and password you use to check for new messages, any security information you need to specify to send messages, the host name of the incoming mail server (typically something like mail.*provider*.com or pop.*provider*.com, where *provider*.com is the domain name of the provider), and the host name of the outgoing mail server (typically either mail.*provider*.com or smtp.*provider*.com). With your account information clutched in your fist, follow these steps to forge a brand-new account on your iPad or iPad mini:

1. **On the Home screen, tap Settings to open the Settings app.**

2. **Tap Mail, Contacts, Calendars.** The Mail, Contacts, Calendars screen appears.

3. **Tap Add Account.** This opens the Add Account screen, as shown in Figure 6.2.

4. **You can proceed in one of the following ways:**

    - **If you're adding an account for iCloud, Microsoft Exchange, Gmail, Yahoo!, AOL, or Outlook.com, tap the corresponding logo.** In the account information screen that appears, type your name, e-mail address, password, and an account description. Tap Save and you're done!

    - **If you're adding another account type, tap Other and continue with step 5.**

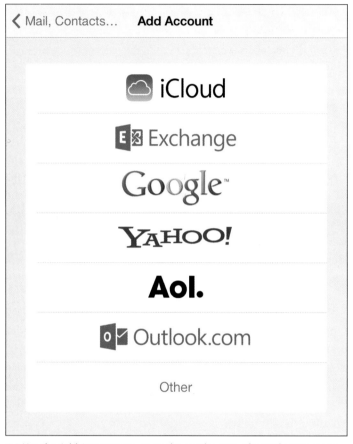

6.2 Use the Add Account screen to choose the type of e-mail account you
want to add.

5. **Tap Add Mail Account to open the New Account screen.**

6. **Use the Name, Email, Password, and Description text boxes to type the corresponding account information, and then tap Next.**

7. **Tap the type of account you're adding: IMAP or POP.**

8. **In the Incoming Mail Server section, use the Host Name text box to type the host name of your provider's incoming mail server, as well as your username and password.**

9. **In the Outgoing Mail Server section, use the Host Name text box to type the host name of your provider's outgoing (SMTP) mail server.** If your provider requires a username and password to send messages, type those as well.

10. **Tap Save.** Your iPad or iPad mini verifies the account info (which might take a minute or three), and then returns you to the Mail settings screen with the account added to the Accounts list.

Specifying the default account

If you've added two or more e-mail accounts to your tablet, Mail specifies one of them as the default account. This means that Mail uses this account when you send a new message, when you reply to a message, and when you forward a message. The default account is usually the first account that you add to your iPad or iPad mini. However, you can change this by following these steps:

1. **On the Home screen, tap Settings to launch the Settings app.**

2. **Tap Mail, Contacts, Calendars.** The Settings app displays the Mail, Contacts, Calendars screen.

3. **In the Mail section of the screen, tap Default Account.** This opens the Default Account screen, which displays a list of your accounts. The current default account is shown with a check mark beside it.

4. **Tap the account that you want to use as the default.** The Settings app places a check mark beside it.

Temporarily disabling an account

The Mail app checks for new messages at a regular interval (I show you how to configure this interval a bit later in this chapter). If you have several accounts configured in Mail, this incessant checking can put quite a strain on your tablet battery. To ease up on the juice, follow these steps to temporarily disable an account and prevent Mail from checking it for new messages:

1. **On the Home screen, tap Settings to open the Settings app.**

2. **Tap Mail, Contacts, Calendars to see the Mail settings.**

3. **Tap the account you want to disable.** The Settings app displays the account settings.

4. **Depending on the type of account, you can use one of the following techniques to temporarily disable it:**

   - **iCloud, Exchange, Gmail, Yahoo!, AOL, or Outlook.com.** Tap the Mail switch to Off. If the account syncs other types of data, such as contacts and calendars, you can also turn those switches off.

   - **POP or IMAP.** Tap the Account switch to Off, as shown in Figure 6.3.

5. **Tap Done to return to the Mail settings screen.**

When you're ready to work with the account again, repeat these steps to turn the Mail or Account switch back to On.

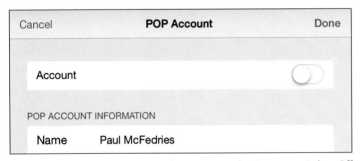

6.3 To temporarily disable an e-mail account, tap the Account switch to Off in the account settings screen.

Deleting an account

If an e-mail account has grown tiresome and boring (or you just don't use it anymore), you should delete it to save storage space, speed up sync times, and save battery power. Follow these steps to delete an account:

1. **On the Home screen, tap Settings to get the Settings app on-screen.**

2. **Tap Mail, Contacts, Calendars to get to the Mail settings.**

3. **Tap the account you want to delete.** This opens the account settings.

4. **Tap Delete Account.** The Settings app asks you to confirm.

5. **Tap Delete.** The Settings app returns you to the Mail settings screen and the account no longer graces the Accounts list.

Switching to another account

When you open the Mail app (by tapping Mail in the Dock), you usually see the Inbox folder of your default account. If you have multiple accounts set up on your iPad or iPad mini, and you want to see what's going on with a different one, follow these steps to make the switch:

1. **On the Home screen, tap Mail to open the Mail app.**

2. **In landscape mode, tap the mailbox button in the top-left corner of the screen (but below the status bar).** If you're in portrait mode, tap Inbox and then tap the mailbox button. The Mail app displays the Mailboxes screen, as shown in Figure 6.4.

3. **Tap the account with which you want to work based on one of the following criteria:**

   - **If you only want to see the account's Inbox folder, tap the account name in the Inboxes section of the Mailboxes screen.**

Mailboxes	Edit
✉ All Inboxes	3 >
✉ iCloud	1 >
✉ Exchange	>
✉ POP Account	2 >
★ VIP	>
ACCOUNTS	
☁ iCloud	1 >
E Exchange	>
@ POP Account	2 >

6.4 Use the Mailboxes screen to choose the e-mail Inbox or account to which you want to switch.

   - **If you want to see all of the account's available folders, tap the account name in the Accounts section of the Mailboxes screen.** Mail displays a list of the account's folders, and you then tap the folder with which you want to work.

Genius

In iOS 7 Mail, you can customize the Mailboxes screen by tapping Edit. You can then use the check boxes that appear on the left side of the screen to toggle specific mailboxes on and off (including general mailboxes such as Unread, which displays only the messages you haven't yet read, and Attachments, which displays only messages that have files attached. You can also change the order of the mailboxes and even add your own mailboxes.

123

Configuring E-mail Accounts

Setting up an e-mail account on your iPad or iPad mini is one thing, but making it do useful things (or sometimes, anything at all) is quite another. The next few sections take you through a few useful settings that help you get more out of e-mail and troubleshoot e-mail problems.

Leaving messages on the server

In today's increasingly mobile world, it's not unusual to find you need to check the same e-mail account from multiple devices. For example, while commuting or traveling, you may want to check your business account using not only your work computer, but also your home computer or your tablet.

If you need to check e-mail on multiple devices, you can take advantage of how POP e-mail messages are delivered over the Internet. When someone sends you a message, it doesn't come directly to your computer. Instead, it goes to the server that your Internet service provider (or your company) has set up to handle incoming messages. When you ask your e-mail client to check for new messages, it communicates with the POP server to see if any messages are waiting in your account. If so, the client downloads those messages to your computer and then instructs the server to delete the copies of the messages that are stored on the server.

The trick, then, is to configure the e-mail program so that it leaves a copy of the messages on the POP server after you download them. This way, the messages are still available when you check messages using another device. Fortunately, the intuitive folks who designed the Mail app must have understood this because the program automatically sets up POP accounts to do just that. Specifically, after you download any messages from the POP server to your iPad or iPad mini, the Mail app leaves the messages on the server.

The following is a good overall strategy to ensure that you can download messages on all of your devices, while preventing messages from piling up on the server:

- **Let your main computer be the computer that controls deleting the messages from the server.** In Mac OS X, the default Mail setting is to delete messages from the server after one week and that's fine.

- **Set all of your other devices — particularly your iPad or iPad mini — not to delete messages from the server.**

To leave messages on the server in the desktop version of Microsoft Outlook, choose File ➪ Account Settings, click the account, click Change, and then click More Settings. Click the Advanced tab, and then select the Leave a Copy of Messages on the Server check box. In Outlook Express or Windows Live Mail, choose File ➪ Options ➪ Email Accounts, click your e-mail account, and then click Properties. Click the Advanced tab, and then select the Leave a Copy of Messages on Server check box.

It's a good idea to check your POP accounts to ensure they're not deleting messages from the server. To do that (or to use a different setting, such as deleting messages after a week or when you delete them from your Inbox), follow these steps:

1. **On the Home screen, tap Settings to open the Settings app.**

2. **Tap Mail, Contacts, Calendars.** The Settings app opens the Mail, Contacts, Calendars settings screen.

3. **Tap the POP account with which you want to work.** The account settings dialog appears.

4. **Tap Advanced.** The Settings app displays the Advanced dialog.

5. **Tap Remove.** The Remove dialog appears.

6. **Tap Never.** If you prefer that your tablet delete messages from the server after a set period of time, tap After one day, After one week, or After one month.

Using a different server port

For security reasons, some Internet service providers (ISPs) insist on routing all of their customers' outgoing mail through their Simple Mail Transfer Protocol (SMTP) servers. This usually isn't a big deal if you're using an e-mail account maintained by the ISP, but it can lead to the following problems if you're using an account provided by a third party (such as your website host):

- Your ISP might block messages sent using the third-party account because it thinks you're trying to relay the message through the ISP server (a technique often used by spammers).

- You might incur extra charges if your ISP allows only a certain amount of SMTP bandwidth per month or a certain number of sent messages, whereas the third-party account offers higher limits or no restrictions at all.

- You might have performance problems, such as the ISP server taking much longer to route messages than the third-party host.

You may think that you can solve the problem by specifying the third-party host's SMTP server in the account settings. However, this usually doesn't work because outgoing e-mail is sent by default through port 25. When you use this port, the outgoing mail goes through the ISP's SMTP server. To work around this problem, many third-party hosts offer access to their SMTP servers via a port other than the standard port 25. For example, the iCloud SMTP server (smtp.icloud.com) also accepts connections on ports 465 and 587.

Follow these steps to configure an e-mail account to use a nonstandard SMTP port:

1. **On the Home screen, tap Settings to launch the Settings app.**

2. **Tap Mail, Contacts, Calendars.** The Mail, Contacts, Calendars settings screen appears.

3. **Tap the POP account with which you want to work.** The account settings dialog appears.

4. **Tap SMTP.** The Settings app displays the SMTP dialog.

5. **In the Primary Server section, tap the name of your server.** The Settings app displays the server settings.

6. **Tap Server Port.** The Settings app displays a keypad so that you can type the port number, as shown in Figure 6.5.

6.5 Tap Server Port to type the new port number for outgoing messages.

Configuring authentication for outgoing mail

Because spam is such a big problem these days, many ISPs now require SMTP authentication for outgoing mail. This means that you must log on to the SMTP server to confirm that you're the person sending the mail (as opposed to some spammer spoofing your address). If your ISP requires authentication on outgoing messages, you need to configure your e-mail account to provide the proper credentials.

If you're not sure about any of this, check with your ISP. If that doesn't work out, by far the most common type of authentication is to specify a username and password (this happens behind the scenes when you send messages). Follow these steps to configure your iPad or iPad mini e-mail account with this kind of authentication:

1. **On the Home screen, tap Settings to get the Settings app on-screen.**

2. **Tap Mail, Contacts, Calendars.** The Mail, Contacts, Calendars settings screen appears.

3. **Tap the POP account with which you want to work.** The account settings dialog appears.

4. **Tap SMTP.** The Settings app displays the SMTP dialog.

5. **In the Primary Server section, tap the server name.** The Settings app displays the server settings.

6. **In the Outgoing Mail Server section, tap Authentication.** The Settings app displays the Authentication dialog.

7. **Tap Password.**

8. **Tap the server address to return to the server settings screen.**

9. **In the Outgoing Mail Server section, type your account username in the User Name box and the account password in the Password box.**

10. **Tap Done.**

Configuring E-mail Messages

The rest of this chapter takes you through a few useful and timesaving techniques for handling e-mail messages on your iPad or iPad mini.

Creating e-mail VIPs

Somebody once said that the world doesn't have an information overload problem, it has a filter problem. In other words, the tsunami of information that comes your way every day wouldn't be such a headache if you had the tools to separate the important from the trivial, the useful from the pointless, the steak from the sizzle.

iOS Mail offers one such tool: the VIP List. This is a simple list of people that you designate as important. From an e-mail perspective, "important" means these are people whose messages you want to read right away because they always contain information that's useful or interesting to you. To find messages from these people, you normally have to wade through the sea of messages in your various account inboxes (or the All Inboxes mailbox, which combines all your accounts). With the VIP List, however, Mail sets up a special VIP inbox that only shows messages from your VIPs, so they're easily located. Additionally, the VIP feature is part of the Notification Center, so you see a special banner alert whenever you receive a message from one of your VIPs. Take that, information overload!

Follow these steps to set up your VIP List:

1. **On the Home screen, tap Mail to open the Mail app.**

2. **If you're currently viewing an inbox, tap Mailboxes to return to the Mailboxes screen.**

3. **Tap VIP.** Mail displays the VIP List screen.

4. **Tap Add VIP.** Mail opens the All Contacts screen.

5. **Tap the contact you want to designate as a VIP.** Mail adds the contact to the VIP List.

6. **Repeat steps 4 and 5 until you've added all of your VIPs.** Figure 6.6 shows the VIP List with a few names added. Note that if you need to delete a VIP, you can tap Edit, and then tap the red Delete button beside the contact.

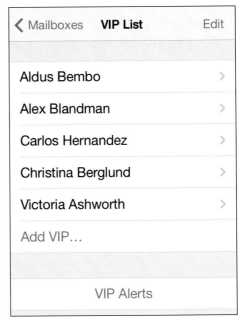

6.6 Use the VIP List to filter your incoming mail and display messages from important people in the VIP mailbox.

Note

Formatting an e-mail

We're all used to rich text e-mail messages by now, where formatting such as bold and italics is used to add pizzazz or emphasis to our e-musings. iOS Mail gives you a limited set of formatting options for text: bold, italics, and underline. It's not much, but it's a start, so follow these steps to format text in the Mail app:

1. **In your e-mail message, tap within the word or phrase you want to format.** The Mail app displays the cursor.

2. **Tap the cursor.** Mail displays a set of options.

3. **Tap Select.** Mail selects the word closest to the cursor.

4. **If needed, drag the selection handles to select the entire phrase you want to format.** Mail displays a set of options for the selected text.

5. **Tap the arrow on the right side of the options.** Mail displays more options.

6. **Tap the BIU button.** Mail displays the Bold, Italics, and Underline buttons, as shown in Figure 6.7.

7. **Tap the formatting you want to apply.** Mail leaves the formatting options on the screen, so feel free to apply multiple formats if needed.

8. **Tap another part of the screen to hide the formatting options.**

Cancel	**Notes from (the London) Underground**	Send

To: Victoria Ashworth

Cc/Bcc, From: paulm@mcfedries.com

Subject: Notes from (the London) Underground

Hi Vicky,

| Bold | Italics | Underline |

Let me begin by counting the ways that London is amazing.

6.7 You can now format e-mail text.

Genius

If you're composing a message on your computer and decide to work on it later, your mail program stores it as a draft that you can reopen. The Mail app doesn't *appear* to have this option, but it does. In the message window, tap Cancel (counterintuitive, I know!), and then tap Save Draft. When you're ready to resume editing, open the account in the Mailboxes screen, tap Drafts, and then tap your saved message.

E-mailing a link

The web is all about finding content that's interesting, educational, and, of course, fun. If you stumble across a page that meets one or more of these criteria, the only sensible thing to do is share your good fortune with someone else, right? So, how do you do that? Some pages are kind enough to include an E-mail This Page link (or something similar), but you can't count on having one of those around. Instead, the usual method is to copy the page address, switch to your e-mail program, paste the address into the message, choose a recipient, and then send it.

And, yes, with the iOS copy-and-paste feature, you can do all that, but boy, it sure seems like a ton of work. So are you stuck using this unwieldy method? Not a chance (you probably knew that). Your iPad or iPad mini includes a great little feature that enables you to plop the address of the current Safari page into an e-mail message with just a couple of taps. You then ship out the message and make the world a better place.

Follow these steps to quickly add a link to an e-mail:

1. **Use Safari to navigate to the page you want to share.**

2. **Tap the Actions button (the one with the arrow) in the status bar.** Safari displays a dialog with several options.

3. **Tap Mail.** This opens a new e-mail message. As you can see in Figure 6.8, the new message already includes the page title as the Subject and the page address in the message body.

4. **Choose a recipient for the message.**

5. **Edit the message text as you see fit.**

6. **Tap Send.** Mail fires off the message and returns you to Safari.

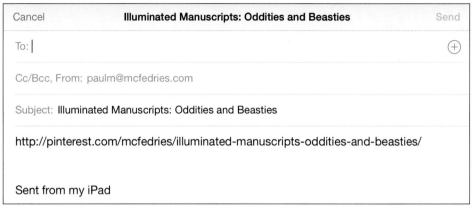

Cancel	**Illuminated Manuscripts: Oddities and Beasties**	Send

To: |

Cc/Bcc, From: paulm@mcfedries.com

Subject: Illuminated Manuscripts: Oddities and Beasties

http://pinterest.com/mcfedries/illuminated-manuscripts-oddities-and-beasties/

Sent from my iPad

6.8 Your iPad or iPad mini can create a new e-mail message with a web page's title and address already inserted.

Creating iCloud message folders

In your e-mail program on your computer, you've no doubt created lots of folders to hold different types of messages that you want or need to save: projects, people, mailing list gems, and so on. This is a great way to reduce Inbox clutter and organize the e-mail portion of your life.

Of course, these days the e-mail portion of your life extends beyond your computer and probably includes a lot of time spent on your iPad or iPad mini. Wouldn't it be great to have that same folder convenience and organization on your favorite tablet? Happily, you can. If you have an iCloud account, any folders (technically, Apple calls them *mailboxes*) that you create on your iCloud account — either on your computer or on the iCloud site — are automatically mirrored on the Mail app.

Even better, you can create new iCloud message folders right from the comfort of your tablet. Follow these steps to create a new folder:

1. **On the Home screen, tap Mail to open the Mail app.**

2. **In landscape mode, tap the mailbox button in the top-left corner of the screen (but below the status bar).** If you're in portrait mode, tap Inbox, and then tap the mailbox button. The Mail app displays the Mailboxes screen.

3. **In the Accounts section, tap your iCloud account.** Mail displays the iCloud folders list.

131

4. **Tap Edit.** Mail opens the iCloud folders list for editing.

5. **Tap New Mailbox.** The Edit Mailbox screen appears.

6. **Type a name for the new folder.**

7. **Tap the Mailbox Location, and then tap the folder in which you want to store your new folder.**

8. **Tap Save.** Mail adds the folder, and iCloud propagates the change to the cloud.

9. **Tap Done.**

Note

To move a message to your new folder, display the iCloud Inbox folder, tap the message, tap the Move button (the folder icon), and then tap the new folder.

Creating a custom signature

E-mail signatures can range from the simple — a signoff such as "Cheers," or "All the best," followed by the sender's name — to baroque masterpieces filled with contact information, snappy quotations, or even some text-based artwork! The Mail app takes the simple route by adding the following signature to all of your outgoing messages (new messages, replies, and forwards):

```
Sent from my iPad
```

I like this signature because it's short, simple, and I, *of course*, want my recipients to know that I'm using my iPad. If the default signature doesn't rock your world, you can follow these steps to create one that does:

1. **On the Home screen, tap Settings to open the Settings app.**

2. **Tap Mail, Contacts, Calendars.** You see the Mail, Contacts, Calendars settings screen.

3. **In the Mail section, tap Signature.** The Signature screen appears.

4. **If you have multiple accounts and you prefer to create a unique signature for each one, tap Per Account and then tap the account you want to work with.** If, instead, you leave the All Accounts item selected, Mail will use the same signature for all your accounts.

5. **Type the signature you want to use.** Mail saves your new signature as you type.

Disabling remote images

Lots of messages nowadays come not just as plain text, but also with fonts, colors, images, and other flourishes. This fancy formatting, called either *rich text* or *HTML*, makes for a more pleasant e-mail experience, particularly with images in messages. Who doesn't like a bit of eye candy to brighten his day?

Note

HTML stands for Hypertext Markup Language and is a set of codes that folks use to put together web pages.

Unfortunately, getting images in your e-mail messages can sometimes be problematic for the following reasons:

- **A cellular connection may cause trouble.** It may take a long time to load the images or, if your data plan has an upper limit, you may not want a bunch of e-mail images taking a big bite out of that limit.

- **Not all e-mail images are benign.** A web bug is an image that resides on a remote server and is added to an HTML-formatted e-mail message by referencing an address on the remote server. When you open the message, Mail uses the address to download the image for display within the message. That sounds harmless enough, but if the message is junk e-mail, it's likely that the address also contains either your e-mail address or a code that points to it. When the remote server gets a request to load the image, it knows not only that you've opened the message, but also that your e-mail address is legitimate. So, not surprisingly, spammers use web bugs all of the time because, for them, valid e-mail addresses are like gold.

The Mail app displays remote images by default. To disable remote images, follow these steps:

1. **On the Home screen, tap Settings.** Your iPad or iPad mini opens the Settings app.

2. **Tap Mail, Contacts, Calendars.** You see the Mail, Contacts, Calendars settings screen.

3. **In the Mail section, tap the Load Remote Images switch to the Off position.** Mail saves the setting and hides remote images in your e-mail messages.

Note that Mail now *hides* remote images, which means that the images are still available if you want to display them when you have a fast connection or when you're dealing with a message that you know is benign. In Mail, display the message, scroll to the bottom, and then tap Load All Images.

Preventing Mail from organizing messages by thread

The Mail app groups your messages by thread, which means the original message and all of the replies you receive are grouped together in the account Inbox folder. This is usually remarkably handy, because it means you don't have to scroll through a million messages to locate the reply you want to read.

Mail indicates a thread by displaying a double arrow (>>) instead of a single arrow (>) to the right of the first message in the thread, as shown in Figure 6.9. Tap the message to see a list of the messages in the thread, and then tap the one that you want to read.

Organizing messages by thread is not always convenient. As you view and scroll through your messages (by tapping the Next (downward-pointing arrow) and Previous (upward-pointing arrow) buttons), Mail jumps into a thread when you come to one. You then scroll through each message in the thread, which can be a real hassle if there are a large number of replies.

If you find that threads are more of a hassle than they're worth, you can follow these steps to configure Mail not to organize messages by thread:

1. **On the Home screen, tap Settings.**
2. **Tap Mail, Contacts, Calendars.** You see the Mail, Contacts, Calendars settings screen.
3. **Tap the Organize By Thread switch to the Off position.** The Settings app saves the setting and no longer organizes your images by thread.

Marking all messages as read

If veteran iOS users had a complaint about the Mail app, it would be how hard it was to manage Inboxes. For example, it was tedious to mark messages as read in a second Mail app. Say you'd already read all your messages on your computer: you obviously wouldn't need to reread them on your iPad or iPad mini, but the only way to mark them as having been read was to open each one. No big whoop for five or ten messages, but a very big whoop indeed for dozens, or even hundreds, of messages.

Happily, that annoyance can be crossed off the iOS gripe list because the Mail app now gives you a simple way to mark everything as read in one (more of less) fell swoop:

1. **In the Mail app, open the mailbox you want to manage.**

2. **Tap Edit.** Mail puts the mailbox into edit mode.

3. **Tap Mark All.** Mail asks what you want marked.

4. **Tap Mark as Read.** Mail marks every message in the mailbox as having been read. Sweet!

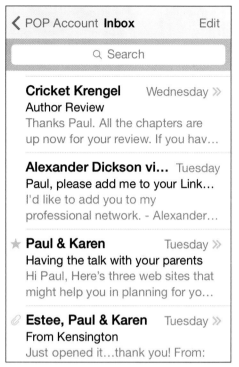

6.9 A double arrow (>>) on the right side of a message tells you there are multiple messages in the thread.

Configuring the Exchange ActiveSync settings

If you have an account on a Microsoft Exchange Server network, and that server has deployed Exchange ActiveSync, you're all set to have your tablet and Exchange account synchronized automatically. That's because ActiveSync supports wireless push technology, which means that if anything changes on your Exchange server account, that change is immediately synced with your tablet. This occurs with all of the following:

- **E-mail.** If you receive a new message on your Exchange account, ActiveSync immediately displays it in the Mail app.

- **Contacts.** If someone at work adds or edits data in the server address book, those changes are immediately synced to your Contacts list.

- **Calendar.** If someone at work adds or edits an appointment in your calendar, or requests a meeting with you, that data is immediately synced with the Calendar application.

- **Reminder.** If someone at work adds or edits a reminder, that data is immediately synced with the Reminders app.

- **Notes.** If you or a colleague adds or edits a note, that change is immediately synced with the Notes app.

ActiveSync works both ways, too. If you send e-mail messages, add contacts or appointments, or accept meeting requests, your server account is immediately updated with the changes. And all this data whizzing back and forth is safe, because it's sent over a secure connection.

Your iPad or iPad mini also gives you a few options for controlling ActiveSync. The following steps show you how to set them up:

1. **On the Home screen, tap Settings to open the Settings app.**

2. **Tap Mail, Contacts, Calendars to open the Mail, Contacts, Calendars settings.**

3. **Tap your Exchange account.** The Exchange account settings screen appears, as shown in Figure 6.10.

4. **To sync your Exchange e-mail account, tap the Mail On/Off switch to the On position.**

5. **To sync your Exchange address book, calendars, reminders, and Notes, tap the Contacts, Calendars, Reminders, and Notes On/Off switches, respectively, to the On position.** In each case, if the Settings app asks what you want to do with the local content on your device, tap Keep on My iPad.

6. **To control the amount of time that gets synced on your e-mail account, tap Mail Days to Sync, and then tap the number of days, weeks, or months you want to sync.**

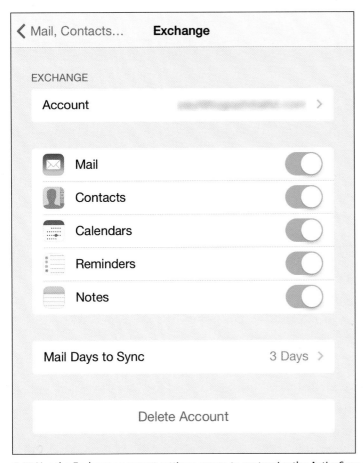

6.10 Use the Exchange account settings screen to customize the ActiveSync support.

Controlling e-mail with Siri voice commands

You can use the Siri voice recognition app to check, compose, send, and reply to messages, all with simple voice commands. Tap and hold the Home button (or press and hold the Mic button of the iPhone headphones, or the equivalent button on a Bluetooth headset) until Siri appears. To check for new e-mail messages on your iCloud account, you need only say "Check e-mail" (or just "Check mail"). You can also view a list of the following iCloud messages:

- **Displaying unread messages.** Say "Show new e-mail."
- **Displaying messages where the Subject line contains a specified topic.** Say "Show e-mail about *topic*," where *topic* is the topic you want to view.
- **Displaying messages from a particular person.** Say "Show e-mail from *name*," where *name* is the name of the sender.

To start a new e-mail message, Siri gives you the following options:

- **Creating a new message addressed to a particular person.** Say "E-mail *name*," where *name* is the name of the recipient. This name can be a name from your Contacts list, or someone with a defined relationship, such as "Mom" or "my brother."
- **Creating a new message with a particular subject line.** Say "E-mail *name* about *subject*," where *name* defines the recipient and *subject* is the Subject line text.
- **Creating a new message with a particular body.** Say "E-mail *name* and say *text*," where *name* is the recipient, and *text* is the message body text.

In each case, Siri creates the new message, displays it, and then asks if you want to send it. If you do, you can either say "Send" or tap the Send button. If you have a message displayed, you can send back a response by saying "Reply." If you want to add some text to the response, say "Reply *text*," where *text* is your response.

You can also use Siri within Mail to dictate a message. Dictation supports American English, British English, Australian English, French, German, and Japanese. When you tap inside the body of a new message, the keyboard that appears shows a Mic button beside the spacebar. Tap it, and then start dictating. The following are some tips about using Dictation:

- For punctuation, you can say the name of the mark you need, such as "comma" (,), "semicolon" (;), "colon" (:), "period" or "full stop" (.), "question mark" (?), "exclamation point" (!), "dash" (-), or "at sign" (@).
- You can enclose text in parentheses by saying "open parenthesis," then the text, and then "close parenthesis."

- To surround text with quotation marks, say "open quote," then the text, and then "close quote."

- To render a word in all uppercase letters, say "all caps," and then say the word.

- To start a new paragraph, say "new line."

- You can have some fun by saying "smiley face" for :-), "wink face" for ;-), or "frown face" for :-(.

When you're finished, pause for a few seconds to let the Dictation feature know that you're done. Dictation then processes your speech and converts it to text within the message window.

How Do I Manage My E-book Library?

Chances are good that, as you read these words, you're holding a physical book in your hands. Physical books are an awesome invention: they're portable and fully showoffable. Books aren't going away anytime soon, but the age of e-books is upon us. The Amazon Kindle lit a fire under the e-book category, but it's clunky and tied to Amazon. The iPhone and iPod touch are actually the most popular eReaders, but they're a bit too small. The iPad and iPad mini fill in these gaps by supporting an open e-book format and having screens that are tailor-made for reading.

Understanding E-book Formats

If there was one reason why e-books took a long time to take off (in the same way that, say, digital music now rules the planet), it would be because the e-book world started out as hopelessly, headachingly confusing. At its worst, at least two dozen (yes, two *dozen*!) e-book formats were available, and new formats jumped on the e-book bandwagon with distressing frequency.

That was bad enough, but it got worse when you considered that some of these formats required a specific eReading device or program. For example, the Kindle e-book format required either the Kindle eReader or the Kindle app. Similarly, the Microsoft LIT format required the Microsoft Reader program. Finally, things turned positively chaotic when you realized that some formats came with built-in restrictions that prevented you from reading e-books on other devices or programs, or sharing e-books with other people.

What the e-book world needed was the simplicity and clarity that comes with having a near-universal e-book format (such as the MP3 format in music). Well, I'm happy to report that one format has emerged from the fray: EPUB. This is a free and open e-book standard created by the International Digital Publishing Forum (IDPF; see www.idpf.org/). EPUB files (which use the .epub extension) are supported by most eReader programs and by most eReader devices (with the Amazon Kindle being the very noticeable exception). EPUB is leading the way, not only because it's free and nonproprietary, but also because it offers the following cool features:

- **Text is resizable, so you can select the size that's most comfortable for you.**

- **The layout and formatting of the text are handled by Cascading Style Sheets (CSS).** This is an open and well-known standard that makes it easy to alter the look of the text, including changing the font.

- **Text is *reflowable*.** When you change the text size or the font, the text wraps naturally on the screen to accommodate the new character sizes (as opposed to some e-book formats that simply zoom in or out of the text).

- **A single e-book can have alternative versions in the same file.**

- **E-books can include high-resolution images right on the page.**

- **Publishers can protect book content by adding digital rights management (DRM) support.** DRM refers to any technology that restricts the usage of content to prevent piracy. Of course, depending on where you fall in the "information wants to be free" spectrum, DRM may not be cool and may not even be considered a feature.

So the first bit of good news is that the iBooks app supports the EPUB format, so all of the features in the previous list are available in the iBooks app.

Note

For the record, I should also mention that you can use the iBooks app to read books in three other formats: plain text, HTML, and PDF.

The next bit of good news is that iBooks' support for EPUB means that a vast universe of public domain books is available to you. On its own, the Books section of Google Play (https://play. google.com/store/books) offers more than a *million* public-domain e-books. Several other excellent EPUB sites exist on the web, and I tell you about them, as well as how to get them onto your iPad or iPad mini, a bit later in this chapter.

By definition, public-domain e-books are DRM-free, and you can use them any way you see fit. However, lots of the EPUB books you find come with DRM restrictions. In the case of iBooks, the DRM scheme of choice is called FairPlay. This is the DRM technology that Apple used on iTunes for many years. Apple phased out DRM on music a while ago, but still uses it for other content, such as movies, TV shows, and audiobooks.

FairPlay means that many of the e-books you download through iBooks face the following restrictions:

- You can access your books on a maximum of five computers, each of which must be authorized with your iTunes Store account info.
- You can read your e-books only on your iPhone, iPad or iPad mini, iPod touch, or a computer that has iTunes installed.

It's crucial to note the following two restrictions that you trip over with DRM-encrusted e-books:

- FairPlay e-books do not work on other eReader devices that support the EPUB format, including the Sony Reader and the Barnes & Noble NOOK.
- EPUB-format books that come wrapped in some other DRM scheme do not work on iPad or iPad mini.

However, remember that DRM is an optional add-on to the EPUB format. Although it's expected that most publishers will bolt FairPlay DRM onto books they sell in the iBookstore, it's not required. So, you should be able to find DRM-free e-books in the iBookstore (and elsewhere).

Note If you have an Amazon Kindle, I'm afraid it uses a proprietary e-book format, so Kindle e-books won't transfer to the iBooks app (or any other eReader). However, Amazon does offer a Kindle app for the iPad and iPad mini that you can use to download and read any Kindle book, even those you purchased earlier.

Syncing E-books

If you've used your computer to grab an e-book from the iBookstore or to add a downloaded e-book to the iTunes library, you probably want to get that book onto your iPad or iPad mini as soon as possible. Similarly, if you've downloaded a few e-books on your tablet, it's a good idea to back them up on your computer.

Syncing via iTunes

You can do both by following these steps to sync e-books between your computer and your tablet:

1. **Connect your iPad or iPad mini to your computer.** iTunes opens and accesses the device. If you added e-books to your tablet, be sure to wait until iTunes syncs them to your computer.

2. **In iTunes, click your iPad or iPad mini in the Devices list.**

3. **Click the Books tab.**

4. **Select the Sync Books check box.**

5. **To sync only some of your books, select the Selected books option.**

6. **In the book list, select the check box beside each book that you want to sync.**

7. **Click Apply.** iTunes syncs the iPad or iPad mini.

Syncing via iCloud

If you purchase an e-book on your iPhone, Mac, or PC, getting it onto your tablet requires a lot of connecting and syncing. This all seems a tad primitive in this modern age. However, if you have an iCloud account, you can configure it to automatically download any new e-book purchases directly to your tablet, without a cable or your computer's iTunes application in sight.

Follow these steps to sync your e-books via iCloud:

1. **On your iPad or iPad mini, tap Settings in the Home screen to launch the Settings app.**

2. **Tap iTunes and App Store.**

3. **If you haven't signed in to the iTunes Store, enter your iCloud username and password, and then tap Sign In.**

4. **Tap the Books switch to On, as shown in Figure 7.1.**

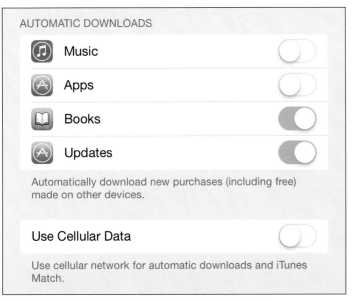

7.1 Tap the Books switch to On to sync e-books via iCloud.

5. **If you have a cellular iPad or iPad mini, and you want iCloud to sync e-books even when you have a cellular-only connection, tap the Use Cellular Data switch to On.**

Now, each time that you purchase an e-book via iTunes on another device, that book is automatically sent to the iBooks library on your tablet, usually within a few seconds.

Managing Your iBooks Library

In this chapter, I concentrate on iBooks, which is the Apple eReader app. However, it's important to stress right off the bat that you're not restricted to using iBooks for reading e-books on your tablet. Tons of great e-book apps are available (I mention a few of them at the end of this chapter), so feel free to use any or all of them in addition to (or even instead of) iBooks.

The iBooks app comes with a virtual wooden bookcase, as shown in Figure 7.2. It's a nice bit of eye candy, for sure, but it's certainly no more than that because the real point is to fill it with your favorite digital reading material. So, your first task is to add a few titles to the bookcase and the next few sections show you how to do just that.

7.2 The iBooks library is designed to mimic a real bookcase.

Note

Unlike the other apps I talk about in this book, iBooks isn't part of the default iOS app collection. Instead, you have to install it (it's free) from the App Store.

Browsing books in the iBookstore

What if you're out and about with your iPad or iPad mini, you have a bit of time to kill, and you decide to start a book? That's no problem, because iBooks has a direct link to the Apple book marketplace, the iBookstore. Your tablet can establish a wireless connection to the iBookstore anywhere that you have Wi-Fi access or a cellular signal (ideally LTE or 3G for faster downloads, assuming that you have a cellular version of the iPad or iPad mini).

You can browse or search for books, read reviews, and purchase any book you want (or grab a title from the large collection of free books). The e-book downloads to your tablet and adds itself to the iBooks bookcase. You can start reading within seconds! To access the iBookstore, display the iBooks library. If you haven't yet loaded the app, tap the iBooks icon to open it. If you're in the iBooks app reading a book, tap the screen to display the controls, tap Library, and then tap the Store button.

As you can see in Figure 7.3, iBooks organizes the iBookstore similar to the App Store. That is, you get four browse buttons in the menu bar located at the bottom of the screen — Featured, Top Charts, Top Authors, and Purchased. You use these buttons to navigate the iBookstore.

Here's a summary of what each browse button does for you:

- **Featured.** Tap this button to display a list of books picked by the iBookstore editors. The list shows each book's cover, title, author, category, star rating, number of reviews, and price. Tap the categories at the top of the screen to browse books by subject (tap More to see the full list).

- **Top Charts.** Tap this button to see charts for the Top Paid books and the Top Free books. You can also tap All Categories to see the top paid and free books in a specific category, such as Non-Fiction.

- **Top Authors.** Tap this button to browse through the bookstore using an alphabetical list of author names that is also divided into the Paid and Free lists.

- **Purchased.** Tap this button to see a list of the books you've purchased using your iTunes account. Tap the cloud icon beside any book to download it to your iPad or iPad mini.

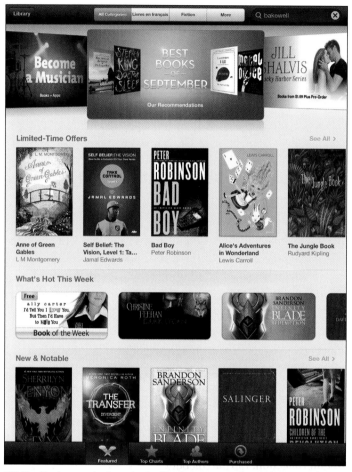

7.3 Use the browse buttons in the iBookstore menu bar to locate and manage e-books for your iPad or iPad mini.

The iBookstore also includes a Search box in the upper-right corner so you can search for the book you want.

Note

Tap a book to get more detailed information about it. The Info screen that appears is divided into three tabs: The Details section shows standard book data, such as the title, author, cover, publisher, number of pages, and a description of the book; the Ratings and Reviews tab offers user ratings and reviews of the book; and the Related tab offers more books by the same author, as well as a list of related books.

Adding a PDF attachment to your library

If you receive an e-mail with an attached PDF file, you can open the attachment right from the Mail app. However, the iBooks app now supports PDFs, so if you'd prefer to read the file in the friendly confines of iBooks (where you can search the PDF and bookmark your current location), you can follow these steps to transfer it to your iBooks Library:

1. **In the Mail app, open the message that contains the PDF attachment.**
2. **Tap and hold the PDF attachment.** Mail displays a menu of commands.
3. **Tap Open in iBooks.** Your iPad or iPad mini opens the iBooks app and displays the PDF.

Working with collections

iBooks supports both e-books and PDF documents. In a welcome burst of common sense, the iBooks programmers decided not to combine e-books and PDFs on the same part of the library. Instead, iBooks supports separate library sections called *collections*. It comes with three default collections: One for e-books (called Books), one for your purchased items (called Purchased Books), and one for PDF documents (called PDFs).

You can use the following techniques to work with your iBooks collections:

- **Switch to another collection.** Tap the Collections button and then tap the name of the collection you want to use.
- **Create a new collection.** Tap the Collections button, tap New, type the name of your collection (such as Fiction or Nonfiction), and then tap Done.
- **Move an item to a different collection.** Tap the Edit button, tap the item you want to move, and then tap the Move button. In the list of collections that appears, tap the collection you want to use as the item's new iBooks home.
- **Delete a collection.** Tap the Collections button, tap Edit, tap the red Delete button beside the collection you want to remove, and then tap Delete. If the collection isn't currently empty, tap Remove when iBooks asks you to confirm. For a nonempty collection, iBooks returns the items to their original locations (for example, e-books to the Books collection).

Adding EPUB e-books to your library

With the apparent ascendance of the EPUB format, publishers and book packagers are tripping over each other to make their titles EPUB-friendly. As a result, the web is awash in EPUB books, so you don't have to get all of your iPad or iPad mini e-book content from the iBookstore. The following is a short list of some sites where you can download EPUB files to your computer:

- **epubBooks: www.epubbooks.com.** This is a terrific site for all things related to the EPUB format. It offers a wide selection of public-domain EPUB books.

- **eBooks.com: www.ebooks.com.** This site has a variety of books in various e-book formats. However, most won't work in the iBooks app because most of the EPUB books use the DRM scheme from Adobe. You can go to the Search Options page and search for the Unencrypted EPUB file format to see the iBooks-friendly titles it offers.

- **Feedbooks: www.feedbooks.com.** This site offers public-domain titles in several formats, including EPUB.

- **Books on Google Play: https://play.google.com/store/books.** This site offers more than a million public-domain titles (many of which are free), plus lots of current releases that you can buy.

- **ManyBooks.net: http://manybooks.net.** This site offers a nice collection of free e-books in a huge variety of formats. When you download a book, be sure to choose the EPUB (.epub) format in the Select Format drop-down list.

- **Smashwords: www.smashwords.com.** This intriguing site offers titles by independent and self-published authors. All e-books are DRM-free and available in the EPUB format.

- **Snee: www.snee.com/epubkidsbooks.** This site offers lots of children's picture books in the EPUB format.

After you download an EPUB title to your computer, import the book into iBooks or iTunes using the Add to Library dialog:

- **In OS X Mavericks.** Open iBooks, choose File ⇨ Add to Library (or press ⌘+Shift+O), locate and click the EPUB file you downloaded, and then click Add. iBooks adds the e-book to the All Books section of the library.

- **In earlier versions of OS X; all versions of Windows.** Open iTunes, choose File ⇨ Add to Library (or press ⌘+O), locate and click the EPUB file you downloaded, and then click Open. iTunes adds the e-book to the Books section of the library.

Editing the library

When you add a book to the iBooks library, the app clears a space for the new title on the left side of the top shelf of the bookcase. The rest of the books are shuffled to the right and down.

This is a sensible way to go about things if you read each book as you download it because it means the iBooks library displays your books in the order that you read them. Of course, life isn't always that orderly and you might end up reading your e-books more haphazardly, which means that the order that the books appear in the library won't reflect the order in which you read them.

Similarly, you may have one or more books in your iBooks library that you refer to frequently or are reading piecemeal (such as a book of poetry or a collection of short stories). In that case, it would be better to have such books near the top of the bookcase where they're slightly easier to find and open.

For these and similar library maintenance chores, iBooks lets you shuffle the books around to get them into the order that you prefer. Follow these steps to rearrange your iBooks library:

1. **Display the iBooks library in one of the following ways:**

   - **If you haven't yet loaded the app, tap the iBooks icon to open the iBooks app.**

   - **If you're in the iBooks app reading a book, tap the screen to display the controls, and then tap Library.**

2. **Tap Edit.** iBooks opens the library for editing, as shown in Figure 7.4.

3. **Tap and drag the book covers to the bookcase positions you prefer.**

4. **If you want to remove a book from your library, tap Edit, tap the book cover, tap the Delete button, and then tap either Delete This Copy (to remove it from just your tablet) or Delete From All Devices (to remove it from every device that has a copy).**

5. **Tap Done.** iBooks closes the library for editing.

Note   To organize books by list, tap the Lists button (the three horizontal lines to the right of the Search box) in the library screen. Tap the buttons on the bottom of the screen to organize your books by Titles, Authors, or Categories. Tap Bookshelf to view your books in the order in which they appear in the library. Tap the Bookshelf button (the four squares to the right of the Search box) to return to the Bookshelf view.

7.4 With the library open for editing, you can move and remove books.

Creating a custom e-book cover

If you've obtained any free books from the iBookstore or if you've downloaded public-domain books to iTunes, you've no doubt noticed that many (or really, most) of these books use generic covers. That's no big deal for a book or two, but it can get monotonous if you have many such books in your iBooks library (as well as making it hard to find the book you want). To work around this, you can create custom book covers from your own photos.

Caution

Creating a custom e-book cover only works if you're using a version of iTunes that supports e-books. If you are using OS X Mavericks, e-books are handled by the new iBooks application, which doesn't support custom e-book covers.

Your first task is to convert a photo (or any image) to something that's usable as a book cover. This involves loading the image into your favorite image-editing program, and then doing the following three things:

- **Crop the image so that it's 420 pixels wide and 600 pixels tall.**
- **Use the text tool in the image-editing program to add the book title to the image.**
- **Save the image as a JPEG file.** If the image is already a JPEG, be sure to save it under a different name so you don't overwrite the original.

Now you're ready to use the new image as a book cover. Follow these steps to import the cover image into iTunes on your computer:

1. **In iTunes, click the Books category.** iTunes displays your e-books.
2. **Right-click the book you want to customize, and then click Get Info.** iTunes displays the book Info dialog.
3. **Click the Artwork tab.** This tab includes a large box for the book cover image.
4. **Use Finder (on a Mac) or Explorer (on a Windows PC) to locate the new cover image.** On a Mac, you can also locate the image in iPhoto.
5. **Click the new image and drop it inside the large box in the Artwork tab.**
6. **Click OK.** iTunes applies the new image as the book cover.

Reading with iBooks

If you're a book lover like me, and your iBooks library is groaning under the weight of all of your e-books, you may want to spend some time looking at all the covers sitting prettily in the bookcase. Or not. If it's the latter, then it's time to get some reading done. The next few sections show you how to control e-books and modify the display for the best reading experience.

Controlling e-books on the reading screen

When you're ready to start reading a book using iBooks, getting started couldn't be simpler. First, you just need to display the iBooks library. If you haven't loaded the app yet, tap the iBooks icon to open it. If you're in the iBooks app reading a book, tap the screen to display the controls, and then tap library. Next, tap the book you want to read and iBooks opens it.

The following is a list of techniques you can use to control an e-book while reading it:

- **View one page at a time.** Orient the tablet in portrait mode.

- **View two pages at a time.** Orient the tablet in landscape mode.

- **Flip to the next page.** Tap the right side of the screen.

- **Flip to the previous page.** Tap the left side of the screen.

- **Manually turn a page.** Flick the page with your finger. Flick left to turn to the next page; flick right to turn to the previous page.

- **Access the iBooks controls.** Tap the middle of the screen. To hide the controls, tap the middle of the screen again.

- **Access the Table of Contents.** Display the controls and tap the Contents button, pointed out in Figure 7.5. You can then tap an item in the Table of Contents to jump to that section of the book.

- **Go to a different page in the book.** Display the controls and tap a dot at the bottom of the screen.

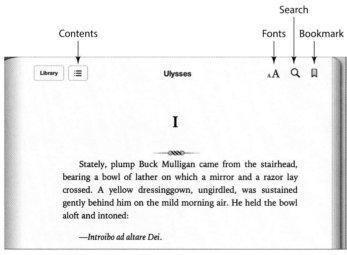

7.5 Tap the middle of the screen to display the controls.

Genius Rather than flipping left and right through the pages, you might prefer to scroll the pages up and down. To set this up, tap the screen to reveal the controls, tap Fonts, tap Themes, and then tap Scroll.

- **Search the book.** Display the controls, tap the Search button in the upper-right corner, type your search text, and then tap Search. In the search results that appear, tap a result to display that part of the book.

- **Return to the iBooks library.** Display the controls, and then tap Library in the upper-left corner.

Formatting e-book text

I mentioned near the top of the show that the EPUB format supports multiple text sizes and multiple fonts, and that the text reflows seamlessly to accommodate the new text size. In the iBooks app, you can take advantage of EPUB features by following these steps:

1. **While reading an e-book, tap the middle of the screen to display the controls.**

2. **Tap the Fonts icon (see Figure 7.5).** iBooks displays the Font options.

3. **Drag the slider to decrease or increase the screen brightness.**

4. **Tap the larger A to increase the text size.** Tap the smaller A to reduce it.

5. **Tap Fonts.** iBooks displays a list of typefaces, as shown in Figure 7.6.

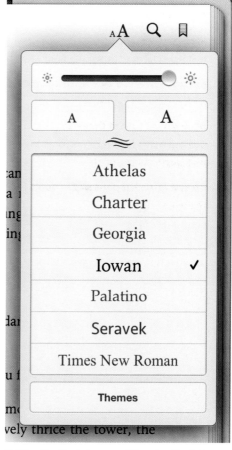

7.6 Tap the Fonts icon, and then tap Fonts to display the iBooks typefaces.

6. **Tap the typeface you want to use.** iBooks reformats the e-book for the new typeface.

7. **Tap Themes, and then tap the color scheme that you want to use.** For example, tap Sepia to switch to a sepia-colored background, or tap Night to switch to white text on a black background for easier reading in the dark.

8. **To remove the book interface elements that appear on the top, right, and bottom edges of the iBooks app, tap the Full Screen switch to On.**

9. **Tap the middle of the screen to hide the controls.**

Adding a bookmark

Reading an e-book with the iBooks app is so pleasurable you may not want to stop! However, you have to eat at some point. So, when it's time to set your book aside, follow these steps to mark your spot with a bookmark:

1. **Navigate to the spot you want to mark.**

2. **Tap the screen to display the controls.**

3. **Tap the Bookmark button (see Figure 7.5).** iBooks saves your spot by creating a book-mark at the current page.

To return to your place, follow these steps:

1. **Tap the page.** iBooks displays the reading controls.

2. **Tap the Contents button (see Figure 7.5).** iBooks displays the Table of Contents.

3. **Tap the Bookmarks tab.** iBooks offers a list of the saved bookmarks.

4. **Tap the bookmark.** iBooks returns you to the bookmarked page.

Looking up a word in the dictionary

As you peruse an e-book, you may come across an unfamiliar word. You can look it up using any of the umpteen online dictionaries but there's no need for that with iBooks. To look up a definition:

1. **Tap and hold the word that has you furrowing your brow.** iBooks displays a set of options.

2. **Tap Define.** iBooks looks up the word and then displays its definition.

3. **Tap outside of the definition to close it.**

156

Highlighting text or adding a note

If you come across a word, phrase, sentence, paragraph, or section of text that strikes your fancy, you might want to return to it later on. The easiest way to do that is to highlight the text. This not only makes it stick out from the surrounding prose by displaying it with a yellow background, but iBooks also bookmarks it, so you can quickly find it again by using the same steps I described earlier to return to a regular bookmark.

Follow these steps to highlight text in iBooks:

1. **Tap and hold a word in the text you want to highlight.** iBooks selects the word and displays a set of options. If the word is all you want to highlight, skip to step 3.

2. **Use the selection controls to expand the selection to include all the text you want to highlight.**

3. **Tap Highlight.** iBooks adds a yellow background to the text and creates a note for it.

4. **Tap the highlight color you want to use or tap the Note button to enter a note for the text.**

Genius

If you change your mind about the highlight background color, you can change it. Tap the highlight and then tap the color you prefer.

Sometimes when you're reading a book you feel an irresistible urge to provide your own two cents. With a paper book, you can grab the nearest writing implement and jot a margin note, but that's not going to work too well with an e-book! Fortunately, the iBooks programmers have taken pity on inveterate margin writers and provided a Note feature. This allows you to add your own comments and asides. Even better, iBooks also creates a bookmark for each note, so you can quickly find your additions.

Follow these steps to create a note with iBooks:

1. **Tap and hold a word in the text on which you want to comment.** iBooks selects the word and displays a set of options. If the word is all you want to work with, skip to step 3.

2. **Use the selection controls to expand the selection to include all of the text you want to use.**

3. **Tap Note.** iBooks displays a text box that looks like a sticky note.

4. **Type your note.**

5. **Tap outside the note.** As shown in Figure 7.7, iBooks adds a yellow background to the text, displays a note icon in the margin, and creates a bookmark for the text.

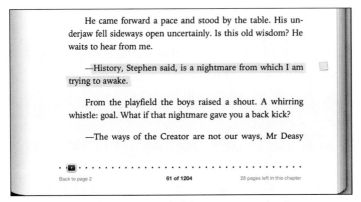

He came forward a pace and stood by the table. His un-
derjaw fell sideways open uncertainly. Is this old wisdom? He
waits to hear from me.

—History, Stephen said, is a nightmare from which I am
trying to awake.

From the playfield the boys raised a shout. A whirring
whistle: goal. What if that nightmare gave you a back kick?

—The ways of the Creator are not our ways, Mr Deasy

Back to page 2   61 of 1204   28 pages left in this chapter

7.7 You can highlight passages and add notes to your e-books.

Reading e-books is no exception to the inevitable social network component that now gets applied to every activity under the sun. If you come across a passage that's particularly funny, witty, profound, or downright shareable, follow these steps to pass it along to either your Twitter followers or Facebook friends:

1. **Tap and hold a word in the text that you want to share.** iBooks selects the word and displays a set of options.

2. **Use the selection controls to expand the selection to include all of the text that you want to share.**

3. **Tap Share.** For some reason, the first time you do this, iBooks asks permission to access your photos. This is a head-scratcher, for sure, so tap Don't Allow.

4. **Tap either Twitter or Facebook.** iBooks opens a new tweet or post and adds the selected text in quotation marks, as well as a link to the book in the iBookstore.

5. **Type an optional note to accompany the quotation.**

6. **Tap Send.** iBooks posts the tweet or status update.

Reading Other E-books

In this chapter, I focus on the iBooks app. This is mostly because it's an excellent app that is optimized for the iPad or iPad mini, and integrates seamlessly with iTunes. However, the iPad and iPad mini are, arguably, the best eReaders available, so it seems a shame to ignore the massive universe of e-books that aren't iBooks-compatible. If you want to turn your tablet into an ultimate eReader — capable of reading practically *any* e-book in practically *any* format — then just head for the App Store and install the appropriate eReader apps.

A complete list of eReader apps would extend for pages, so the following list just hits the highlights:

- **eBookMobi.** This powerful app (it costs $1.99) supports an amazing variety of e-book formats, including EPUB, PDF, and Mobipocket.
- **eReader.** This app supports the eReader format.
- **i2Reader.** This app supports EPUB books and PDF documents.
- **iSilo.** This app (which costs $9.99) supports the iSilo and Palm Doc formats.
- **Kindle.** Amazon's Kindle app is the way to go if you want to read Kindle e-books on your iPad or iPad mini.
- **Kobo.** This app is supplied by the same folks who make the Kobo eReader, and it supports both EPUB books and PDF documents.

Reading Magazines with Newsstand

The iPad just might be the perfect medium for reading magazines. It's just a bit smaller than a regular print magazine, so the pages look natural and uncluttered on the iPad screen. The iPad mini is a bit smaller, of course, but it's still a great device for perusing digital magazines. Plus magazine publishers have been coming up with all kinds of innovative new tools and techniques that make reading a digital version of a magazine a more interactive and media-rich experience than reading the print version.

If there's a problem with tablet-based magazines, it's that you have to manage a different app for each magazine, which gets clumsy once you have more than a half dozen or so magazine apps scattered around your Home screens. You can try plopping all your magazine apps into a single folder, but then it makes it hard to see the icon badges that tell you a new issue is available.

To solve these kinds of problems, iOS offers Newsstand, an app specifically designed to manage magazines. Newsstand is really a special folder, and when you tap it you see a replica of a magazine shelf, as shown in Figure 7.8. For magazine apps that know how to work with Newsstand (in the App Store, open the Newsstand category), when you install such an app, it loads the most recent issue in the Newsstand, which lets you browse your available issues in a single spot. As I write this, a number of magazine publishers have signed on to support Newsstand, including Condé Nast (*Wired, The New Yorker, Vanity Fair,* and many more), National Geographic, Hearst, Bloomberg, and Disney. Newsstand also supports newspaper subscriptions, so you'll also see the likes of *The New York Times, The Wall Street Journal,* and other major newspapers.

7.8 Use the Newsstand app to organize your iOS magazine subscriptions.

How Can I Have Fun with Photos?

The sharp display on the iPad and iPad mini make them the perfect portable photo album. No more whipping out wallet shots of your kids — just show people your on-screen photo albums. The iPad and iPad mini also come with some great features that make it a breeze to browse photos and run slide shows. However, your tablet is capable of more than just viewing photos. It's actually loaded with cool features that enable you to manipulate and take photos, and use them to enhance other parts of your digital life. This chapter is your guide to these features.

Syncing and Importing Photos

No iPad or iPad mini media collection is complete without a few choice photos to show off around the water cooler. If you have some good pics on your computer, you can use iTunes to send those images to the tablet. Note that Apple supports a number of image file types — the usual TIFF and JPEG formats that you normally use for your photos as well as BMP, GIF, JPG2000 or JP2, PICT, PNG, PSD, and SGI.

Syncing computer photos to your tablet

If you use your computer to process a lot of photos and you want to take copies of some (or all) of those photos with you on your tablet, then follow these steps to get synced:

1. **Connect your iPad or iPad mini to your computer.**
2. **In iTunes, click your tablet in the Devices list.**
3. **Click the Photos tab.**
4. **Select the Sync Photos from check box.**

Note

If you have another photo-editing application installed on your computer, chances are good that it also appears in the Sync Photos from list.

5. **Choose one of the following options from the drop-down menu:**

    - **iPhoto (Mac only).** Choose this item to sync the photos, albums, and events you've set up in iPhoto.

    - **Choose Folder.** Choose this command to sync the images contained in a folder you specify.

    - **Pictures (or My Pictures in some versions of Windows).** Choose this item to sync the images in the Pictures (or My Pictures) folder.

6. **Select the photos you want to sync.** The controls you see depend on which of the following options you chose in step 5:

    - **Pictures (or My Pictures) or Choose folder.** If you chose either of these, select either the All photos option or the Selected Folders option. If you select the latter, select the check box beside each subfolder you want to sync.

- **iPhoto.** If this is what you chose, you get two additional options: Select the All photos, albums, Events, and Faces option to sync your entire iPhoto library. Select the Selected albums, Events, and Faces, and automatically include option, and then select the check box beside each item that you want to sync, as shown in Figure 8.1. Choose the number of events from the pop-up menu you want automatically synced.

7. **Click Apply.** iTunes syncs the photos using the new settings.

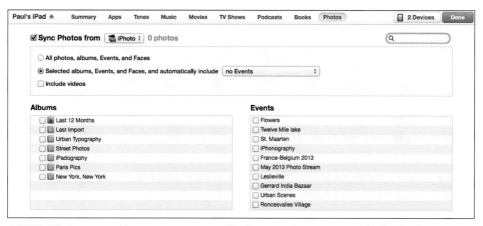

8.1 With iPhoto on your Mac, you can sync specific albums and events to your iPad or iPad mini.

Note   iTunes doesn't sync exact copies of your photos to the tablet. Instead, it creates what Apple calls TV-quality versions of each image. These are copies of the images that have been reduced in size to match the iPad or iPad mini screen size. This makes syncing faster and the photos take up much less room on your tablet.

Syncing iPad or iPad mini photos to your computer

If you create a Safari bookmark on your iPad or iPad mini, and then sync with your computer, that bookmark is transferred from the tablet to the default web browser on your computer. That's a sweet deal that also applies to contacts and appointments. Unfortunately, it doesn't apply to media files which, with two exceptions, travel along a one-way street from your computer to your iPad or iPad mini.

Ah, but then there are those two exceptions, and they're good ones. If you take any photos using the built-in cameras in your iPad or iPad mini, or if you receive any photos on your tablet (via, say, an e-mail message or AirDrop), the sync process reverses itself and enables you to send some (or all) of those images to your computer. Sign me up!

The tablet-to-computer sync process bypasses iTunes entirely. Instead, your computer deals directly with the iPad or iPad mini, and treats it just as though it's some garden-variety media storage device. How this works depends on whether your computer is a Mac or a Windows PC, so I'll use separate sets of steps.

To sync your tablet photos to your Mac, follow these steps:

1. **Connect your iPad or iPad mini to your Mac.** iPhoto opens, adds your tablet to the Devices list, and then displays the photos from your Camera Roll album, as shown in Figure 8.2.

2. **Use the Event Name text box to name the event that these photos represent.**

8.2 When you connect your iPad or iPad mini to your Mac, iPhoto shows up to handle importing photos.

Genius

If you've imported some of your iPad or iPad mini photos in the past, you probably don't want to import them again. That's very sensible of you, and you can prevent that by hiding those photos. Select the Hide Photos Already Imported check box.

3. **Choose from the following import options:**

   - **If you want to import every photo, click Import X Photos, where X is the number of images in your tablet's Camera Roll album.** Technically, *X* is the number of Camera Roll photos that you have not yet imported.

   - **If you want to import only some of the photos, select those that you want to import, and then click Import Selected.**

4. **In the dialog that appears after the import is complete, choose which of the following options you want iPhoto to perform with the photos on your iPad or iPad mini:**

   - **If you want to leave the photos on your tablet, click Keep Photos.**

   - **If you prefer to clear the photos from your tablet, click Delete Photos.**

Follow these steps if you're syncing with a Windows 8.1 PC:

1. **Connect your tablet to your Windows 8 PC.** If Windows 8.1 displays a notification, ignore it.

2. **Open File Explorer and click This PC.** In the Devices and Drives section, File Explorer displays an icon for your iPad or iPad mini.

3. **Right-click the icon for your iPad or iPad mini, and then click Import pictures and videos.** The Import Pictures and Videos dialog box appears.

4. **Select the Import all new Items now option.** If you prefer to select the photos you want to Import, select the Review, organize, and group Items to import option. Click Next, use the dialog box to choose the photos that you want, and then go to step 6.

5. **Type a tag for the photos.** A tag is a word or short phrase that identifies the photos.

6. **Click Import.** Windows 8.1 imports the photos.

Follow these steps if you're syncing with a Windows 8 PC:

1. **Connect your tablet to your Windows 8 PC.** When Windows 8 detects the device, it displays a notification.

2. **Click the notification.** Windows 8 displays a list of actions that you can take.

3. **Click Import Photos and Videos.** Windows 8 opens the Photos app and displays a list of the photos on the tablet's Camera Roll.

4. **Click Clear Selection.**

5. **Select each photo that you want to import.** The Photos app adds a check mark to the upper-right corner of each selected photo.

6. **Use the text box at the bottom of the screen to type a name for the folder that Windows 8 will use to store the photos.**

7. **Click Import.** Windows 8 imports the photos to your PC.

Follow these steps if you're syncing with a Windows 7 PC and have installed Windows Live Photo Gallery from the Windows Live Essentials site:

1. **Connect your tablet to your Windows 7 PC.** If you see the AutoPlay dialog box, click Import pictures and videos using Windows Live Photo Gallery and skip to step 5.

2. **Open Windows Live Photo Gallery.**

3. **Choose Home ⇨ Import.** The Import Photos and Videos dialog box appears.

4. **Click the icon for your iPad or iPad mini, and then click Import.** Windows Live Photo Gallery connects to your device to gather the photo information.

5. **Select the Import all new Items now option.** If you prefer to select the photos you want to Import, select the Review, organize, and group Items to import option. Click Next, use the dialog box to choose the photos that you want, and then go to step 7.

6. **Type a tag for the photos.** A tag is a word or short phrase that identifies the photos.

7. **Click Import.** Windows Live Photo Gallery imports the photos.

Genius

You can also access your iPad or iPad mini photos in Windows 8.1, 8, or 7 directly. In Windows 8.1 or 8, click Desktop, click File Explorer, and then click either This PC (Windows 8.1) or Computer (Windows 8). In Windows 7, choose Start ⇨ Computer, and then double-click your tablet in the Portable Devices group. Open the Internal Storage folder, the DCIM folder, and then the folder that appears (which has a name like 800AAAAA) to display your Camera Roll photos.

Preventing your tablet from sending photos to your computer

Each and every time that you connect your tablet to your computer, you see iPhoto (on your Mac) or the AutoPlay dialog box (in Windows 8.1, 8, or 7 without iTunes installed). This is certainly con-venient if you actually want to send photos to your computer, but you may find that you do that only once in a blue moon. In that case, having to deal with iPhoto or a dialog every time could cause even the most mild-mannered among us to start pulling out our hair. If you prefer to keep your hair, you can configure your computer not to pester you about getting photos from your iPad or iPad mini.

Follow these steps to set this up on your Mac:

1. **Connect your tablet to your Mac.**

2. **Choose Launchpad ⇨ Other ⇨ Image Capture.** The Image Capture application opens.

3. **Click your iPad or iPad mini in the Devices list.**

4. **Click the Connecting this iPad opens menu, and then click No application, as shown in Figure 8.3.**

5. **Choose Image Capture ⇨ Quit Image Capture.** Image Capture saves the new setting and shuts down. The next time that you connect your tablet, iPhoto ignores it.

8.3 Choose No application to prevent iPhoto from starting when you connect your iPad or iPad mini.

Note Configuring your computer not to download photos from your iPad or iPad mini means that in the future, you either need to reverse the setting or manually import your photos.

Follow these steps to convince Windows 8 or Windows 7 not to open the AutoPlay dialog box each time that you connect your iPad or iPad mini:

1. **Open the Default Programs window and perform one of the following steps:**

   - **Windows 8.1 or 8.** In the Start screen, type **default**, and then click Default Programs.
   - **Windows 7.** Choose Start ⇨ Default Programs to open the Default Programs window.

2. **Click Change AutoPlay Settings.** The AutoPlay dialog box appears.

3. **In the Devices section, open the list beside your tablet's name and choose Take No Action.**

4. **Click Save.** Windows saves the new setting.

Syncing photos via iCloud

Syncing photos from your computer isn't difficult, but it seems more than a little old-fashioned in this increasingly wireless age. Fortunately, if you have an iCloud account you can place your feet firmly in the modern era by using the Photo Stream feature to sync photos without even looking at a USB cable. Photo Stream automatically syncs photos you take with your iPad or iPad mini camera to your iCloud account, which then downloads them to your computer, your iPhone, or any other device associated with your account. Similarly, if you upload photos to iCloud using another device, those photos are automatically synced to your tablet.

Follow these steps to activate Photo Stream on your iPad or iPad mini:

1. **In the Home screen, tap Settings to open the Settings app.**
2. **Tap Photos and Camera.**
3. **Tap the My Photo Stream switch to On.**

Importing photos from a camera

If you have a stack of photos on a digital camera or iPhone, you may think the only way to get them onto your tablet is to first sync the photos to your Mac or PC, and then sync them from your computer to your tablet. And you'd be right — *most* of the time. However, Apple offers a way to avoid this time-consuming route by using an adapter designed to get photos directly from a camera on to an iPad or iPad mini. Apple offers the following two adapters:

- **Lightning to USB Camera Adapter.** Connect this adapter's Lightning connector to the Lightning port on the iPad or iPad mini, and then connect the USB connector to the USB port on the digital camera.

- **Lightning to SD Card Camera Reader.** Connect this adapter's Lightning connector to the Lightning port on the iPad or iPad mini, and then insert the digital camera's SD (Secure Digital) card. Actually, if you have photos on another SD card — for example, one from another camera, one someone else has given you, or one you've used to copy photos from a computer — you can also insert that card into the reader.

The Photos app recognizes the connection, and you can then import some (or all) of the photos to the iPad or iPad mini.

Browsing and Viewing Your Photos

After you dump a bucketful of photos onto your iPad or iPad mini, you can start messing around with them by tapping the Photos icon on the Home screen. In the Photos app, you use the three tabs at the bottom of the screen — Photos, Shared, and Albums — to view your photos from different angles, so to speak. However, there are lots of other browsing and viewing tricks up your tablet's sleeve, and I cover them in the next few sections.

Scrolling, rotating, zooming, and panning

You can do so much with your photos after they're on your iPad or iPad mini, and it isn't your normal photo-browsing experience. You aren't just a passive viewer because you can actually take some control over what you see and how the pictures are presented.

You can use the following techniques to navigate and manipulate your photos:

- **Scroll.** You view your photos by flicking. If you're in landscape mode, flick left to view the next photo and flick right to view the previous shot. If you're in portrait mode, flick up to see the next image and flick down to display the previous image. Alternatively, tap the screen to display a sequence of thumbnails at the bottom of the Photos app window and run your finger along those thumbnails to quickly peruse the photos.

- **Rotate.** When a landscape shot shows up in the Photos app, it is letterboxed at the top (that is, you see black space above and below the image). To get a better view, rotate the screen into the landscape position and the photo rotates right along with it, filling the entire screen. When you come upon a photo with a portrait orientation, rotate the tablet back to the upright position for best viewing.

- **Flip.** To show a photo to another person, flip the iPad or iPad mini so that the back is toward you and the bottom is now the top. The Photos app automatically flips the photo right-side up.

- **Zoom.** Zooming magnifies the shot that's on the screen. You can do this in either of the following ways:

  - **Double-tap the area of the photo on which you want to zoom in.** The Photos app doubles the size of the portion you tapped. Double-tap again to return the photo to its original size.

- **Spread and pinch.** To zoom in, spread two fingers apart over the area you want magnified. To zoom back out, pinch two fingers together.

- **Pan.** After you zoom in on the photo, drag your finger across the screen to move it along with your finger.

Note You can scroll to another photo if you're zoomed in, but it takes much more work to get there because the Photos app thinks you're trying to pan. For faster scrolling, return the photo to its normal size and then scroll.

Creating a custom photo slide show

In the Photos app, you can open the Camera Roll or an album, tap Slideshow, and then tap Start Slideshow to run through the album images automatically. The basic slide show is pretty cool, but the Photos app also offers a few settings for creating custom slide shows. For example, you can set how long each photo lingers on-screen and you can configure the slide show to display your photos randomly.

To customize your slide show settings, tap the Settings icon in the Home screen. When the Settings app opens, tap Photos & Camera to display the Photos & Camera settings. You can configure your custom slide show to perform in any of the following ways:

- **Play Each Slide For.** Use this setting to set the amount of time that each photo appears on-screen. Tap Play Each Slide For, and then tap a time: 2 Seconds, 3 Seconds (this is the default), 5 Seconds, 10 Seconds, or 20 Seconds.

- **Repeat.** This setting determines whether the slide show repeats from the beginning after the last photo is displayed. To turn on this setting, tap the Repeat switch to the On position.

- **Shuffle.** You use this setting to display the album photos in random order. To turn on this setting, tap the Shuffle switch to the On position.

Creating a photo album

If you have been taking a lot of pictures on your iPad or iPad mini, the Photos app enables you to create your own photo albums right on your device. These albums aren't transferred to your computer when you sync, but they're handy if you need to organize your photos quickly.

Follow these steps to create a photo album:

1. **In the Photos app, tap Albums.**

2. **Tap New Album (the + icon).** The Photos app prompts you for an album name.

3. **Type the name, and then tap Save.** The Photos app displays a list of all of your tablet images.

4. **Tap each image that you want to include in your new album.** The Photos app adds a check mark to each selected photo.

Note

To remove an album you no longer need, tap Albums, tap Edit, and then tap the X button in the upper-left corner of the album.

5. **Tap Done.** The Photos app creates the new album and adds it to albums.

Streaming photos to Apple TV

If you have an Apple TV that supports AirPlay, you can use AirPlay to stream your photos or a photo slide show from your tablet to your TV.

Follow these steps to stream photos to Apple TV:

1. **Make sure your Apple TV is turned on.**

2. **Using the Photos app, display the album that you want to stream.**

3. **Open the first photo you want to stream.**

4. **Swipe up from the bottom of the screen.** The Control Center appears.

5. **Tap the AirPlay button, which appears to the left of the Brightness slider.** The Photos app displays a menu of output choices, as shown in Figure 8.4.

6. **Tap the name of your Apple TV device.** The Photos app streams the photo to that device, and hence, to your TV.

To stream a slide show, make sure your Apple TV is on, tap Actions, and then tap Slideshow. In the Slideshow Options dialog that appears, tap your Apple TV in the list of output devices, and then configure and start the slide show.

8.4 In the Control Center, tap the AirPlay button to stream photos to your Apple TV.

Getting More Out of Photos

Working with Photos on your iPad or iPad mini seems quite straightforward: you take some shots with the cameras or import photos, and then you view those photos. Enough said, right? Actually, no. Your tablet is bristling with photo-related features, so there's plenty more to explore. The next few sections take you through a few of the more interesting features of the Photos app.

Adding an existing photo to a contact

You can assign a photo to a contact in two ways: straight from a photo album or through the Contacts app. Follow these steps to assign a photo from a photo album:

1. **Tap Photos in the Home screen.** The Photos app appears.

2. **Locate the image you want to use and tap it.** The Photos app opens the photo and reveals the photo controls.

3. **Tap the Actions button.** The Actions button is the arrow that appears on the left side of the menu bar. If you don't see it, tap the screen to reveal the controls. The Photos app displays a list of actions you can perform.

4. **Tap Assign to Contact.** A list of all of your contacts appears.

5. **Tap the contact you want to associate with the photo.** The Move and Scale screen appears.

6. **Drag the image so it's positioned on the screen the way you want.**

7. **Pinch or spread your fingers over the image to set the zoom level you want.**

8. **Tap Choose.** The Photos app assigns the photo to the contact and returns you to your photo album.

To assign a photo using the Contacts app, follow these steps:

1. **On the Home screen, tap the Contacts icon to open the Contacts app.**

2. **Tap the contact to which you want to add a photo.** The Contacts app displays the contact's Info screen.

3. **Tap Edit to put the contact into Edit mode.**

4. **Tap Add Photo, and then tap Choose Photo.** You see a list of photo albums.

5. **Tap the album that contains the photo you want to use.**

6. **Tap the photo you want.** The Move and Scale screen appears.

7. **Drag the image so it's positioned on the screen the way that you want.**

8. **Pinch or spread your fingers over the image to set the zoom level you want.**

9. **Tap Choose.** The Contacts app assigns the photo to the contact and returns you to the Info screen.

10. **Tap Done.** The Contacts app saves your changes.

Taking screenshots

You might come across a situation in which you need to take a picture of your iPad or iPad mini screen. For example, you might see an error message while using an app. Instead of writing down the error message, it's easier to take a screenshot of it and then send it to the app's technical support department. Similarly, if you're playing a game and achieve a high score or pull off some spectacular feat, take a screenshot to show off to your friends and fellow gamers.

To take a screenshot, press and hold the Sleep/Wake button, press the Home button, and then release Sleep/Wake. Your iPad or iPad mini captures the screen, and then saves it as a PNG file in the Camera Roll.

Deleting a photo

If you mess up a photo using one of the cameras, you should delete it before people think you have shoddy camera skills (because we all know it was the tablet's fault, right?).

You might think that deleting a photo would be a straightforward proposition. Nope, not even close. That's because your tablet differentiates between the following two types of photos:

- Photos that you add to the iPad or iPad mini via syncing with iTunes.
- Photos that you create directly on the iPad or iPad mini by using the cameras, taking a screenshot, saving a photo from an e-mail or web page, and so on.

Synced photos *can't* be deleted directly, but photos that you create on the iPad or iPad mini *can* be deleted. Clear as mud, I know. To delete a photo, follow these steps:

1. **Tap Photos in the Home screen.** The Photos app appears.
2. **Locate the image you want to blow away.** For example, if you know the photo is part of a particular event, open that event stack.
3. **Tap the doomed photo.** The Photos app opens the photo.
4. **Tap the screen to reveal the controls.**
5. **If you see the Delete button (the trash can icon), tap it.** If you don't see the Delete button, it means that you can't delete the photo directly. Otherwise, the Photos app asks you to confirm the deletion.
6. **Tap Delete Photo.** The Photos app tosses the photo into the trash, wipes its hands, and returns you to the photos.

Genius

What happens if you have duplicate synced photos on your iPad or iPad mini and you can't delete the copies? The way to fix this is to connect the tablet to your computer, click the device in iTunes, click the Photos tab, deselect Sync Photos, and then click Apply. This removes all synced photos from the tablet. You then reselect Sync Photos and click Apply. You should end up with no duplicates on the iPad or iPad mini.

Printing a photo with AirPrint

How do you print an iPad or iPad mini photo? The obvious answer would be to sync the photo to your Mac or Windows PC, and then print it from there. That works, of course, but it seems like a lot of extra work, and what if you don't have a Mac or PC handy? The better answer is that, if you have a printer that supports the AirPrint standard for wireless printing, you can follow these steps to send a photo directly from your tablet to that printer:

1. **Use the Photos app to display the photo you want to print.**

2. **Tap the screen to display the controls.**

3. **Tap Actions.** A menu of web page actions appears.

4. **Tap Print.** The Printer Options dialog appears. If the Printer field already shows the printer you want to use, you can skip to step 7.

5. **Tap Printer.** The Photos app looks for wireless printers on your network, and then displays a list of any that are available.

6. **Tap the printer that you want to use.** The Photos app adds the printer to the Printer Options dialog, and then enables the other controls, as shown in Figure 8.5.

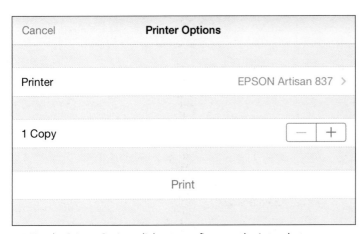

Cancel	**Printer Options**	
Printer	EPSON Artisan 837 >	
1 Copy	—	+
	Print	

8.5 Use the Printer Options dialog to configure and print a photo.

7. **In the Copy field, tap the plus sign (+) to set the number of copies you want to print.**

8. **Configure the other printer options as needed.** Note that the options you see vary from printer to printer.

9. **Tap Print.** The Photos app sends the photo to the printer.

Editing Photos

The iPad and iPad mini aren't the easiest devices in the world to use as cameras — the iPad is a bit too big and unwieldy to hold steady, and the iPad mini is only a bit easier to use thanks to its lighter weight. As a result, you might end up with a few less-than-perfect shots. There's not much you can do to fix blurry images (the biggest iPad or iPad mini photo faux pas), but other problems can be fixed by enhancing the color or brightness, removing red-eye, and cropping out extraneous elements.

In the old days, you first had to sync your photos to your computer, make the fixes using iPhoto, the Windows 8 Photos app, or Photo Gallery, and then sync the fixed photos back to your tablet. Now, however, iOS lets you make these kinds of adjustments right on your iPad or iPad mini. The next three sections provide the details.

Enhancing a photo

If you have a photo that's too bright in some spots or if the color is washed out in others, the Photos app comes with an Enhance tool that can automatically adjust the color and brightness. Follow these steps to use the Enhance tool:

1. **In the Photos app, open the photo that you want to fix.**
2. **Tap the photo to display the controls.**
3. **Tap Edit.** The Photos app displays its editing tools at the bottom of the screen.
4. **Tap Enhance.** The Photos app adjusts the color and brightness.
5. **Tap Save.** The Photos app saves your changes.

Removing red eye

When you use a flash to take a picture of one or more people, in some cases the flash may reflect off the subjects' retinas. The result is the common phenomenon of red eye, where each person's pupils appear red instead of black. Some cameras come with a red-eye reduction feature, which is usually a double flash: one to make the pupils contract before the shot and then another for the actual picture.

If you have a photo on your iPad or iPad mini in which one or more people have red eye because of the camera flash, you can use the Photos app to remove it and give your subjects a more natural look.

Follow these steps to remove red eye:

1. **In the Photos app, open the photo that contains the red eye you want to remove.**

2. **Tap the photo to display the controls.**

3. **Tap Edit.** The Photos app displays its editing tools.

4. **Tap Red-Eye.**

5. **Tap the red eye that you want to remove.** The Photos app removes the red eye.

6. **Repeat step 5 until you've removed all of the red eye in the photo.**

7. **Tap Apply.** The Photos app applies the changes to the photo.

Cropping and straightening

If you have a photo containing elements that you do not want or need to see, you can often cut them out. This is called *cropping* and you can use the Photos app to do this. When you crop a photo, you specify a rectangular area of it that you want to keep. The Photos app then discards everything outside of the rectangle. Cropping is a useful skill because it can help you give focus to the true subject of a photo. Cropping is also useful for removing extraneous elements that appear on or near the edges of a photo.

As you probably know from hard-won experience, getting your iPad or iPad mini camera perfectly level when you take a shot is very difficult. It requires lots of practice and a steady hand. Despite your best efforts, you might still end up with a photo that is not quite level. To fix this problem, you can also use the Photos app to rotate the photo clockwise or counterclockwise so that the subject appears straight.

Genius

If your iPad photos are consistently askew, turn on the Camera grid, which adds lines that divide the Camera screen into nine rectangles (that is, a 3 × 3 grid). Open the Settings app, tap Photos & Camera, and then tap the Grid switch to On. The grid is also useful for composing pictures using the Rule of Thirds, where you place your subject on one of the grid lines instead of in the middle of the screen.

Follow these steps to crop and straighten a photo:

1. **In the Photos app, open the photo that you want to edit.**

2. **Tap the photo to display the controls.**

3. **Tap Edit.** The Photos app displays its editing tools.

4. **Tap Crop.** The Photos app displays a grid for cropping and straightening, as shown in Figure 8.6.

8.6 Tap Crop to display the cropping and straightening tools.

5. **Tap-and-drag a corner of the grid to set the area you want to keep.**

6. **To straighten the photo, place two fingers on the screen and rotate them clockwise or counterclockwise until the image is level.**

7. **Tap Crop.** The Photos app applies the changes to the photo.

Genius The fastest way to crop some photos is to tell the Photos app the dimensions you want to use for the resulting photo. Tap Aspect Ratio, and then tap either a specific shape (Original or Square), or a specific ratio (such as 5 × 7 inches or 8 × 10 inches). You then drag the photo (not the grid!) so that the portion you want to keep is within the grid.

Applying a filter

The stunning popularity of the Instagram app and similar apps such as Hipstamatic has created a mania for applying filters to photos. A *filter* is a special effect applied to a photo's colors to give it a different feel. The iOS 7 version of the Camera app comes with a Filters icon, as does the Photos app in Edit mode. When you tap Filter, you see nine effects that you can apply to your photo, including Mono (which gives you a black-and-white photo) and Instant (which makes the photo look as though it was taken by an old Polaroid film camera). Here's how to apply a filter to a photo using the Photos app:

1. **Open the photo you want to edit.**

2. **Tap the photo to display the controls.**

3. **Tap Edit.** The Photos app displays its editing tools.

4. **Tap Filters.** Photos displays thumbnail versions of the photo that demonstrate each effect.

5. **Tap the effect you want to use.**

6. **Tap Apply.** The Photos app applies the filter to the photo.

Sharing Photos

You probably use the Photos app most often for personal trips down Memory Lane, and there's nothing wrong with that. However, photos are for sharing, and with the big, bright iPad or iPad mini screen, it's easy to gather a few nearby folks and show off your digital masterpieces. That's fine for nearby victims, uh, people, you can cajole into huddling around your tablet, but far-flung folks are another matter. How can you share your photo goodness with people across town or across the country? There are lots of ways, actually: You can send a photo via e-mail, include one in a text message, beam it via AirDrop, or post it to a social network.

Sending a photo via e-mail

More often than you'd think, being able to send photos from your iPad or iPad mini to someone's e-mail is a handy trick. This is particularly true if it's a photo you've just taken with one of the cameras or received on your tablet (say, via an e-mail message), because then you can share the photo pronto without having to trudge back to your computer. You can e-mail any existing photo from one of your photo albums.

Follow these steps to send one or more photos from your iPad or iPad mini via e-mail:

1. **If necessary, use the Camera app to take the photo you want to send, then tap the Camera Roll button to open the Camera Roll photo album.** Otherwise, open Photos and then display the photo album that has the image you want to send.
2. **Tap Select.** The Photos app displays the Select Photos screen.
3. **Tap each photo that you want to send.** The Photos app selects each photo.

Note

If you're just sending a single photo, a quicker way to attach it to an e-mail message is to open the photo using the Photos app, tap the Actions button, and then tap Mail.

4. **Tap Actions, and then tap Mail.** In the New Message screen that appears, the photo appears in the body of the message.
5. **Choose your message recipient and type a Subject line.**
6. **Tap Send.** The Mail app sends the message and returns you to the Photos app.

Saving a photo from an e-mail

If someone sends you a nice photo in an e-mail message, you might want to save it to your iPad or iPad mini, so you can check it out whenever you want, assign it to a contact, sync it to your computer, and so on. Follow these steps to save a photo from an e-mail message:

1. **On the Home screen, tap Mail.** The Mail app appears.
2. **Tap the mailbox that contains the photo message.** The Mail app opens the mailbox.
3. **Tap the message that contains the photo.** The Mail app opens the message for viewing.

4. **Tap and hold the image.** After a couple of seconds, the Mail app displays a list of actions you can perform for the image.

5. **Tap Save to Camera Roll.** If the message contains multiple images, tap Save Image instead. If you want to save all of the images, tap Save *X* Images (where *X* is the number of images in the message). The Mail app saves the image (or images) to the Camera Roll.

Sending and receiving a photo via AirDrop

Sharing a photo via e-mail or text message works well, but it has a slightly primitive feel to it. After all, your iPad or iPad mini is the ultimate wireless device, so surely there must be some way to send a photo directly from one device to another? Happily, the answer to that question is now a resounding "Yes!" An iOS 7 feature called AirDrop, a Bluetooth service that lets two nearby devices — specifically, an iPhone 5s, 5c, or 5; a fourth-generation iPad or later; an iPad mini; or a fifth-generation iPod touch or later — now enables you to exchange photos directly. Here are the steps to follow:

1. **Use the Photos app to open the photo you want to share.**

2. **Tap the Actions icon.** The AirDrop section shows an icon for each nearby device.

3. **Tap the icon for the person with whom you want to share the photo.** The other person sees a dialog asking for permission to accept the photo. When she taps Accept, her version of the Photos app loads and displays the photo.

Posting a photo to Facebook

If you set up your Facebook account on your iPad or iPad mini (which I cover in Chapter 3), you can follow these steps to post a photo:

1. **In the Photos app, open the photo you want to post.**

2. **Tap the Actions button.**

3. **Tap Facebook.** The Photos app displays the Facebook dialog.

4. **Type your post text in the large text box, as shown in Figure 8.7.**

8.7 Include a bit of explanatory text with your Facebook photo.

5. **To change the Facebook album in which the photo will appear, tap Album to open the Choose Album dialog, and then tap the album you want to use.**

6. **If you want to include your present whereabouts as part of the post, tap Location.**

7. **To choose who can see the photo, tap Audience to open the Audience dialog, and then tap the group you want to use.**

8. **Tap Post.** The Photos app posts the photo to your Facebook Timeline.

Tweeting a photo

If you set up your Twitter account (or accounts) on your tablet (again, see Chapter 3), you can follow these steps to tweet a photo to your followers:

1. **In the Photos app, open the photo you want to tweet.**

2. **Tap the Actions button.**

3. **Tap Twitter.** The Photos app displays the Twitter dialog.

4. **If you added more than one account to the Twitter settings, tap the username in the Account section, and then tap the name of the account that you want to use to send the tweet.**

5. **Type your tweet text in the large text box.**

6. **If you want to include your present whereabouts as part of the tweet, tap Location.**

7. **Tap Post.** The Photos app posts the photo as a tweet.

Texting a photo

The Messages app sends text messages outside of a cellular provider's messaging system. This means that you can use the Messages app to send unlimited (yes, that's right: *unlimited*) text messages via Wi-Fi or a cellular connection to other people using iOS devices, including iPhones, iPod touches, and other iPads, as well as Macs running OS X Mountain Lion or later. You can also follow these steps to send a photo in a text message:

1. **On the Home screen, tap Messages.** The Messages screen appears.

2. **Tap New Message.**

3. **Select your recipient.**

4. **Tap the Photo button that appears to the left of the text box.**

5. **Select or take a photo by performing one of the following actions:**

   - **If you want to send a photo that's already on your tablet, tap Choose Existing.** Locate and tap the photo, and then tap Use.

   - **If you want to take a new photo, tap Take Photo or Video.** Take the shot and then tap Use Photo.

6. **Type your message text.**

7. **Tap Send.** The Messages app sends the message with the photo attached.

Saving a photo from a text message

If someone sends you a nice photo in a text message, you might want to save it to your iPad or iPad mini, so that you can check it out whenever you want, assign it to a contact, sync it to your computer, and so on. Follow these steps to save a photo from a text message:

1. **On the Home screen, tap Messages.** The Messages screen appears.

2. **Tap the conversation that contains the photo message.** The Messages app opens the conversation screen.

3. **Tap the photo.** Your iPad or iPad mini opens it for viewing.

4. **Tap the screen and then tap the Actions button.** The Actions options appear.

5. **Tap Save Image.** The Messages app saves the image to the Camera Roll.

Using the Cameras

Your iPad or iPad mini comes with a couple of built-in digital cameras that you can use while you're running around town. Taking a picture is straightforward. First, on the Home screen, tap Camera. (Alternatively, from any screen, swipe up from the bottom to display the Control Center, and then tap the Camera icon.)

Genius

When your iPad or iPad mini is locked, you can get to the Camera app in seconds flat by double-pressing the Home button and then dragging up the Camera icon that appears in the bottom-right corner of the Lock screen.

185

If this is the first time you've opened the Camera app, it asks if it can use your current location. This is an excellent idea because it tags your photos with your present whereabouts, so be sure to tap OK.

When the Camera app appears, make sure that the Mode switch (see Figure 8.8) is set to Photo instead of Video. Next, just line up your shot and tap either the Shutter button (see Figure 8.8) or the Volume Up switch, which appears on the top edge of the tablet when you hold it in the landscape position with the Home button on the left. To view your photo, tap the Camera Roll button, which appears in the lower-right corner of the Camera app screen.

Understanding the iPad or iPad mini camera features

While using the camera itself may be simple, what you can do with photos on your iPad or iPad mini is pretty cool. For example, you can take a photo to use as wallpaper, or you can shoot a portrait of a friend or family member and use it as that person's contact photo. Before getting to those tasks, though, take a second to go over the following list of the iPad and iPad mini camera features:

- **Rear- and front-facing cameras.** The iPad and iPad mini come with two cameras: a 5-megapixel FaceTime HD camera on the back for regular shots, and a 1.2-megapixel camera on the front for taking self-portraits. In the Camera app, tap the Switch Camera button, shown in Figure 8.8, to switch between the front and rear cameras.

- **Autofocus.** The rear camera automatically focuses on whatever subject is in the middle of the frame.

- **Tap to focus.** If the subject you want to focus on is not in the middle of the frame, tap it, and the rear camera automatically moves the focus onto that object. It also automatically adjusts the white balance and exposure.

- **Face detection.** This feature balances focus and exposure across any face that it detects in the frame; it works on both cameras.

- **5X digital zoom.** You can zoom using the rear camera. Pinch two fingers together on the screen to display the zoom slider, as shown in Figure 8.8. Then, drag the slider right to zoom in or left to zoom out.

- **Geotagging.** The iPad or iPad mini can use its built-in GPS sensor to add location data to each photo, a process called *geotagging*. This means that you can organize your photos by location, which is great for vacation snaps and other trip-related photos.

Caution

Geotagging makes it easy to map your photos, but it also raises privacy issues because it means that each photo comes with its location embedded in the photo data. This can be a big problem if you post photos online (especially of kids) because it means that strangers might be able to extract the photo location. You can control whether the Camera app uses your location by launching the Settings app, tapping Privacy, tapping Location Services, and then tapping the Camera switch On or Off.

Switch Camera icon

HDR switch

Shutter button

Mode switch

Camera Roll

Zoom slider

8.8 The features of the Camera app.

187

Taking a wallpaper photo

You can create an on-the-fly wallpaper image using one of the iPad or iPad mini cameras by following these steps:

1. **On the Home screen, tap Camera.** The Camera app appears.

2. **Line up your subject and tap the Shutter button to take the picture.**

3. **Tap the Camera Roll button in the lower-left corner.** The Camera app opens the Camera Roll photo album and displays a preview of the photo.

4. **Tap the Actions button.** The Actions button is the button to the right of the Slideshow button in the menu bar (if you don't see the menu bar, tap the screen). You see a list of actions you can perform.

5. **Tap Use as Wallpaper.** The Move and Scale screen appears.

6. **Drag the image so that it's positioned on the screen the way that you want.**

7. **Pinch or spread your fingers over the image to set the zoom level you want.**

8. **Tap either Set Lock Screen or Set Home Screen.** If you prefer to see the photo on both screens, tap Set Both.

Taking a contact's photo

If you don't have a picture of a contact handy, that's not a problem because you can take advantage of the rear camera on your iPad or iPad mini and snap his image the next time you get together.

To take and assign a photo from the Camera app, follow these steps:

1. **In the Home screen, tap the Camera button to enter the Camera app.** A shutter appears on the screen.

2. **If necessary, tap the Switch Camera button to activate the rear camera.**

3. **Frame the person on your screen.**

4. **Tap the Shutter button (or the Volume Up button, if that's easier) to snap the picture.**

5. **Tap the Camera Roll button in the bottom-left corner.** This opens the Camera Roll screen and displays the photo you just took.

6. **Tap the Actions button.** The Photos app displays a list of actions that you can perform.

7. **Tap Assign to Contact.** A list of all of your contacts is displayed.

8. **Tap the contact you want to associate with the photo.** The Move and Scale screen appears.

9. **Drag the image so that it's positioned on the screen the way that you want.**

10. **Pinch or spread your fingers over the image to set the zoom level you want.**

11. **Tap Choose.** The Photos app assigns the photo to the contact and returns you to the photo.

12. **Tap Done.** The Photos app returns you to the Camera app.

How Can I Get More Out of Listening to Audio?

The Music app is built with audio in mind. It lets you crank music, music videos, audiobooks, and podcasts. If you have a fast Wi-Fi (or even a cellular) connection, you can use your iPad or iPad mini to purchase music from the iTunes Store. Playing a track is a snap on your tablet: tap Music, tap a browse button, and then tap the song. However, your iPad or iPad mini is more than a simple tap-and-play device. This chapter shows you how to take advantage of some of the more useful audio features.

Preparing iTunes Audio for Your Tablet

Although you can purchase and download songs directly from the iTunes Store on your iPad or iPad mini, I'm going to assume that the vast majority of your music library is cooped up on your Mac or PC, and that you're going to want to transfer that music to your tablet. Actually, perhaps I should say that you're going to want to transfer *some* of that music to the tablet. Most of us now have multigigabyte music collections, so depending on the storage capacity of your iPad or iPad mini (and the amount of other content you've stuffed into it, particularly videos and movies), it's likely that you want to copy only a subset of your music library.

If that's the case, then iTunes gives you four choices when it comes to selecting which tunes to transfer: artists, genres, albums, and playlists. The first three are self-explanatory (and, in any case, I give you the audio syncing details a bit later in this chapter), but it's the last one that allows you to take control of syncing music to your iPad or iPad mini.

A *playlist* is a collection of songs that are related in some way. You can use your iTunes library to create customized playlists that include only the songs that you want to hear. For example, you might want to create a playlist of upbeat or festive songs to play during a party or celebration. Similarly, you might want to create a playlist of your current favorite songs.

Playlists are the perfect way to control music syncing for the iPad or iPad mini, so before you start transferring tunes, consider creating a playlist or three in iTunes. As the next two sections show, you can create two types of playlists: standard and Smart.

Building a standard playlist

A standard playlist is one where you manually control which songs are in the playlist (as opposed to the automatic Smart and Genius playlists that I talk about in the next two sections). A standard playlist is a bit more work to maintain, but it gives you complete control over the contents. Follow these steps to build a standard playlist:

1. **Choose File ⇨ New ⇨ Playlist.** You can also press ⌘+N (Ctrl+N in Windows) or click Playlists, click Add (+), and then click the New Playlist button. iTunes adds a new item to the Playlists section with an edit box around it.

2. **Type the name you want to give the playlist, and then press Return (or Enter in Windows).**

3. **In the iTunes Music library, right-click the song, album, artist, or genre that you want to include in the playlist, click Add to Playlist, and then select the playlist.**

4. **Repeat step 3 to populate the playlist.**

Genius

If you're looking for a faster way to create and populate a standard playlist, iTunes offers another technique that lets you select some or all of the songs in advance. Press and hold the ⌘ key (the Ctrl key in Windows) and then click each song that you want to include in your playlist. When you're done, choose File ➪ New ➪ Playlist from Selection or press ⌘+Shift+N (Ctrl+Shift+N in Windows).

Building a Smart Playlist

A standard playlist gives you a satisfying amount of control over the contents, but it can often be a hassle. For example, if you've created a playlist for a particular genre, then every time you add new music from that genre you must then drag the new tunes to the playlist. Similarly, if you assign a particular album or artist to a genre that's different than the one in your playlist, you have to manually remove the album or artist from the playlist.

To avoid this kind of digital music drudgery, you can create a *Smart Playlist* where the songs that appear in the list have one or more properties in common, such as the genre, rating, artist, or text in the song title. The key here is iTunes populates and maintains a Smart Playlist automatically. For example, if you build a Smart Playlist based on a particular genre, then every time you add new music from that genre, iTunes automatically includes it in the playlist. Similarly, if you change the genre of some music in your playlist, iTunes automatically removes it from the playlist.

Follow these steps to build a Smart Playlist:

1. **Choose File ➪ New ➪ Smart Playlist.** You can also press ⌘+Option+N (Ctrl+Alt+N in Windows) or click Playlists, click Add (+), and then click New Smart Playlist. iTunes displays the Smart Playlist dialog.

2. **Set up the conditions for the playlist by performing the following actions:**

   ● **Use the first pop-up menu to choose the field you want to use for the first condition.**

   ● **Use the second pop-up menu to choose an operator for the condition.** Your choices here depend on the field you selected in the first pop-up menu. For example, if you chose a text field, the available operators include contains, is, and starts with. For a numeric field, the operators include is greater than, is less than, and is in the range.

- **Use the third control (or set of controls) to enter the details of the condition.**
Again, the controls you see depend on the type of field, although in most cases you
see a single text box. If you chose is in the range as the operator, you see two text
boxes so that you can enter the beginning and end values for the range.

3. **If you want to add another condition, click the Add button (+) to the right of the
controls.** iTunes adds another set of condition controls to the dialog.

4. **Repeat step 2 to specify the settings for the new condition.**

5. **Repeat steps 3 and 4 to add as many conditions as you need.** Figure 9.1 shows an
example of the Smart Playlist dialog with four conditions added.

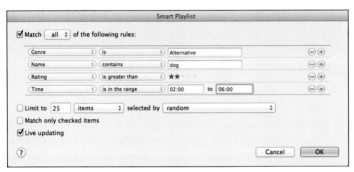

9.1 Use the Smart Playlist dialog to add the conditions that define your
new playlist.

6. **If you want to limit the playlist to a certain length or number of songs, select the
Limit to check box, and then perform the following actions to specify the limit:**

   - **Type the number in the first box, and then choose minutes, hours, MB, GB, or
   items in the first pop-up menu.**

   - **In the second pop-up menu, choose how to select the songs.** Your choices include
   by least often played, by highest rating, or at random.

7. **Select the Match only checked items check box if you want to include only songs
with check boxes you've selected.** This setting lets you clear a song's check box and
make sure it won't show up in your Smart Playlists.

8. **Select the Live updating check box if you want iTunes to automatically update the
Smart Playlist for you.**

9. **Click OK.** iTunes creates the playlist and displays an edit box around its name.

10. **Type the name you want to give the playlist, and then press Return (or Enter).**

Syncing Audio

The brainy iBooks e-reader and the sleek Safari browser may get the lion's share of app kudos, but many people reserve their rave reviews for the Music app. The darn thing is just so versatile: It can play music, of course, but it also happily cranks out audiobooks and podcasts on the audio side, and music videos, movies, and TV shows on the video side. Ear and eye candy in one package!

If there's a problem with this digital largesse, it's that the Music app might be too versatile. Even if you have a big, 64GB iPad, you may still find its confines a bit cramped — particularly if you're also loading it up with photos, contacts, calendars, e-books, and apps. All of this means that you probably have to pay a bit more attention when it comes to syncing audio to your tablet. The following sections show you how to do just that.

Syncing music and music videos

The Music app is a digital music player at heart, so you've probably loaded it up with lots of audio content and music videos. To get the most out of your tablet's music and video capabilities, you need to know all of the different ways you can synchronize these items. For example, if you use the Music app primarily as a music player, and the iPad or iPad mini has more hard drive capacity than you need for all of your digital audio, feel free to throw all of your music onto your tablet.

On the other hand, your tablet may not have much free space, or you may want only certain songs and videos on the player to make it easier to navigate. Not a problem! You can configure iTunes to sync only the songs or playlists that you select.

Genius

Something I like about syncing playlists is that you can estimate in advance how much space your selected playlists will usurp on the tablet. In iTunes, click the playlist and examine the status bar, which tells you the number of songs in the playlist, the total duration of the playlist, and, most significantly for your purposes, the total size of the playlist.

195

Before getting to the specific sync steps, you should know that you can manually sync music and music videos in the following three ways:

- **Playlists.** With this method, you specify the playlists you want iTunes to sync. Those playlists also appear on the Music app. This is by far the easiest way to manually sync music and music videos, because you usually just have a few playlists to select. The downside is that if you have large playlists and you run out of space on your iPad or iPad mini, the only way to fix the problem is to remove an entire playlist. Another bummer: With this method, you can only sync *all* or *none* of your music videos.

- **Check boxes.** With this method, you specify which songs and music videos get synced by selecting the little check boxes that appear beside every song and video in iTunes. This is fine-grained syncing for sure, but because your tablet can hold thousands of songs, it's also lots of work.

- **Individual tracks.** With this method, you select individual songs and music videos and send them directly to your iPad or iPad mini. This is an easy way to get a bunch of tracks on your device quickly, but iTunes doesn't give you any way of tracking which files you've added.

Genius

What do you do if you want to select only a few tracks from a large playlist? Waste a big chunk of your life deselecting a few hundred check boxes? Pass. Here's a better way: Press ⌘+A (Mac) or Ctrl+A (Windows) to select every track, right-click any track, and then click Uncheck Selection. Voila! iTunes deselects every track in seconds flat. Now you can select only the tracks you want. You're welcome.

Follow these steps to sync music and music videos using playlists:

1. **Connect your iPad or iPad mini to your computer.**
2. **In iTunes, click your tablet in the Devices list.**
3. **Click the Music tab.**
4. **Select the Sync Music check box.**
5. **If iTunes asks you to confirm that you want to sync music, click Sync Music.**
6. **Select the Selected playlists, artists, albums, and genres option.**

7. **Select the check box beside each playlist, artist, album, and genre you want to sync, as shown in Figure 9.2.**

8. **Select the Include music videos check box if you also want to add your music videos into the sync mix.**

9. **Select the Include voice memos check box if you also want to sync voice memos that you recorded on your iPhone or iPod touch.**

10. **If you want iTunes to fill any remaining free space on your iPad or iPad mini with a selection of related music from your library, select the Automatically fill free space with songs check box.**

11. **Click Apply.** iTunes syncs your tablet using the new settings.

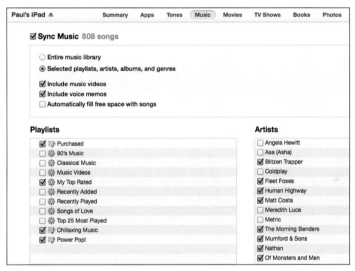

9.2 Select the Selected playlists, artists, albums, and genres option, and then select the items that you want to sync.

Follow these steps to sync using the check boxes that appear beside each track in your iTunes Music library:

1. **Click your iPad or iPad mini in the Devices list.**

2. **Click the Summary tab.**

3. **Select the Sync only checked songs and videos check box.**

4. **Click Apply.** If iTunes starts syncing, click Cancel (the X) in the iTunes status window to stop it.

5. **Either click Music in the Library list or click a playlist that contains the tracks you want to sync.** If a track's check box is selected, iTunes syncs the track with your tablet. If a track's check box is deselected, iTunes doesn't sync the track with your tablet. If a track is already on your iPad or iPad mini, iTunes removes it.

6. **In the Devices list, click your iPad or iPad mini.**

7. **Click the Summary tab.**

8. **Click Sync.** iTunes syncs only the selected tracks.

You can follow these steps to configure iTunes to let you send tracks from the Music library (or any playlist) directly to your iPad or iPad mini:

1. **Click your tablet in the Devices list.**

2. **Click the Summary tab.**

3. **Select the Manually manage music and videos check box.**

Note

When you select the Manually manage music and videos check box, iTunes automatically deselects the Sync Music check box in the Music tab. However, iTunes doesn't mess with the music on your iPad or iPad mini. Even when it syncs after a drag and drop, it only adds the new tracks; it doesn't delete any of your tablet's existing music.

4. **Click Apply.** If iTunes starts syncing, click Cancel (the X) in the iTunes status window to stop it.

5. **Either click Music in the Library list or click a playlist that contains the tracks you want to sync.**

6. **Choose the tracks you want to sync in one of the following ways:**

   - **If all of the tracks are together, Shift+click the first track, hold down Shift, and then click the last track.**

   - **If the tracks are scattered all over the place, hold down ⌘ (Mac) or Ctrl (Windows) and click each track.**

7. **Right-click the selected tracks, click Add to Playlist, and then select your iPad or iPad mini in the list that appears.** iTunes syncs the selected tracks.

Caution If you decide to return to playlist syncing by selecting the Sync Music check box in the Music tab, iTunes removes all of the tracks that you added to your tablet via the direct-send method.

Syncing music via iCloud

As covered earlier, if you purchase a song or album on your Mac or PC, getting that music onto your tablet requires that you connect the tablet to your computer, and then run a sync. Even worse, if you purchase music on another device, such as your iPhone, getting that music on your iPad or iPad mini means that you first have to sync the other device with your computer, and *then* sync your tablet. Too much work!

You can avoid all of that hassle if you have an iCloud account because you can configure it to automatically download any new music purchases — whether they are bought on your Mac, PC, iPhone, iPod touch, or even another iPad — directly to your tablet.

This is called *automatic downloading*. Follow these steps to set it up:

1. **On your iPad or iPad mini, tap Settings in the Home screen to open the Settings app.**
2. **Tap iTunes & App Stores.**
3. **If you haven't signed in to the iTunes Store, type your iCloud username and password, and then tap Sign In.**
4. **Tap the Music switch to On.**

Now, each time that you purchase music via iTunes on another device, it is automatically sent to your iPad or iPad mini.

Syncing podcasts

In many ways, podcasts are the most problematic of the various media you can sync with your iPad or iPad mini. It's not that podcasts themselves pose any concern. Quite the contrary: They're so addictive that it's not unusual to collect them by the dozens. Why is that a problem? Because most professional podcasts are at least a few megabytes in size and many are tens of megabytes. A large-enough collection can put a serious dent in the storage space on your tablet, which is all the more reason to follow these steps and take control of the podcast-syncing process:

Note

Bear in mind that as of iOS 7, the Music app does not play podcasts. Instead, you need to download Apple's free Podcasts app from the App Store (or, of course, any podcast player that you prefer).

1. **Connect your iPad or iPad mini to your computer.**

2. **In iTunes, click your tablet in the Devices list.**

3. **Click the Podcasts tab.**

4. **Select the Sync Podcasts check box.**

5. **If you want iTunes to choose some of the podcasts automatically, select the Automatically include check box and proceed to steps 6 and 7.** If you prefer to manually choose all the podcasts, deselect the Automatically include check box and skip to step 8.

6. **Use the first pop-up menu to choose the number and type of podcasts to include in the sync.**

Note

A podcast episode is *unplayed* if you haven't yet played at least part of it, either in iTunes or on your iPad or iPad mini. If you play an episode on your tablet, the player sends this information to iTunes when you next sync. Even better, your tablet also lets iTunes know if you paused in the middle of an episode; when you play that episode in iTunes, it starts at the point where you left off. To mark a podcast episode as unplayed, in iTunes choose the Podcasts library, right-click the episode, and then choose Mark as Unwatched.

7. **Select one of the following options from the second pop-up menu:**
   - **All podcasts.** Choose this option to apply the option from step 6 to all of your podcasts.
   - **Selected podcasts.** Choose this option to apply the option from step 6 to only the podcasts that you select, as shown in Figure 9.3.

8. **Select the check box beside any podcast or podcast episode you want to sync.**

9. **Click Apply.** iTunes syncs the iPad or iPad mini using your new podcast settings.

9.3 To sync specific podcasts, choose the selected podcasts option, and then select the check boxes for each podcast that you want to sync.

Syncing audiobooks

The iTunes sync settings for your iPad or iPad mini have tabs for Music, Photos, Podcasts, and Video, but not one for Audiobooks. What's up with that? It's not, as you might think, some sort of antibook conspiracy or even forgetfulness on Apple's part. Instead, iTunes treats audiobook content as a special type of playlist which, confusingly, doesn't appear in the iTunes Playlists section. To get audiobooks on your iPad or iPad mini, follow these steps:

1. **Connect your iPad or iPad mini to your computer.**
2. **In iTunes, click your tablet in the Devices list.**
3. **Click the Books tab.**
4. **Scroll down and select the Sync Audiobooks check box.**
5. **Select the Selected audiobooks option.**
6. **Select the check box beside each audiobook you want to sync.**
7. **Click Apply.** iTunes syncs your audiobooks to your iPad or iPad mini.

If you've opted to manually manage your music and video, you need to choose the Audiobooks category of the iTunes library. Next, drag and drop the audiobooks that you want to sync on your iPad or iPad mini.

Working with the Music App

Your iPad or iPad mini is a full-fledged music player thanks to its Music app, which you can fire up any time you want by tapping the Music icon in the Home screen Dock. You navigate the Music app using the *browse buttons* on the bottom of the screen — Radio, Playlists, Artists, Songs, Albums, Audiobooks, Genres, Compilations, and Composers — each of which represents a collection of media files organized in some way. For example, tapping the Songs browse button displays a list of all of the songs on your tablet or in the currently selected playlist. (In some cases, you see a More button instead of Composers, and you tap More to see a few extra browse buttons.)

In the next couple of sections, I cover a few useful techniques that help you get more out of the Music app.

Creating a playlist on your tablet

The playlists on your iPad or iPad mini are those you've synced via iTunes. These playlists are either generated automatically by iTunes or they're playlists you've cobbled together yourself. However, when you're out in the world and listening to music, you might come up with an idea for a different collection of songs. It might be girl groups, boy bands, or songs with animals in the title.

Whatever your inspiration, don't do it the hard way by picking out and listening to each song one at a time. Instead, you can use your iPad or iPad mini to create a playlist on the fly. To create a playlist using the Music app, follow these steps:

1. **Open the Music app.**
2. **Tap the Playlists browse button.**
3. **Tap New Playlist.** The Music app displays the New Playlist dialog.
4. **Type the name of your playlist, and then tap Save.** The Music app displays the Songs screen, which contains a list of all of your songs. You can also click one of the browse buttons to find your music.
5. **Scroll through the list and tap each song you want to add to your playlist.** The Music app turns a song gray when you add it, as shown in Figure 9.4.
6. **When you've added all the songs you want, tap Done.** The Music app displays the playlist in Edit mode.
7. **Tap Done.**

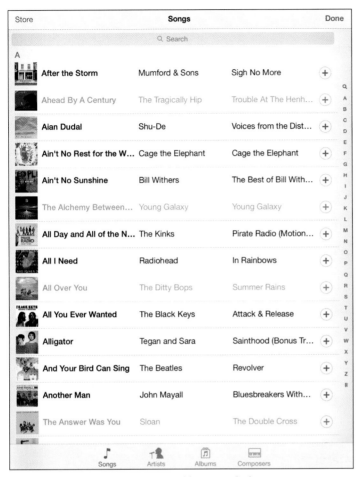

9.4 Tap each song that you want to add to your playlist.

Your playlist isn't set in stone by any means. You can perform the following steps to get rid of songs, change the song order, or add more songs:

1. **Open the Music app.**

2. **Tap the Playlists browse button.**

3. **Tap your playlist.**

4. **Tap Edit.** This changes the list to the editable version, as shown in Figure 9.5.

‹ Playlists	Sunday Morning	+
	Done	

⊖		**Ahead By A Century**	The Tragically Hip	Trouble At The Henh… ≡
⊖		**The Alchemy Between…**	Young Galaxy	Young Galaxy ≡
⊖		**All Over You**	The Ditty Bops	Summer Rains ≡
⊖		**The Answer Was You**	Sloan	The Double Cross ≡
⊖		**Beautiful Dawn**	The Wailin' Jennys	40 Days ≡
⊖		**Beyond Me**	Sloan	Between The Bridges ≡
⊖		**Bobcaygeon**	The Tragically Hip	Phantom Power ≡
⊖		**Casual Viewin'**	54-40	Casual Viewin' ≡
⊖		**Champagne Supernova**	Oasis	(What's The Story)… ≡
⊖		**Chrome Waves**	Ride	Going Blank Again ≡
⊖		**Civil Twilight**	The Weakerthans	Reunion Tour ≡
⊖		**Cold December**	Matt Costa	Songs We Sing ≡
⊖		**Cuddly Toy**	The Bicycles	The Good, the Bad,… ≡
⊖		Drivin' On 9	The Breeders	Last Splash

9.5 A playlist in Edit mode.

5. **To remove a song, tap the red Delete button (–) to the left of it, and then tap the Delete button that appears.** If you change your mind, tap the Delete button again to cancel.

6. **To move a song within the playlist, slide the drag icon (to the right of each song) up or down to the position you prefer.**

7. **To add more tracks, tap Add Songs (+), tap each song you want to add, and then tap Done.**

8. **When you finish editing, tap Done.** This sets the playlist.

Note

If your playlist is a bit of a mess or if your mood suddenly changes, you can delete the entire playlist and start over. Tap the Playlists browse button, tap the playlist, and then tap either Clear (to keep the playlist but remove the songs) or Delete (to remove the playlist entirely).

Creating a Genius playlist on your tablet

You saw earlier how to create a Genius playlist in iTunes. You also can follow these steps to use this seemingly magical feature right on your iPad or iPad mini:

1. **Tap Playlists.**

2. **Tap Genius Playlist.** The Music app opens the Songs list.

3. **Tap the song you want to use as the basis of the Genius playlist.** The Music app selects 24 songs that are similar to the song you tapped and adds those along with the original song to a new playlist.

4. **In the Playlists tab, tap the new Genius playlist.**

5. **Tap Save.** The Music app renames the playlist as the name of the original song. Figure 9.6 shows an example.

9.6 An example of a Genius playlist.

In the Genius playlist screen, you can perform the following actions to mess around with your shiny, new playlist:

- Tap Refresh to re-create the playlist.
- Tap a song to play it.
- Tap Delete to remove the playlist.

Listening to a shared iTunes library

You may be familiar with an iTunes feature called Home Sharing. It enables you to share your iTunes library with other people on your network as long as you're all logged in with the same Apple ID. Home Sharing is also available on the iPad or iPad mini, which means you can use your tablet to get wireless access to an iTunes library that's stored on a Mac or PC.

To set this up, you must first perform the following steps to activate Home Sharing in iTunes:

1. **In iTunes on your Mac or PC, choose File ⇨ Home Sharing ⇨ Turn On Home Sharing.** iTunes prompts you for an Apple ID.
2. **Type your Apple ID and password.**
3. **Click Turn On Home Sharing.** iTunes configures your library for sharing on the network.
4. **Click Done.** iTunes returns you to the library.

With Your iTunes library set up for sharing, your next task is to configure your tablet with the same Home Sharing Apple ID and password. Follow these steps to do so:

1. **Tap Settings to open the Settings app.**
2. **Tap Music to open the Music settings.**
3. **In the Home Sharing section, use the Apple ID and Password boxes to type the same account information that you used to set up Home Sharing in iTunes.**

Now open the Music app, tap More, and then tap Shared. As you can see in Figure 9.7, the Music app displays the Shared dialog, which lists the available shared libraries. Tap the library you want to access and the Music app displays the media in that library instead of the media that's on the tablet.

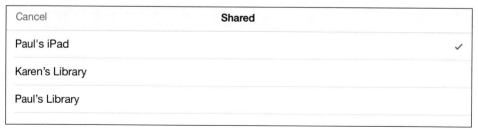

9.7 Tap More, and then tap Shared to see a list of the available shared libraries.

Genius
By default, iTunes shares the library with the name *User's* Library, where *User* is the first name of the current user account. To change that, choose iTunes ⇨ Preferences (on a Mac) or Edit ⇨ Preferences (on a PC), click the General tab, and then use the Library Name text box to type the new name.

Listening to iTunes Radio

I mentioned earlier that the age of the audio CD — indeed, the age of physical music in general — is just about done. In its place comes the age of digital music, and one of the consequences of this conversion from atoms to bits is that most of the world's music is now just a few taps or clicks away. The problem, however, is *discovering* that music. How do you locate new artists and songs, particularly without spending a fortune experimenting with untried bands and genres?

A lot of satellite- and Internet-based services have sprung up in recent years to answer that genuinely musical question, with varying degrees of success. It turns out that most of us are looking for a simple solution to the discovery problem: Given my current musical tastes, as shown by the collection of artists and songs on, say, my iPad, allow me to listen to other artists and songs that are similar.

That, in a nutshell, is the idea behind the new iTunes Radio feature (which, as this book went to press, was only available in the United States, although you can expect that to change very soon). Given a particular song or artist on your tablet, you create a "radio station" that streams similar music. The best news is that it's completely free, although you can use iTunes to purchase songs from the radio station, if something grabs your booty.

If you want, you can use iTunes Radio to listen only to the curated playlists that it offers in genres such as Blues, Classical, and Jazz. However, you can get the most out of iTunes Radio by creating your own stations.

The easiest way to create a new radio station based on your current tastes is to use an existing song or artist on your iPad or iPad mini as the basis of the station. Here's how it works:

1. **In the Music app, play the artist or song you want to use as the basis for the station.**

2. **Tap Create.**

3. **Tap the type of station you want to create:**

   - **New Station from Artist.** Tap this command to create a new radio station with songs that are similar to those of the artist playing the current song.

   - **New Station from Song.** Tap this command to create a new radio station with songs that are similar to the current song.

The Music app creates the new station, switches to iTunes radio, and begins playing the station.

What if you want to create a radio station based on an artist or song you don't own? Sure, not a problem:

1. **In the Music app, tap Radio.** The iTunes Radio screen appears.

2. **Tap New Station to open the New Station screen**.

3. **Use the Search box at the top of the screen to type the name of an artist, song, or genre.**

4. **In the search results, tap the item you want to use as the basis of your playlist.** iTunes Radio creates the new station and begins streaming it.

During station playback (see Figure 9.8), iTunes Radio gives you a lot of options for interacting with the music:

- To skip the current song, tap the fast-forward button (the two right-pointing arrows).

- To mark the current song as a favorite, tap the star icon.

- To purchase the current song from iTunes, tap the price button in the upper-right corner.

- To create a new station from the current song, tap the Info icon in the top middle of the screen, and then tap either New Station from Artist or New Station from Song.

- To let your friends or family know about a station, tap the Info icon, tap Share Station, and then tap the method you want to use: AirDrop, Message, Mail, Twitter, or Facebook.

9.8 During streaming, each iTunes Radio station gives you quite a few options.

Using AirPlay to stream audio from your tablet

If you have an Apple TV that supports AirPlay, you can follow these steps to stream audio from your tablet to your TV or other audio device:

1. **Make sure your Apple TV is turned on.**

2. **On your tablet, start the audio that you want to stream.**

3. **Use four or five fingers to swipe up.** The multitasking bar appears. You can also double-press the Home button.

4. **Swipe the multitasking bar right to see the playback controls.**

5. **Tap the AirPlay button (which appears to the right of the Next/Fast Forward button).** You see a menu of output choices similar to the one shown in Figure 9.9.

9.9 Tap the AirPlay button on the multitasking bar to stream the audio to your Apple TV.

6. **Tap the name of your Apple TV device.** Your iPad or iPad mini streams the audio to that device, and hence, to your TV or receiver.

Rating a song on your tablet

If you use song ratings to organize your tunes, you may come across situations like the following, in which you want to rate a song that's playing on your iPad or iPad mini:

● You used your tablet to download some music from the iTunes Store, and you want to rate that music.

● You're listening to a song on your tablet, and decide that you've given a rating that's either too high or too low, and you want to change it.

In the first case, you could sync the music to your computer and rate it there. In the second case, you could modify the rating on your computer, and then sync with your iPad or iPad mini. However, these solutions are lame because you have to wait until you connect your tablet to your computer. If you're out and about, you want to rate the song *now*, while it's fresh in your mind. Follow these steps to do so:

1. **Locate the song you want to rate, and then tap it to start the playback.** The Music app displays the album art and the name of the artist, song, and album at the top of the screen.

2. **Tap Now Playing.** The Music app displays the album art.

3. **Tap the Details button in the upper-right corner of the screen.** The Music app turns the album art and displays the list of songs on the album.

4. **Tap Rating.** The Music app displays the five rating dots.

5. **Tap the dot that corresponds to the rating you want to give the song.** For example, to give the song a four-star rating, tap the fourth dot from the left.

6. **Tap Done.** The Music app saves the rating and returns you to the album art view.

The next time that you sync your tablet with your computer, iTunes notes your new ratings and applies them to the same tracks in the iTunes library.

Getting More Out of the Audio Features

To close out this tour of your tablet's audio features, the rest of this chapter takes you through a few useful techniques for redeeming iTunes gift cards, using audio accessories, and customizing the audio settings.

Redeeming an iTunes gift card

If you've been lucky enough to receive an iTunes gift card or gift certificate for your birthday or some other special occasion (or just for the heck of it), you normally use the iTunes Store on your computer to redeem it. However, if you're not at your computer and the gift card is burning a hole in your pocket, don't fret — you can follow these steps and redeem it right on your iPad or iPad mini:

1. **Sign in to the iTunes Store on your iPad or iPad mini.** You do this by tapping Settings, tapping iTunes & App Stores, typing your iTunes Store username and password, and then tapping Sign In.

2. **On the Home screen, tap iTunes to open the iTunes app.**

3. **Tap any content-related browse button in the menu bar, such as Music, Movies, or TV Shows.**

4. **Scroll to the bottom of the Music screen, and then tap Redeem.** iTunes then displays the Redeem dialog.

5. **To use the iPhone camera to enter the redeem code, tap Use Camera, and then align the white box onscreen with the box containing the redeem code.** Otherwise, tap You Can Also Enter Your Code Manually and then type the code from the gift card or certificate.

6. **Tap Redeem.** This redeems the gift card and adds the amount to your iTunes store credit.

Genius

To view your current iTunes store credit amount, tap any content-related browse button in the menu bar, and then scroll to the bottom of the screen. Your balance is displayed in the Apple ID button.

Using audio accessories with your tablet

Apple offers a few accessories for the iPad and iPad mini, but third-party vendors also want a piece of the iPad pie. There is now a rather large cottage industry of iPad and iPad mini accessories, including headsets (wired and Bluetooth), external speakers, FM transmitters, and all manner of cases, car kits, cables, and cradles. Many places all over the web sell iPad and iPad mini accessories, but the following sites are my faves:

- **Apple.** http://store.apple.com/us/ipad/ipad_accessories
- **Belkin.** www.belkin.com/us/d/IPAD
- **Griffin.** www.griffintechnology.com/ipad
- **NewEgg.** www.newegg.com
- **EverythingiCafe.** http://store.everythingicafe.com

Keep the following notes in mind when shopping for and using audio-related accessories for your iPad or iPad mini:

- **Look for the logo.** Despite the presence of the Music app, your iPad or iPad mini is not an iPod dressed up in fancy tablet clothes. It's a completely different device that doesn't fit or work with many iPod accessories. To be sure what you're buying is iPad or iPad mini-friendly, look for the *Works with iPad* logo.
- **Headsets, headphones, and earpieces.** The iPad and iPad mini use a standard headset jack, so just about any headset that uses a garden-variety 3.5mm stereo mini-plug fits, without requiring the purchase of an adapter.
- **External speakers.** You can also use the iPad or iPad mini headset jack to connect a set of external speakers. There are also Bluetooth wireless external speakers that you can pair with your tablet.
- **FM transmitters.** These are must-have accessories for car trips because they send the iPad or iPad mini output to an FM station, which you then play through your car stereo. The FM transmitters that work with the iPod don't generally work with iPads or iPad minis, so look for one that's designed for your tablet.

● **Electronic interference.** Because your iPad or iPad mini is a transmitter (of Wi-Fi, Bluetooth and, in some cases, cellular signals), it generates a nice little field of electronic interference, which is why you need to switch it to Airplane mode when you're flying (see Chapter 2). That same interference can wreak havoc on nearby external speakers and FM transmitters, so if you hear static when playing audio, switch to Airplane mode to get rid of it.

Customizing the iPad audio settings

Audiophiles in the crowd don't get much to fiddle with in the iPad, but you can play with a few audio settings. Follow these steps to get at them:

1. **Press the Home button to get to the Home screen.**
2. **Tap the Settings icon to open the Settings app.**
3. **Tap Music.** The Settings app displays the Music settings screen.

You then have the following five settings to try out:

● **Sound Check.** Every track is recorded at different audio levels, so invariably you get some tracks that are louder than others. With the Sound Check feature, you can set your iPad or iPad mini to play all of your songs at the same level. This feature affects only the baseline level of the music and doesn't change any of the other levels, so you still get the highs and lows. If you use it, you don't need to worry about having to quickly turn down the volume when a really loud song comes on. To turn on Sound Check, in the Music settings screen tap the Sound Check switch to the On position.

● **EQ.** This setting controls the built-in equalizer, which is actually a long list of preset frequency levels that affect the audio output. Each preset is designed for a specific type of audio: vocals, talk radio, classical music, rock, hip-hop, and lots more. To set the equalizer, tap EQ, and then tap the preset you want to use (or tap None to turn it off).

● **Volume Limit.** You use this setting to prevent the volume from being turned up too high and damaging your (or someone else's) hearing. You know, of course, that pumping up the volume while you have your earbuds in is an audio no-no, right? I thought so. However, I also know that when a great tune comes on, it's often a little too tempting to go for 11 on the volume scale. If you can't resist the temptation, use Volume Limit to limit the damage. Tap Volume Limit and drag the Volume slider to the maximum allowed volume.

- **Group By Album Artist.** Leave this setting On to group the Artists browse button based on the value in the Album Artist field, as opposed to the Artist field. For most albums, these two fields are the same, but some compilation albums use Various in the Artist field, and the names of the individual track artists in the Album Artist field. If you were to turn off this switch, you'd end up with all such albums listed under Various in the Artists browse button, which probably isn't what you want.

- **Show All Music.** When this setting is On, Music shows not only the albums and songs that you've purchased on or synced to your iPad or iPad mini, but also those tunes that are associated with your iCloud account that currently reside in the cloud. These albums and songs display a cloud icon with a downward pointing arrow, and you tap that icon to download the music to your tablet. If you only want to see the music that is physically on your device, tap this setting to Off.

- **iTunes Match.** If you have an iCloud account and you've shelled out the extra $24.99 per year for the iTunes Match service, tap this switch to On to activate iTunes Match on your tablet. This means that any songs that you own that aren't available via the iTunes Store will be automatically synced to your tablet as soon as you upload them to iCloud.

Genius

If you're setting up an iPad or iPad mini for a younger person, you should set the Volume Limit. To prevent it from being changed, open Settings, tap General, tap Restrictions, and then tap Enable Restrictions. In the Set Passcode screen, tap out a four-digit code, and then tap the code again to confirm. Tap Volume Limit and then tap Don't Allow Changes. This disables the Volume slider in the Volume Limit screen.

Controlling music with Siri voice commands

If you're using your iPad or iPad mini in a hands-free environment, you can still control your music using the handy Siri app, which recognizes a number of music-related voice commands. To get started, tap and hold the Home button (or press and hold the Mic button of the Apple headset or the equivalent button on a Bluetooth headset) until the Siri screen appears.

The most basic music voice commands mimic the on-screen controls you see when you play a song. That is, while a song is playing, you can speak any of the following commands to control the playback:

- Pause
- Play
- Next track (or next song)
- Previous track (or previous song)

In each case, Siri repeats the command back to you so you know whether it heard you correctly. You can also get more sophisticated by speaking commands that use roughly the following format: *verb object subject*

Here, *verb* is the action you want the Music app to take, which will most often be play; *object* is the type of item you want to work with, such as a song, album, or playlist; and *subject* is the particular item you want included in the action, such as the name of a song, album, playlist, or artist. The following examples should help you get the hang of it:

- Play songs by the Submarines
- Play album Blue Horse
- Play some blues
- Play playlist My Top Rated

Again, Siri confirms the command by saying it back to you (for example, "Playing songs by the Submarines"). The following list includes a few more voice commands to play with:

- **Shuffle.** Activates the Music app's Shuffle mode.
- **Shuffle *playlist*.** Plays the specified playlist in Shuffle mode.
- **Skip.** Skips to the next track.
- **What song is this?** Tells you the name of the current song and artist. Siri responds, "Now playing (*name of song*) by (*name of artist*)."
- **Play more songs like this.** Creates a playlist of songs that are similar to the current song. Siri responds, "Playing similar songs." This is called a Genius playlist, which is explained in more detail earlier in this chapter.

How Can I Work with Video on My iPad or iPad mini?

The iPod touch and the iPhone solve the audio part of the hunt for the perfect portable media player rather nicely. However, the video mission is more problematic. Single-purpose video players are too, well, single-purpose. The more versatile tools, such as the iPod touch and the iPhone, are too small for proper viewing. Now, the iPad and iPad mini are making a bid for portable media perfection, and their case is strong given the high-resolution touch-screen interface, HD video recording capabilities, and FaceTime video calling. This chapter puts that case to the test.

Syncing Videos

Although you can use the iTunes app on your iPad or iPad mini to rent or purchase movies, TV shows, and music videos, it's more likely that the bulk of your video content resides on your computer. If watching any of that video on your computer while sitting in your office chair is unappealing, then you need to transfer it to your tablet for viewing in more comfy circumstances. The next few sections provide the not-even-close-to-gory details.

Making a video compatible with iPad or iPad mini

Your iPad or iPad mini is very video friendly, but only the following formats are compatible with it:

- **H.264 video.** Features: Up to 1080 pixels; 30 frames per second; H.264 High Profile Level 4.1 with AAC-LC audio up to 160 Kbps, 48 kHz, stereo audio in M4V, MP4, and MOV file formats.

- **MPEG-4 video.** Features: Up to 2.5 Mbps; 640 × 480 pixels; 30 frames per second; Simple Profile with AAC-LC audio up to 160 Kbps, 48 kHz, stereo audio in M4V, MP4, and MOV file formats.

- **Motion JPEG video.** Up to 35 Mbps, 1280 × 720 pixels, 30 frames per second, audio in u-law PCM stereo audio using the AVI file format.

If you have a video file that doesn't match any of these formats, you may think you're out of luck. Not so. You can follow these steps to convert that video to a tablet-friendly MPEG-4 file in iTunes:

1. **If the video file isn't already in iTunes, choose File ⇨ Add to Library or press ⌘+O.** In Windows, choose File ⇨ Add File to Library or press Ctrl+O. The Add To Library dialog box appears. If the file is already in iTunes, skip to step 3.

2. **Locate and choose your video file, and then click Open.** iTunes copies the file into the library, which may take a while depending on the size of the file. In most cases, iTunes adds the video to the Movies section of the library.

3. **In iTunes, click your movie.**

4. **Choose File ⇨ Create New Version ⇨ Create iPad or Apple TV Version.** iTunes begins converting the video to the MPEG-4 format. This may take some time for even a relatively small video. When the conversion is complete, a copy of the original video appears in the iTunes library.

Note

Because the converted video has the same name as the original, you should probably rename one of them so you can tell them apart when it comes to syncing your
iPad or iPad mini. If you're not sure which file is which, right-click one of the videos
and then click Get Info. In the Summary tab, read the Kind value. The tablet-friendly
file has a Kind setting of MPEG-4 Video File.

Syncing movies

The iPad screen is a good size (9.7 inches on the diagonal) and it has a super-sharp Retina display
(2048 × 1536 resolution at 264 pixels per inch), which makes it ideal for watching a flick while sitting on the front porch with a mint julep. The second-generation iPad mini screen also boasts a
Retina display, but it's a bit smaller than the iPad (7.8 inches measured diagonally). The major
problem with movies is that their file size tends to be quite large — even short films lasting only a
few minutes weigh in at dozens of megabytes, and full-length movies are several gigabytes.
Clearly, there's a compelling need to manage your movies to avoid filling up your tablet, leaving
no room for the latest album from your favorite band.

Syncing rented movies

If you've rented a movie from iTunes, you can move it to your iPad or iPad mini and watch it there.
Note that you're *moving* the rented movie, not copying it. You can store rented movies in only one
location at a time, so if you sync it to your tablet, it is no longer available on your computer.

Follow these steps to sync a rented movie to your iPad or iPad mini:

1. **Connect your tablet to your computer.**

2. **In iTunes, click your iPad or iPad mini in the Devices list.**

3. **Click the Movies tab.**

4. **In the Rented Movies section, shown in Figure 10.1, click Move beside the rented
   movie you want to shift to your tablet.** iTunes adds the movie to the On *iPad* list
   (where *iPad* is the name of your iPad or iPad mini).

5. **Click Apply.** iTunes syncs the rented movie to your iPad or iPad mini.

| Paul's iPad ⏏ | Summary | Apps | Tones | Music | (Movies) | TV Shows | Podcasts | Books | Photos | | 📱 2 Devices | Done |

Rented Movies

The Mexican Suitcase
89 minutes
2.74 GB
Expires in 30 days
[HOT RATED]

Move ▷

On "Paul's iPad"

You must be connected to the Internet to transfer a rented movie.

10.1 Click Move to move a rented movie to your tablet.

Syncing purchased or downloaded movies

If you've purchased a movie from iTunes or added a video to your iTunes library, follow these steps to sync some (or all) of them to your iPad or iPad mini:

1. **Connect your tablet to your computer.**

2. **In iTunes, click your iPad or iPad mini in the Devices list.**

3. **Click the Movies tab.**

4. **Select the Sync Movies check box.**

5. **If you want iTunes to choose some of the movies automatically, select the Automatically include check box and proceed to step 6.** If you prefer to choose all of the movies manually, deselect the Automatically include check box and skip to step 7.

6. **Choose one of the following options from the pop-up menu:**

   - **All.** Choose this item to sync every movie.

   - **X Most Recent.** Choose this item to sync the X most recent movies you've added to iTunes.

   - **All Unwatched.** Choose this item to sync all of the movies you haven't yet played.

Note

A movie is unwatched if you haven't yet viewed it either in iTunes or on your tablet. If you watch a movie on your tablet, the player sends this information to iTunes when you next sync.

   - **X Most Recent Unwatched.** Choose this item to sync the X most recent movies you haven't yet played.

   - **X Least Recent Unwatched.** Choose this item to sync the X oldest movies you haven't yet played.

7. **Select the check box beside any other movie you want to sync, as shown in Figure 10.2.**

8. **Click Apply.** iTunes syncs the movies to your iPad or iPad mini.

Genius

To mark a movie as unwatched in iTunes, choose the Movies library, right-click the movie, and choose Mark as Unwatched.

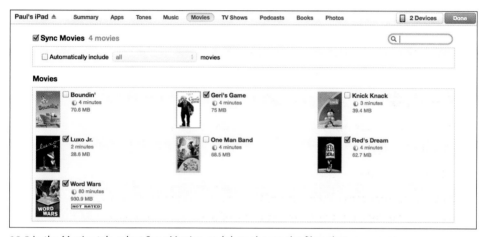

10.2 In the Movies tab, select Sync Movies, and then choose the films that you want to sync.

Syncing TV shows

If the average iPad or iPad mini is at some risk of being filled up by a few large movie files, it's probably also at grave risk of being overwhelmed by a large number of TV show episodes. A single half-hour episode eats up approximately 250MB, so even a modest collection of shows consumes multiple gigabytes of precious hard drive space on your tablet.

This means that it's crucial to monitor your collection of TV show episodes and keep your tablet synced with only those that you need.

Fortunately, iTunes gives you a decent set of tools to handle this — follow these steps to get it set up:

1. **Connect your tablet to your computer.**

2. **In iTunes, click your iPad or iPad mini in the Devices list.**

3. **Click the TV Shows tab.**

4. **Select the Sync TV Shows check box.**

5. **If you want iTunes to choose some of the episodes automatically, select the Automatically include check box, and proceed to steps 6 and 7.** If you prefer to choose all of the episodes manually, deselect the Automatically include check box and skip to step 8.

6. **Choose one of the following options from the drop-down menu:**

   - **All.** Choose this item to sync every TV show episode.

   - *X* **Most Recent.** Choose this item to sync the *X* most recent episodes.

   - **All Unwatched.** Choose this item to sync all of the episodes you haven't yet viewed.

Note A TV episode is unwatched if you haven't yet viewed it either in iTunes or on your tablet. If you watch an episode on your tablet, the player sends this information to iTunes when you next sync.

   - *X* **Most Recent Unwatched.** Choose this item to sync the *X* most recent episodes you haven't yet viewed.

   - *X* **Least Recent Unwatched.** Choose this item to sync the *X* oldest episodes you haven't yet viewed.

7. **Select one of the following options from the second pop-up menu:**

   - **All shows.** Choose this option to apply the choice from step 6 to all of your TV shows.

   - **Selected shows.** Choose this option to apply the choice from step 6 to only the TV shows you select.

8. **Select the check box beside any TV show or episode you want to sync.**

9. **Click Apply.** iTunes syncs the TV shows to your iPad or iPad mini.

Genius To mark a TV episode as unwatched, in iTunes, choose the TV Shows library, right-click the episode, and choose Mark as Unwatched.

Other Ways to Watch Video

With a few movies and TV shows finally residing on your iPad or iPad mini, you get to kick back and watch some moving pictures in comfort. Your commute (meaning, of course, your commute as a *passenger*) doesn't have to be boring anymore. Just connect your headphones and fire up a show. The next few sections take you through a few techniques and tips to help you get a bit more out of your tablet's video capabilities.

Playing videos on your TV

You can carry a bunch of videos with you on your iPad or iPad mini, so why shouldn't you be able to play them on a TV if you want? Well, you can. First, if you have an Apple TV that supports AirPlay, you can use AirPlay to stream a video from your tablet to your TV. On your iPad or iPad mini, start the video, tap the

10.3 While playing back a video, tap the screen, and then tap the Output button to stream it to your Apple TV.

screen to display the controls, and then tap the Output button (which appears to the right of the Volume bar). As shown in Figure 10.3, you can then tap your Apple TV to stream the video to that device and, hence, to your TV.

If you don't have an Apple TV (or if you have an older Apple TV that doesn't support AirPlay), you have to buy another cable. However, that's the only investment you have to make to watch iPad or iPad mini videos right on your TV. To hook your iPad or iPad mini up to your TV, you have the following two choices:

- **Lightning Digital AV Adapter.** This $49 cable has a Lightning connector on one end that connects to the iPad or iPad mini. The other end has another Lightning connector, so you can connect your tablet to a power outlet, and an HDMI (High-Definition Multimedia Interface) connector that enables you to make a connection to the corresponding HDMI input on your HDTV.

- **Lightning to VGA Adapter.** This $49 cable has a Lightning connector on one end that plugs into the iPad or iPad mini. The other end has another Lightning connector, so you can connect your tablet to a power outlet, and a VGA (video graphics array) connector that enables you to make a connection to the corresponding VGA input on your TV.

The cable you choose depends on the type of TV or screen that you have. If you're using an HDTV or projector that has at least one HDMI port, then the Lightning Digital AV Adapter is the way to go. If you're using a TV, projector, or monitor that has a VGA port, then you want the Lightning to VGA Adapter. After connecting your cables, set your TV to the corresponding input (HDMI or VGA) and play your videos as you normally would.

Mirroring your tablet's screen on your TV

iOS, in one of its most outstanding features, offers wireless AirPlay mirroring through Apple TV. As long as you have a second-generation Apple TV (and it has been updated with the latest software), you can use AirPlay mirroring not only to send videos to your TV, but also to view photos, slide shows, websites, apps, games, and anything else that you can display on your tablet.

Follow these steps to start mirroring the iPad or iPad mini screen on your TV:

1. **Turn on your Apple TV device.**

2. **On your tablet, swipe up from the bottom of the screen to display the Control Center.**

3. **Tap the AirPlay button.** The AirPlay dialog appears, offering a menu of output choices.

4. **Tap the name of your Apple TV device.**

5. **Tap the Mirroring switch to On, as shown in Figure 10.4.** Your iPad or iPad mini streams the screen to Apple TV and indicates that AirPlay is active by displaying the AirPlay icon in the status bar, as shown in Figure 10.5.

10.4 Use the multitasking bar to tap AirPlay, tap your Apple TV, and then tap the Mirroring switch to On.

Customizing the video settings

Your iPad or iPad mini offers a few video-related settings that you can try on for size. Follow these steps to get at them:

AirPlay icon

10.5 When AirPlay mirroring is on, you see the AirPlay icon in the status bar.

1. **Press the Home button to get to the Home screen.**

2. **Tap Settings to open the Settings app.**

3. **Tap Videos to open the Videos screen.**

In addition to the Home Sharing options that I mentioned earlier in this chapter, you also get the following settings to meddle with:

- **Start Playing.** This setting controls what your tablet does when you stop and restart a video. You have two choices: Where Left Off (the default), which picks up the video from the same point where you stopped it; and From Beginning, which always restarts the video from scratch. Tap Start Playing, and then tap the setting you prefer.

- **Show All Videos.** When this switch is On (as it is by default), the Videos app shows not only the videos that you've synced from iTunes, but also those videos that have been synced to your iCloud account. You can then download any iCloud video to your iPad or iPad mini by tapping the cloud icon in the lower-right corner of the video icon. If you don't want to see iCloud videos in the Videos app, tap this switch to Off.

Recording and Editing Video

The fifth-generation iPad is a bit lighter and quite a bit thinner than the original iPad, but it's still too big and heavy for regular use as a digital video camera. The iPad mini is smaller (it's about half the weight of the iPad), but it's still a slightly odd choice to use as a camcorder. You probably won't find yourself using your tablet to record video all that often. On the other hand, the rear camera in each tablet supports recording 1080p HD at 30 frames per second, so if a must-record event suddenly arises and you don't have your digital camera (or iPhone) with you, then iPad or iPad mini video will certainly do in a pinch.

Recording video with an iPad or iPad mini

Of course, this being an iPad and all, it's no surprise that recording a video is almost criminally easy. Follow these steps to do so:

1. **On the Home screen, tap the Camera button to launch the Camera app.**

2. **On the right side of the screen, slide the Mode switch to Video.**

3. **Tap the screen to focus the video if necessary.**

4. **Tap the Switch Camera button (at the top-right corner of the screen) if you want to use the front camera rather than the rear one.**

5. **Tap the Record button.** The Camera app starts recording video and displays the total recording time on the right side of the screen.

6. **When you're done, tap the Record button again to stop recording.** The Camera app saves the video to the Camera Roll.

Genius

If you have an AirPlay-friendly device, such as an Apple TV, you can stream your recorded videos to that device. Make sure that your AirPlay device is on, open the recorded video on your iPad or iPad mini, and then tap the Output button in the upper-right corner. In the menu that appears, tap the AirPlay device name (such as Apple TV) and away you go.

Editing a recorded video

Okay, being able to record video at the tap of a button is pretty cool, but your iPad or iPad mini tops that by also letting you perform basic editing chores right on the device. It's nothing fancy — basically, you can trim video from the beginning and end of the file — but it sure beats having to first sync the video to your computer, and then fire up iMovie or some other video-editing software.

Follow these steps to edit a video right on your tablet:

1. **Open the Camera Roll album in one of the following ways:**
   - **Camera app.** Tap the Camera Roll button in the lower-left corner of the screen.
   - **Photos app.** Display the Albums screen, and then tap Camera Roll. You can also tap the Videos album for a more direct route to your recorded videos.

2. **Tap the video you want to edit.** The Photos app displays the video and a timeline of the video along the top of the screen.

Note

Video thumbnails show a video camera icon in the lower-left corner and the duration of the video in the lower-right corner.

3. **Tap and drag the left edge of the timeline to set the starting point of the video.**

4. **Tap and drag the right edge of the timeline to set the ending point of the video.**

   The trimmed timeline appears surrounded by orange, as shown in Figure 10.6.

Genius If you need more precision when trimming the timeline, tap and hold either the start trim control or the end trim control. The Photos app expands the timeline to show more frames, which enables you to make more precise edits.

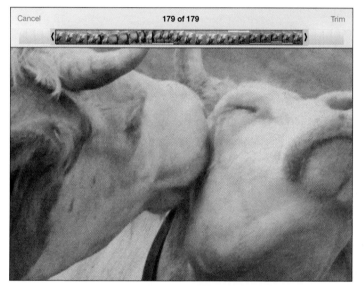

Cancel | 179 of 179 | Trim

10.6 Use the video timeline to set the start and end points of the footage that you want to keep.

5. **Tap Play to ensure that you've set the start and end points correctly.** If not, repeat steps 5 and 6 to adjust the timeline as needed.

6. **Tap Trim.** The Photos app trims the video, and then saves your work.

Uploading a video to YouTube

Of course, the real reason you want to be able to instantly record something is because you want to upload it to YouTube and share it with the world.

Your iPad or iPad mini is happy to help here, too, as shown by the following steps:

1. **Open the Camera Roll album in one of the following ways:**

   - **Camera app.** Tap the Camera Roll button in the lower-left corner of the screen.

   - **Photos app.** Display the Albums screen, and then tap Camera Roll or Videos.

2. **Tap the video you want to share.** The Photos app opens the video.

3. **Tap the Actions button in the menu bar.** The Action button appears in the bottom-left corner of the screen. If you don't see the menu bar, tap the screen to display the controls. The Share options appear.

4. **Tap YouTube.** The Photos app compresses the video and prompts you to log in to your YouTube account.

5. **Type your YouTube username and password, and then tap Sign In.** The Publish Video screen appears.

6. **Tap a title, description, and tags for your video, and then choose a category.**

7. **If you want to upload a high-definition (HD) version of the video, tap HD.** HD versions of iPad or iPad mini videos are more than three times larger than standard-definition versions, so uploading them takes longer.

8. **Tap Publish.** The Videos app publishes the video to your YouTube account. This may take several minutes, depending on the size of the video. When the video is published, you see a dialog with a few options.

9. **Tap one of the following options:**

   - **View on YouTube.** Tap this option to cue up the video on the YouTube site.

   - **Tell a Friend.** Tap this option to send an e-mail message that includes a link to the video on YouTube.

   - **Close.** Tap this option to return to the video.

Video Calling with FaceTime

One of the most welcome features of the iPad or iPad mini is the front-mounted camera. This means you can take advantage of the amazing Apple FaceTime feature, which lets you make HD (720p) video calls on your tablet, and actually see the other person face to face. It's an awesome feature, but to use it the other person must also be using an iPad mini, an iPad 2 or later, an iPhone 4 or later, a fourth-generation or later iPod touch, or a Mac with a video camera and the FaceTime application installed. You must also both be signed in either to an Internet-connected Wi-Fi network or to a cellular network.

The good news about FaceTime (besides how cool it is) is that the app is already installed on your iPad or iPad mini, and it doesn't require anything for use other than an Apple ID.

Configuring FaceTime

If you didn't sign in to your Apple ID when you configured your iPad or iPad mini, then the first time that you launch FaceTime you need to run through a one-time configuration procedure. Follow these steps to get FaceTime set up:

1. **In your Home screen, tap FaceTime.** The FaceTime app appears.
2. **Type your Apple ID and password.**
3. **Tap Sign In.** FaceTime asks which e-mail address you want other people to use to call you.
4. **Tap to deselect any address that you don't want to use for FaceTime.**
5. **Tap Next.** FaceTime verifies your Apple ID, and then displays the FaceTime screen.

Initiating a FaceTime call

To initiate a FaceTime call, tap the FaceTime button (if the app isn't open already), and then use either of the following techniques:

- **If the other person is in your Contacts list, tap Contacts, and then tap the person you want to call.** If the person has multiple contact items (phone numbers and e-mail addresses), tap the item you want to use to place the call.

- **If you've recently made a FaceTime call to someone, tap the Recents button, and then tap the FaceTime call.**

Genius

If you FaceTime call someone frequently, add that person to the FaceTime app Favorites list. Tap the Favorites button, tap the plus sign (+), tap the contact, and then tap the phone number or e-mail address you want to use.

If another FaceTime user calls you, you see the message "*Name* would like FaceTime" (where *Name* is the caller's name if she is in your Contacts list), as shown in Figure 10.7.

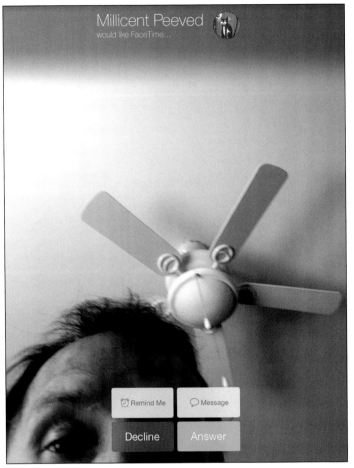

10.7 When a FaceTime user calls you, tap Answer to initiate a FaceTime video call.

Tap Answer and your video call connects, just like that. You see your caller's (hopefully) smiling face in the full iPad or iPad mini screen, and your own mug in a picture-in-picture (PIP) window, as shown in Figure 10.8.

Genius

Your PIP window appears by default in the upper-right corner. If you prefer a different position, tap and drag it to any corner of the screen.

10.8 Face-to-face calling on the iPad.

The FaceTime calling screen includes the following three buttons in the menu bar:

- **Mute.** Tap this button (it's the one on the left) to mute the sound from your end of the conversation. You can still hear sound from the other person's end.

- **End.** Tap this button (it's the one in the middle) to end the call.

- **Switch cameras.** Tap this button to switch your video output to the rear camera (for example, to show your caller something in front of you).

Disabling FaceTime

There are times when you simply don't want a face-to-face conversation, no matter who's calling. Perhaps you're in a secret location or you just don't look your best that day. Whatever the reason, you can follow these steps to turn off FaceTime:

1. **In the Home screen, tap Settings.** The Settings app appears.
2. **Tap FaceTime.** The FaceTime screen appears.
3. **Tap the FaceTime switch to the Off position.**

Now, when people try to call you using FaceTime, they see a message saying that you're not available for FaceTime.

How Do I Manage Contacts?

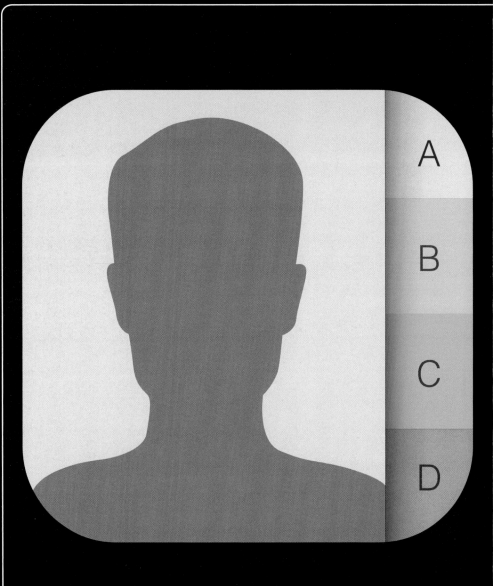

One of life's paradoxes is that as your contact information becomes more important, you store less of it in the easiest database system of all — your memory. Instead of memorizing phone numbers, you now store them electronically. This is because it's no longer just a landline number that you have to remember for each person — there's also a cell number, an e-mail or website address, and more. That's a lot, so it makes sense to go the electronic route. For the iPad and iPad mini, *electronic* means Contacts, which is loaded with useful features to help you organize your contacts.

Syncing Your Contacts

Although you can certainly add contacts directly on your iPad or iPad mini — and I show you how to do just that a bit later in this chapter — adding, editing, grouping, and deleting contacts is a lot easier on a computer. A good way to approach contacts is to manage them on your Mac or PC, and then sync your contacts with your tablet.

Note The version of iTunes that comes with OS X Mavericks does *not* support syncing contacts accounts directly between iTunes and an iPad or iPad mini. Instead, you must configure your Mac to sync this data to your iCloud account, and then configure your tablet to have this data synced from your iCloud account. See Chapter 4 for the details.

Creating contact groups

However, do you really need to sync *all* of your contacts? For example, if you only use your iPad or iPad mini to reach out to friends and family, why clog your Contacts app with work colleagues and clients? You can control which contacts are sent to your tablet by creating groups of contacts, and then syncing only the groups that you want. Here are some quick instructions for creating groups:

- **Contacts (OS X Mountain Lion) or Address Book (earlier versions of OS X).** Choose File ⇨ New Group, type the group name, and then press Return. Now populate the new group by dragging and dropping contacts onto it.

- **Windows Contacts (Windows 8, Windows 7, and Windows Vista).** Click New Contact Group, type the group name, and then click Add to Contact Group. Choose all of the contacts you want in the group, and then click Add. Click OK.

Note If you're an Outlook user, note that iTunes doesn't support Outlook-based contact groups, so you're stuck syncing everyone in your Outlook Contacts folder. Also note that iTunes doesn't support the Windows 8 People app or Windows Live Mail at all, so you can't use those applications to sync your contacts.

Running the sync

With your group (or groups) all figured out, follow these steps to sync your contacts with your iPad or iPad mini:

1. **Connect your tablet to your computer.**

2. **In iTunes, click your iPad or iPad mini in the Devices list.**

3. **Click the Info tab.** Remember that you will not see the Info tab if you are running iTunes on OS X Mavericks.

4. **Turn on contacts syncing by using one of the following techniques:**

   - **OS X Mountain Lion.** Select the Sync Contacts check box.

   - **Earlier versions of OS X.** Select the Sync Address Book Contacts check box.

   - **Windows.** Select the Sync Contacts With check box, and then use the list to choose the program you want to use (such as Outlook). For Yahoo! contacts, see step 7; for Google contacts, see step 8.

5. **Select one of the following options:**

   - **All contacts.** Select this option to sync all of your Address Book contacts.

   - **Selected groups.** Select this option to sync only the groups you pick. In the Selected groups list, select the check box beside each group that you want to sync, as shown in Figure 11.1.

11.1 You can sync selected contact groups to your iPad or iPad mini.

6. **If you want to make the sync a two-way street, select the Add contacts created outside of groups on this iPad to check box, and then choose a group from the menu.**

7. **In Windows, use the Sync Contacts with list to select Yahoo! Address Book.** Click Agree, type your Yahoo! ID and password, and then click OK.

8. **In OS X, if you have a Google account and you also want your Google Contacts in on the sync, select the Sync Google Contacts check box.** In Windows, use the Sync Contacts with list to select Google Contacts. In either case, you then click Agree, type your Google ID and password, and click OK.

9. **Click Apply.** iTunes syncs your tablet using your new contacts settings.

Getting Started with Contacts

You need Contacts up and running for this chapter, so head for the Home screen and tap the Contacts icon. Figure 11.2 shows Contacts.

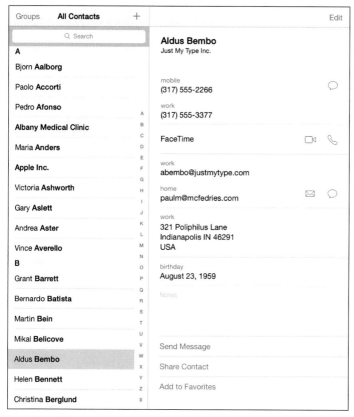

11.2 The iOS 7 version of the Contacts app.

Contacts displays the All Contacts list on the left and the data for the currently selected contact on the right. If you have a healthy number of contacts, you need to know how to navigate the list. You have the following four choices:

- **By default, Contacts displays the All Contacts list.** To view a group of contacts, tap Groups in the upper-left corner of the screen, and then tap the group you want to view.
- **Flick up and down to scroll through the list.**
- **Tap a letter to leap directly to the contacts whose last names begin with that letter.**
- **Use the Search box at the top of the All Contacts list to type a few letters of the name of the contact with which you want to work, and then tap the contact in the search results.**

Creating and Editing Contacts

Syncing your computer's contacts program (such as OS X Contacts or the Outlook Contacts folder) is, by far, the easiest way to populate Contacts with a crowd of people. However, it might not include everyone in your posse. If someone's missing and you're not around your computer, you can add that person directly to Contacts.

Similarly, you might be messing around with Contacts and notice an error or old info for someone. No problem — you can edit a contact right on the iPad or iPad mini. Best of all, any changes that you make within Contacts are automatically synced back to your computer the next time your tablet and iTunes get together for a sync session.

Creating a new contact

The next time you realize someone's missing from your contacts, you can fire up your trusty tablet and follow these steps to tap that person's vital statistics right into Contacts:

1. **In the Home screen, tap the Contacts icon to open Contacts.**
2. **Tap the plus sign (+) at the top of the contacts list.** The New Contact screen appears, as shown in Figure 11.3.

3. **Tap the First box, and then type the person's first name.** If you're jotting down the contact data for a company or some other inanimate object, skip to step 5.

4. **Tap the Last box, and then type the person's last name.**

5. **If you want to note where the person works (or if you're adding a business), tap the Company box and type the company name.**

Yup, I know there are still plenty of other fields to fill in, and we get to those in a second. For now, though, I want to interrupt your regularly scheduled programming to show you how to edit an existing contact. It will all make sense soon, trust me.

Editing an existing contact

Now that your new contact is off to a flying start, you can go ahead and fill in details, such as phone numbers, addresses (e-mail, web, and snail mail), and anything else you want to add (or have the patience to enter into the Info screen). The next few sections take you through the steps for each type of data. However, the steps I show also apply to any contact that's already residing in your iPad or iPad mini.

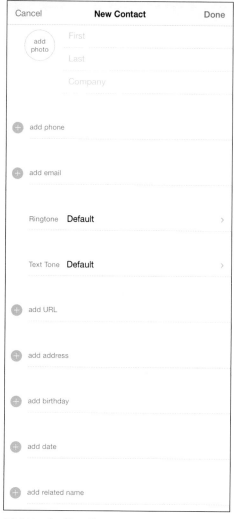

11.3 Use the New Contact screen to tap in the details of your contact.

Note The one technique that I don't get into here is how to spruce up your contact with a photo. That's because I cover that in Chapter 8.

These are the steps required to open an existing contact for editing:

1. **Open Contacts and tap the contact you want to edit.**

2. **Tap Edit.** Contacts displays the contact's data.

3. **Make your changes, as described in the next few sections.**

4. **Tap Done.** Contacts saves your work and returns you to the list of contacts.

Assigning phone numbers to a contact

Everyone has a phone number, so you, no doubt, want to augment a contact by entering his phone data. Sure, but *which* number: Work? Home? Cell? Pager? Fax? Fortunately, there's no need to choose just one because Contacts is happy to store all of these, plus a few more if needed.

Follow these steps to add one or more phone numbers for a contact:

1. **With the contact's data open for editing, tap Add Phone.** Contacts creates a new phone field and displays a numeric keypad.

2. **Tap inside the Phone field and then type the phone number with area code first.** Note that you only need to type the numbers — Contacts helpfully adds extra stuff, like parentheses around the area code and the dash. When you begin typing the phone number, Contacts automatically adds another Phone field below the current one.

3. **Examine the label box in the Phone field to see if the default label is the one you want.** If you're okay with the existing label, skip to step 5; otherwise, tap the label to open the Label dialog, shown in Figure 11.4.

Label
radio ✓
home fax
home
company main
work
work fax
car
mobile
assistant

11.4 Tap the label you want to use for a contact's phone number.

4. **Tap the label that best applies to the phone number you're adding, such as mobile, home, or work.** Contacts displays the new label.

5. **Repeat steps 1 to 4 to add any other numbers you want to store for this contact.**

Assigning e-mail addresses to a contact

It makes sense that you might want to add multiple phone numbers for a contact, but would you ever need to enter multiple e-mail addresses? Well, sure you would! Most people have at least a couple of addresses — usually for home and work — and some Type A e-mailers have a dozen or more. Life is too short to type that many e-mail addresses, but you do need at least the important ones if you want to use the iPad or iPad mini Mail app to send a note to your contacts.

Follow these steps to add one or more e-mail addresses for a contact:

1. **With the contact's data open for editing, tap Add Email.** Contacts creates a new e-mail field and displays the keyboard.

2. **Type the person's e-mail address.**

3. **Feel free to repeat steps 1 and 2 to add up to three e-mail addresses for this contact.**

Assigning web addresses to a contact

Who on Earth doesn't have a website these days? It could be a humble home page, a blog, a Tumblr page, a home business site, or it could be someone's corporate website. Whatever web home a person has, it's a good idea to toss the address into her contact data because, later on, you can simply tap the address and Contacts (assuming your tablet can see the Internet from here) immediately fires up Safari, which takes you to the site.

You can add a web address for a contact by making your way through these steps:

1. **Open the contact's data for editing.**

2. **Tap Add URL.** Contacts creates a new URL field and displays the keyboard, as shown in Figure 11.5. Note the . (period) and .com keys in the on-screen keyboard, which come in very handy.

3. **Type the person's web address.**

11.5 Don't forget to take advantage of the on-screen keyboard URL-related keys, such as slash (/) and .com.

Genius

To save some wear and tear on your tapping finger, don't bother adding the http:// stuff at the beginning of a URL. Safari adds those characters automatically anytime that you tap an address to visit a site — same with the www. prefix. So if the full address is http://www.wordspy.com, you need only enter wordspy.com.

Assigning social network data to a contact

These days, many of us are far more likely to contact others via social networks (such as Twitter, Facebook, and LinkedIn) than we are via more traditional methods like e-mail. Contacts reflects this new reality by enabling you to save social network data for each contact, including data for Twitter, Facebook, LinkedIn, Flickr, and Myspace. Here are the steps to follow to add one or more social network details to a contact:

1. **With the contact's data open for editing, tap Add Social Profile.** Contacts creates a new Social Profile field.

2. **If you want to use a different social network, tap the Twitter label to see a list of social networks, as shown in Figure 11.6.**

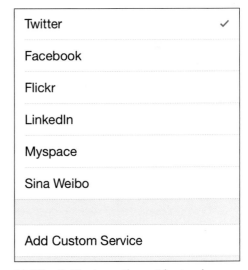

11.6 Tap Twitter to see the social networks supported by Contacts.

3. **Tap the label that suits the social network data you're entering, such as Facebook or Flickr.** Contacts adds the new label.

4. **Tap inside the field, and then tap the person's username for the chosen social network.** Note that as soon as you tap at least one character, Contacts adds a new social network field.

5. **If necessary, repeat steps 1 to 4 to add other social networks, as needed.**

Assigning physical addresses to a contact

With all this talk about cell numbers, e-mail and web addresses, and social networks, it's easy to forget that people actually live and work somewhere. You may have plenty of contacts where the location of that somewhere doesn't much matter, but if you ever need to get from here to there, taking the time to insert a contact's physical address really pays off. Why? Because you need only tap the address and Contacts switches to Maps to show you the precise location. From there you can get directions, see a satellite map of the area, and more. (I talk about all this great map stuff in Chapter 13.)

Tapping out a full address is a bit of work, but as the following steps show, it's not exactly painful:

1. **With the contact's data open for editing, tap Add Address.** Contacts displays the address fields.

2. **Tap the first Street field, and then type the person's street address.** When Contacts realizes you're typing a street address, it automatically adds a second Street field.

3. **If necessary, tap the second Street field, and then type even more of the person's street address.**

4. **Tap the City field, and then type the person's city.**

5. **Tap the State field, and then type the person's state.** Depending on what you later select for the country, this field might have a different name, such as Province.

6. **Tap the ZIP field, and then type the ZIP code.** Again, depending on what you later select for the country, this field might have a different name, such as Postal Code.

7. **Tap the Country field to open the Country list, and then tap the contact's country.**

8. **Examine the label box to see if the default label is the one you want.** If it is, skip to Step 10; if it's not, tap the label box to open the Label screen.

9. **Tap the label that best applies to the physical address you're inserting (Contacts automatically sends you back to the contact's data screen after you tap), such as home or work.**

10. **Repeat steps 1 to 9 if you feel like entering another address for your contact.**

Deleting a contact

It feels good to add new contacts, but you don't get a lifetime guarantee with these things: Friends fall out or fade away, colleagues decide to make a new start at another firm, clients take their business elsewhere, and some of your acquaintances simply wear out their welcome after a while. You move on and so does your Contacts list. The best way to proceed is to delete the contact and keep the list trim and tidy.

Follow these steps to delete a contact:

1. **Tap the contact you want to delete.**

2. **Tap Edit.** The contact's data screen appears.

3. **Tap the Delete Contact button at the bottom of the screen.** Contacts asks you to confirm the deletion.

4. **Tap Delete Contact.** Contacts removes the contact and returns you to the All Contacts screen.

Getting More Out of Contacts

Adding and editing data using Contacts is blissfully linear: Tap a field label to change it and then tap inside a field to add the data. If you remember to take advantage of the on-screen keyboard context-sensitive keys (such as the .com key that materializes when you type a web address), then contact data entry becomes a snap.

Contacts is straightforward on the surface, but if you dig a bit deeper, you find some useful tools and features that can make your contact management duties even easier.

Creating or deleting a custom label

When you fill out your contact data, Contacts insists that you apply a label to each tidbit: home, work, mobile, and so on. If none of the predefined labels fits, you can always just slap on the generic *other* label, but it seems so, well, dull.

If you have a phone number or address that you can't shoehorn into any of the prefab labels, follow these steps to get creative and make one up:

1. **With the contact's data open for editing, tap the label beside the field in which you want to work.** The Label dialog appears.

2. **Tap Add Custom Label.** If you're working with a social network field, tap Add Custom Service instead. Contacts adds a new blank line to the Label dialog.

Note

If you can't see the Add Custom Label command because the keyboard is in the way, tap the Hide Keyboard button that appears in the bottom-right corner of the keyboard.

3. **Type the custom label.**

4. **Tap Return.** Contacts saves your custom label and returns you to the Info screen.

You can apply your custom label to any type of contact data. For example, you can create a label named college and apply it to a phone number, e-mail address, web address, or physical address.

Adding or deleting fields

The New Contact screen (which appears when you add a contact) and the data screen (which appears when you edit an existing contact) display only the fields you need for basic contact info. In addition to the fields I've covered so far, you can click the following items to add more fields to a contact's data:

- **Add Birthday.** Tap this item to add the contact's day, month, and year of birth.

- **Add Data.** Tap this item to add any other date, such as an anniversary.

- **Add Related Name.** Tap this item to specify another contact who is related to the contact you're editing. For example, if you also have the contact's brother in your Contacts list, tap Add Related Name, tap More Info (the *i* icon), tap the brother, tap the field label (the default is *mother*), and then tap the relationship type.

- **Add Instant Message.** Tap this item to add the contact's instant messaging data for a service such as Skype, Google Talk, or AIM.

- **Notes.** Use this field to add general observations or contact data that doesn't fit into any other field.

Despite these additional fields, the contact data screen still lacks quite a few common fields. For example, you might need to specify a contact's prefix (such as Dr. or Professor), suffix (such as Jr., Sr., or III), or job title.

Thankfully, Contacts is merely hiding these and other useful fields where you can't see them. There are 9 hidden fields that you can add to any contact, as shown in Figure 11.7. Contacts is only too happy to let you add as many of these extra fields as you want. Follow these steps to do so:

1. **With the contact's data open for editing, tap Add Field.** The Add Field dialog appears, as shown in Figure 11.7.

2. **Tap the field that you want to add.** Contacts adds the field to the contact.

3. **If the field has a label, tap the label box to choose a new one if needed.**

4. **Type the field data.** In the case of the Related Name field, tap the label (the default value is *mother*), tap the relationship (such as spouse or manager), tap the blue More Info (*i*) icon, and then tap the related contact.

| Prefix |
| Phonetic First Name |
| Middle |
| Phonetic Middle Name |
| Phonetic Last Name |
| Suffix |
| Nickname |
| |
| Job Title |
| Department |

11.7 The Add Field dialog shows the hidden fields that you can add to any contact.

5. **Repeat steps 1 to 4 to add more fields as needed.**

People change, and so does their contact info. Most of the time these changes require you to edit an existing field, but sometimes people actually shed information. For example, they might get rid of a pager or fax machine, or might shutter a website. Whatever the reason, you should delete that data from the contact to keep the data screen tidy and easier to navigate.

To delete a contact field, follow these steps:

1. **In the Contacts list, tap the contact with which you want to work.**

2. **Tap Edit.** The Info screen appears.

3. **Tap the red Delete button to the left of the field you want to trash.** Contacts displays a Delete button to the right of the field.

4. **Tap Delete.** Contacts removes the field.

5. **Tap Done.** Contacts closes the data screen.

Creating a new contact from a vCard

Typing a person's contact data is a tedious bit of business at the best of times, so it helps if you can find a faster way to do it. If you can cajole a contact into sending his or her contact data electronically, then you can add that data with just a couple of taps.

What do I mean when I talk about sending contact data electronically? The world's contact management gurus long ago came up with a standard file format for contact data: the vCard. It's a kind of digital business card that exists as a separate file. People can pass this data along by attaching their (or someone else's) card to an e-mail message.

If you get a message with contact data, you see an icon for the VCF file, as shown in Figure 11.8. To get this data into your Contacts list, follow these steps:

1. **In the Home screen, tap Mail to open the Mail app.**

2. **Tap the message that contains the vCard attachment.**

3. **Tap the attachment's Tap to Download link and then tap the icon for the vCard file.** Mail opens the vCard.

4. **Tap Create New Contact.** If the person is already in your Contacts list, but the vCard contains new data, tap Add to Existing Contact, and then tap the contact.

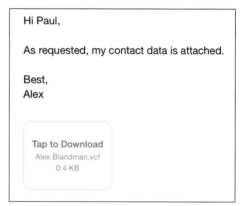

Hi Paul,

As requested, my contact data is attached.

Best,
Alex

Tap to Download
Alex Blandman.vcf
0.4 KB

11.8 If your iPad or iPad mini receives an e-mail message with an attached vCard, an icon for the file appears in the message body.

Sending and receiving a contact via AirDrop

Sharing your contact data using a vCard has worked well for many years, but sharing data via attachments is beginning to feel decidedly old-fashioned. Fortunately, these days of exchanging virtual business cards may soon be over thanks to an iOS 7 feature called AirDrop, which is a Bluetooth service that lets two nearby devices — specifically, an iPhone 5 or 5S, a fourth-generation iPad or later, an iPad mini, or a fifth-generation iPod touch or later — swap contacts directly. Here are the steps to follow:

1. **Use Contacts to open the contact you want to share.**

2. **Tap Share Contact.** The AirDrop section shows an icon for each nearby device.

3. **Tap the icon for the person with whom you want to share the contact.** The other person sees a dialog asking for permission to accept the contact. When she taps Accept, her version of Contacts loads and displays the contact.

Sorting contacts

By default, Contacts displays your contacts sorted by last name (or company name, for businesses) and then by first name (to resolve cases where people have the same last name). That makes sense in most cases, but you might prefer a more friendly approach that sorts contacts by first name and then by last name. Follow these steps to make it so:

1. **Return to the Home screen and tap Settings to launch the Settings app.**

2. **Tap Mail, Contacts, Calendars.** The Mail, Contacts, Calendars screen appears.

3. **Scroll down to the Contacts section.**

4. **Tap Sort Order to display the Sort Order options.**

5. **Tap First, Last.** Contacts now sorts your contacts by first name.

Working with Facebook contacts

If you've signed in to your Facebook account on your iPad or iPad mini, as described in Chapter 3, iOS automatically updates your Contacts with all of your Facebook friends. This means that all of the profile data that each person shares with his friends is automatically available via Contacts. This often includes info such as the person's profile picture, occupation, company name, e-mail address, location, and birthday, but it can also include the following fields:

- **Mobile.** Tap this field to call the friend's cellphone.

- **URL.** Tap this field to visit the friend's website.

- **Facebook.** Tap this field to view the friend's Facebook profile page.

- **IM.** Tap this field to send an instant message to the friend.

Note

Although you can add new data to a Facebook contact, you can't edit any data that comes via Facebook. (When you tap Edit to display the Info screen, you see that each Facebook-generated field appears with a Facebook logo beside it and that the field isn't editable.)

Managing contacts with Siri voice commands

The Siri voice recognition app enables you to locate and query your contacts using simple voice commands. To get started, tap and hold the Home button (or press and hold the Mic button of the Apple headphones, or the equivalent button on a Bluetooth headset) until Siri appears.

To display one or more contacts, use the following techniques within Siri:

- **Displaying a specific contact.** Say "Show (or Display or Find) *First Last*," where *First* and *Last* are the person's first and last names as given in the Contacts list; you can also just say the person's name. If the contact is a business, say "Show (or Display or Find) *company*," where *company* is the business name as given in your Contacts list; you can also just say the company name.

- **Displaying a contact who has a relationship with you.** Say "Show (or Display or Find) *relationship*," where *relationship* is the connection you've defined (such as sister or father).

- **Displaying a contact with a unique first name.** Say "Show (or Display or Find) *First*," where *First* is the person's first name as given in your Contacts list.

- **Displaying multiple contacts who have some information in common.** Say "Find people *criteria*," where *criteria* defines the common data. Examples: "Find people named Stevens" or "Find people who live in New York."

To query your contacts, you can use the following general syntax: *Question contact info*?

Here, *question* can be "What is" (for general data), "When is" for dates, or "Who is" (for people); *contact* specifies the name (or relationship) of the contact; and *info* specifies the type of data you want to retrieve (such as "birthday" or "home phone number"). Here are some examples:

- What is Alex Blandman's mobile phone number?
- When is my sister's anniversary?
- What is David Cutrere's address?
- Who is Kyra's husband?

How Do I Track My Appointments?

Thursday

12

Do you, like the White Rabbit in Lewis Carroll's *Alice's Adventures in Wonderland*, find yourself constantly saying, "Oh my ears and whiskers, how late it's getting"? Well, you've come to the right place, because the iPad can help. Not only can you can use it to read *Alice's Adventures in Wonderland* (that will just make you later than you already are, though), but also you can take advantage of the Calendar app. It turns your tablet into an electronic administrative assistant that stores your appointments, and even reminds you when they're coming up. Oh my ears and whiskers, how punctual you'll be!

Syncing Your Calendars

When you're tripping around town with your trusty iPad or iPad mini, you certainly don't want to be late if you have a date. The best way to ensure that you don't miss an appointment, meeting, or rendezvous is to always have the event details at hand. This means adding those details to the Calendar app. You could add the appointment to Calendar right on the tablet (a technique I take you through later in this chapter), but it's easier to create it on your computer and then sync it to your device. This gives you the added advantage of having the appointment listed in two places, so you're sure to arrive on time.

Note
The version of iTunes that comes with OS X Mavericks does *not* support syncing calendars directly between iTunes and an iPad or iPad mini. Instead, you must configure your Mac to sync calendars to your iCloud account and then configure your tablet to have this data synced from your iCloud account. See Chapter 4 for the details.

Most people sync all their appointments, but it's not unusual to keep track of separate schedules — for example, business and personal. To control which schedule is synced to your iPad or iPad mini, you can create separate calendars and then sync only those that you want by performing one of the following actions:

- **OS X Mavericks or Mountain Lion.** In the Calendar application, choose File ⇨ New Calendar, type the calendar name, and then press Return.

- **Earlier versions of OS X.** In the iCal application, choose File ⇨ New Calendar, type the calendar name, and then press Return.

- **Windows.** In Outlook, click the Calendars tab, choose Folder ⇨ New Calendar, type the calendar name, and then click OK.

Now, follow these steps to sync your calendar with your iPad or iPad mini:

1. **Connect your tablet to your computer.**

2. **In iTunes, click your iPad or iPad mini in the Devices list.**

3. **Click the Info tab.** Remember that you won't see the Info tab if you're running OS X Mavericks.

4. **Turn on calendar syncing by using one of the following techniques:**
   - **OS X Mountain Lion.** Select the Sync Calendars check box.

- **Earlier versions of OS X.** Select the Sync iCal Calendars check box.

- **Windows.** Select the Sync Calendars With check box and use the list to choose the program you want to use (such as Outlook).

Note iTunes doesn't support Windows 8's Calendar app, Windows Live Calendar, or Windows Vista's Calendar program, so you're out of luck if you use any of these applications to manage your schedule.

5. **Select one of the following options:**

   - **All calendars.** Select this option to sync all your calendars.

   - **Selected calendars.** Select this option to sync only the calendars you choose. In the calendar list, select the check box beside each calendar that you want to sync, as shown in Figure 12.1.

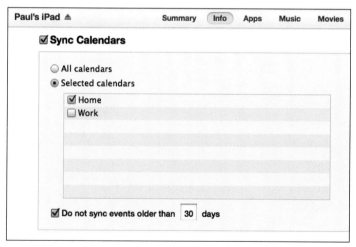

12.1 You can sync selected calendars with your iPad or iPad mini.

6. **To control how far back the calendar sync goes, select the Do not sync events older than X days check box.** Next, type the number of days of calendar history that you want to see on your tablet.

7. **Click Apply.** iTunes syncs the iPad or iPad mini using your new calendar settings.

Getting Started with the Calendar App

These days, when you ask someone how she is, the most common reply is a short one: "Busy!" We're all busy, and that places-to-go, people-to-see feeling is everywhere. All the more reason to keep your affairs in order, and that includes your appointments. iOS comes with a Calendar app that you can use to create items, called *events*, which represent your appointments, meetings, lunch dates, and so on. Calendar keeps track of all this stuff for you, leaving your brain free to concentrate on more important things.

You need the Calendar app up and running for this chapter, so head for the Home screen and tap the Calendar icon. Figure 12.2 shows the Calendar app in portrait mode.

The key to getting around in the Calendar app efficiently is to take advantage of its various views, represented by the following four buttons at the top of the screen:

- **Day.** This view shows the events of a single day. To navigate this view, tap a date near the top of the screen. To see more dates, scroll the displayed dates left or right.

- **Week.** This view shows all your events for the selected week. To navigate this view, scroll the screen left or right.

- **Month.** This view shows the titles of all your events for a given month. You navigate this view by scrolling up or down.

- **Year.** This view shows a full calendar year. The dates on which you have scheduled events appear with a colored background. You navigate this view by scrolling up or down.

12.2 Your tablet's administrative assistant: the beautiful and talented Calendar app.

Tracking Your Events

I showed you how to sync your computer's calendar application (such as Calendar on the Mac, or the Outlook Calendar folder) earlier in this chapter. That's the easiest way to fill your iPad or iPad mini with events. However, something always comes up when you're running around, so you need to know how to add and edit events directly in the Calendar app. The next few sections provide the details.

Adding an event to your calendar

Follow these steps to add a basic event (the more advanced features, such as repeating events and alerts, are covered a bit later in this chapter):

1. **Display the date on which the event occurs.**

2. **Tap and hold the time when the event occurs.** In Month view, tap and hold the date. You can also tap the plus sign (+) in the top-right corner of the screen. The Add Event screen appears, as shown in Figure 12.3.

3. **Tap the Title box and type a title for the event.**

4. **Tap the Location box and type a location for the event.**

5. **Tap Starts, and use the scroll wheels to set the date and time that your event begins.**

6. **Tap Ends, and use the scroll wheels to set the date and time that your event finishes.**

7. **If you have multiple calendars, tap Calendar, and then tap the calendar in which you want this event to appear.**

8. **Tap the Notes box, and type your notes for the event.**

9. **Tap Done.** The Calendar app saves the event info and displays the new event in the calendar.

Cancel	**Add Event**	Done

Title

Location

All-day

Starts Oct 29, 2013 5:00 PM

Ends 6:00 PM

Repeat Never >

Invitees None >

Alert None >

Calendar • Writing >

Show As Busy >

12.3 Use the Add Event screen to create your event.

Genius

If you just want to change the start or end time (or both), switch to either Day or Week view. Then, tap and hold the event until Calendar adds selection handles to it. Tap and drag the top selection handle to change the start time; tap and drag the bottom selection handle to change the end time; tap and drag any other part of the event to move it to a new time.

Editing an existing event

Whether you've scheduled an event by hand or synced it from your computer, the event details might change: a new time, a new location, and so on. Whatever the change, you need to edit the event to keep your schedule accurate.

Follow these steps to edit an existing event:

1. **Display the date that contains the event you want to edit.** In Day view, navigate to the date. In Week or Month view, open the week or month that contains the date.

2. **Tap the event.**

3. **Tap Edit.** Calendar displays the event data in the Edit screen.

4. **Make your changes.**

5. **Tap Done.** Calendar saves your work and returns you to the event details.

Setting up a repeating event

One of the truly great timesavers in Calendar is the repeat feature. This enables you to set up a single event and get Calendar to automatically repeat it at a regular interval.

For example, if you set up an event for a Friday, you can repeat it every week, which means that Calendar automatically sets up the same event to occur on subsequent Fridays. You can continue the events indefinitely or end them after a certain number of repeats or on a specific date.

Follow these steps to configure an existing event to repeat:

1. **Display the date that contains the event you want to edit.** In Day view, navigate to the date. In Week or Month view, open the week or month that contains the date.

2. **Tap the event.** Calendar opens the event info.

3. **Tap Edit.** Calendar displays the event data in the Edit screen.

4. **Tap Repeat.** The Repeat list appears.

5. **Tap the repeat interval you want to use.**

6. **Tap End Repeat.** The End Repeat list appears.

7. **You have the following two choices:**

    - **Tap On Date to have the event repeats stop on a particular day.** Use the scroll wheels to set the day, month, and year that you want the final event to occur.

    - **Tap Never to have the event repeat indefinitely.**

8. **Tap Edit.** Calendar returns you to the Edit Event screen.

9. **Tap Done.** Calendar saves the repeat data and returns you to the event details.

Converting an event to an all-day event

Some events don't really have specific times that you can pin down. These include birthdays, anniversaries, sales meetings, trade shows, conferences, and vacations. What all these types of events have in common is that they last all day. In the case of birthdays and anniversaries, this is literally so, and in the case of trade shows and the like, *all day* refers to the entire workday.

Why is this important? Well, suppose you schedule a trade show as a regular event that lasts from 9 a.m. to 5 p.m. When you examine that day in the Calendar app Day or Week view, you see a big, fat block that covers the entire day. If you also want to schedule meetings that occur at the trade show, Calendar lets you do that, but it shows these new events on top of this existing trade-show event. This makes the schedule hard to read, so you might miss an event.

To solve this problem, configure the trade show (or whatever) as an all-day event. Calendar clears it from the regular schedule and displays it separately, near the top of the Day view or on the top part of the Week view. Follow these steps to configure an event as an all-day event:

1. **Display the date that contains the event you want to edit.** In Day view, navigate to the date. In Week or Month view, open the week or month that contains the date.

2. **Tap the event.** Calendar opens the event info.

3. **Tap Edit.** Calendar switches to the Edit screen.

4. **Tap the All-day switch to the On position.**

5. **Tap Done.** The Calendar app saves the event, returns you to the calendar, and now shows the event as an all-day event, as shown in Figure 12.4.

Adding an alert to an event

One of the truly useful secrets of stress-free productivity in the modern world is what I call the set-it-and-forget-it school of time management. That is, you set up an event elec-

12.4 All-day events appear in the all-day section, near the top of the Day and Week views.

tronically and then get the same technology to remind you when that event occurs. This way, your mind doesn't have to waste energy fretting about missing the event because you know your technology has your back.

The technology of choice for this is the Calendar app and its alert feature. When you add an alert to an event, Calendar automatically displays a reminder of the event, which is a Notification Center alert that pops up on the screen. Your tablet also vibrates and sounds a few beeps to get your attention. You also get to choose when the alert triggers (such as a specified number of minutes, hours, or days before the event).

Follow these steps to set an alert for an event:

1. **Display the date that contains the event you want to edit.** In Day view, navigate to the date. In Week or Month view, open the week or month that contains the date.

2. **Tap the event.** Calendar opens the event info.

3. **Tap Edit.** Calendar displays the event data in the Edit screen.

4. **Tap Alert.** The Event Alert list appears. Figure 12.5 shows the Event Alert list for a regular event; the list that appears for an all-day event offers slightly different choices.

5. **Tap the number of minutes, hours, or days before the event you want to see the alert.** If you're editing an all-day event, you can set the alert for 9 a.m. on the day of the event, 9 a.m. the day before the event, 9 a.m. two days before the event, or a week before the event.

6. **To set up a backup alert, tap the Second Alert option.** Next, tap the number of minutes, hours, or days before the event you want to see the second alert.

7. **Tap Done.** The Calendar app saves your alert choices and returns you to the calendar.

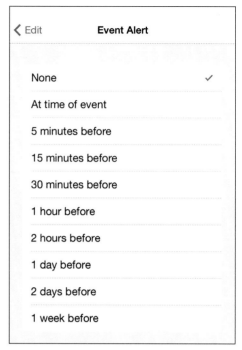

‹ Edit	Event Alert	
None		✓
At time of event		
5 minutes before		
15 minutes before		
30 minutes before		
1 hour before		
2 hours before		
1 day before		
2 days before		
1 week before		

12.5 Use the Event Alert screen to tell Calendar when to remind you about your event.

Genius

You can save yourself some time by setting the default alert time for different types of events. Tap Settings in the Home screen, and then tap Mail, Contacts, Calendars. In the Calendars section, tap Default Alert Times, tap the type of alert you want to configure (Birthdays, Events, or All-Day Events), and then tap the default alert interval.

Note

You can disable the alert chirps if you find them annoying. On the Home screen, tap Settings, tap Sounds, tap Calendar Alerts, and then tap None.

Getting More Out of the Calendar App

The basic features of the Calendar app — multiple views, color-coded calendars, repeating events, all-day events, and event alerts — make it an indispensable time-management tool. But it has a few more tricks up its sleeve that you ought to know about, and these are covered in the rest of this chapter.

Setting the default calendar

If you have multiple calendars on the go, each time you create a new event the Calendar automatically chooses one of your calendars by default. It's no big whoop if every now and then you have to tap the Calendar setting and choose a different calendar. However, if you have to do this most of the time, it gets old in a hurry, particularly when I tell you there's something you can do about it. Follow these steps to configure the Calendar app to use a different default calendar:

1. **Return to the Home screen, and then tap Settings.** The Settings app appears.
2. **Tap Mail, Contacts, Calendars.** The Mail, Contacts, Calendars screen appears.
3. **In the Calendars section, tap Default Calendar.** The Default Calendar screen appears.
4. **Tap the calendar you prefer to use as the default.** The Calendar app now uses that calendar as the default for each new event.

Subscribing to a calendar

If you know someone who has published a calendar, you might want to keep track of it within the Calendar app. You can do that by subscribing to the published calendar. The Calendar app sets up the published calendar as a separate item, so you can easily switch between your own calendars and the published one.

To pull this off, you need to know the web address of the published calendar. This address usually takes the following form: *server.com/calendar.ics*. Here, *server.com* is the address of the calendar server, and *calendar.ics* is the name of the file, which is almost always an iCalendar format file with the extension .ics, preceded (usually) by a folder location.

For calendars published to iCloud, the address always looks like this: *ical.icloud.com/member/ calendar.ics*. Here, *member* is the iCloud member name of the person who published the calendar. Here's an example address: ical.icloud.com/aardvarksorenstam/aardvark.ics.

Follow these steps to subscribe to a published calendar:

1. **On the Home screen, tap Settings.** Your iPad or iPad mini opens the Settings app.
2. **Tap Mail, Contacts, Calendars.** The Mail, Contacts, Calendars screen appears.
3. **Tap Add Account.** The Add Account screen opens.
4. **Tap Other.** The Settings app displays the Other screen.
5. **Tap Add Subscribed Calendar.** You see the Subscription screen.

6. **Use the Server text box to type the calendar address.**

7. **Tap Next.** The Settings app connects to the calendar.

8. **Tap Save.** The Settings app adds an account for the subscribed calendar.

To view the subscribed calendar, tap Calendar on the Home screen to open the Calendar app, and then click Calendars to open the Calendars screen.

Controlling events with Siri voice commands

The Siri personal assistant offers a number of voice commands for creating, editing, and querying your events. To get Siri to schedule an event, you use the following general syntax: *Schedule what with whom at when.*

Here, *schedule* can be any of the following: "schedule," "meet," "set up a meeting," "new appointment."

The *what* part of the command (which is optional) determines the topic of the event, so it could be something like "Lunch" or "Budget review" or "Dentist"; you can also precede this part with "about" (for example, "about expenses"). The *whom* part of the command specifies the person you're meeting with, if any, so it can be a contact name or a relationship (such as "My husband" or "Dad"). The *when* part of the command sets the time and date of the event; the time portion can be a specific time such as "3" (meaning 3 p.m.) or "8 a.m.", or "noon"; the date portion can be "today" or "tomorrow," a day in the current week (such as "Tuesday" or "Friday"), a relative day (such as "next Monday"), or a specific date (such as "August 23rd").

See the following examples:

- "Schedule lunch with Karen tomorrow at noon."
- "Meet with my sister Friday at 4."
- "Set up a meeting about budgeting next Tuesday at 10 a.m."
- "New appointment with Sarah Currid on March 15 at 2:30."

You can also use Siri to modify existing events. For example, you can change the event time by using the verb "Reschedule" or "Move," as shown in the following examples:

- "Reschedule my meeting with Sarah Currid to 3:30."

- "Move my noon appointment to 1:30."

You can also use the verb "Add" to include another person in a meeting or the verb "Cancel" to remove a meeting from your schedule, as shown in the following examples:

- "Add Charles Aster to the budgeting meeting."

- "Cancel my lunch with Karen."

Finally, you can query your events to see what's coming up, as shown in the following examples:

- "When is my next appointment?"

- "When is my meeting with Sarah Currid?"

- "What is on my calendar tomorrow?"

- "What does the rest of my day look like?"

Handling Microsoft Exchange meeting requests

If you've set up a Microsoft Exchange account in your iPad or iPad mini, there's a good chance you're using its push features. This means that the Exchange Server automatically sends incoming e-mail messages to the Mail app, as well as new (or changed) contact and calendar data. If someone back at headquarters adds your name to a scheduled meeting, Exchange generates an automatic meeting request, which is an e-mail message that tells you about the meeting and asks if you want to attend.

How will you know? The Home screen's Calendar icon shows a badge with the number of pending requests. Also, in the Calendar app status bar, the Inbox link in the bottom-right corner tells you how many meeting requests you have waiting for you.

If you don't see the Inbox link, you need to turn on syncing for your Exchange calendar. I show you how to do this in Chapter 6. It's best to handle such requests as soon as you can, so here's what you do:

1. **Tap Inbox in the bottom-right corner of the screen.** Calendar displays your pending meeting requests.

2. **Tap the meeting request.** Calendar displays the meeting details, as shown in Figure 12.6.

3. **Tap your response:**

   - **Accept.** Tap this button to confirm that you can attend the meeting.
   - **Maybe.** Tap this button if you're not sure and will decide later.
   - **Decline.** Tap this button to confirm that you can't attend the meeting.

Working with Reminders

The Calendar app is an excellent tool for tracking appointments, meetings, and other events. By adding an alert to an event you get a digital tap on the shoulder to remind you when and where your presence is required.

However, our days are littered with tasks that could be called *sub-events*. These are things that need to be done at a certain point during your day but don't rise to the level of full-fledged events: returning a call, taking the laundry out of the dryer, turning off the sprinkler. If you need to be reminded to perform such a sub-event, it seems like overkill to crank out an event using the Calendar app.

Logophilia Website Working Group
Third floor conference room

Tuesday, Oct 15, 2013   3 PM to 4 PM

Calendar   • Calendar

From   Karen Hammond >

Invitees   >
Paul McFedries

Alert   15 minutes before >

Notes
Hi all,

The next meeting of the Website Working Group will occur on October 15 at 3PM in the 3rd floor conference room. Bring an open mind and lots of good ideas!

See you then.

K.

Show As   Busy >

Accept   Maybe   Decline

12.6 The details screen for an Exchange meeting request.

Fortunately, iOS offers a better solution: the Reminders app. You use this app to create *reminders*, which are simple nudges that tell you to do something, to be somewhere, or whatever. These nudges come in the form of Notification Center banners that appear on your screen at a time that you specify or when your tablet reaches a particular location. If you have an iCloud account, you can sync your reminders among your tablet, your Mac, your iPhone, and any other supported device.

Setting a reminder

Follow these steps to set up a reminder that alerts you at a specific time:

1. **On the Home screen, tap Reminders.** The Reminders app appears.
2. **On the left side of the screen, tap the list you want to use to store the reminder.**
3. **On the right side of the screen, tap the first empty line in the list.** Reminders creates a new reminder.
4. **Type the reminder text.**
5. **To add details, tap the More Info icon (*i*).** The Details dialog appears, as shown in Figure 12.7.
6. **Tap the Remind Me On a Day switch to On.**
7. **Tap Alarm, and then use the scroll wheels to set the date and time of the reminder.**
8. **Use the Repeat setting to set up a repeat interval for the reminder.**
9. **Use the Priority setting to assign a priority to the reminder: None, Low (!), Medium (!!), or High (!!!).**
10. **Use the Notes text box to add some background text or other information about the reminder.**
11. **Tap Done.**

Setting a reminder for a specific location

Getting an alert at a specific time is the standard way of working with reminders, but Reminders supports a second type of criterion: location. That is, when you specify a particular location for a reminder, the app sets up a *geofence* — a kind of virtual border — around that location. When your iPad or iPad mini crosses that geofence, the associated reminder appears on your screen. So, for example, if you're on your way to a meeting with a client, you could create a reminder that includes notes about the meeting or the client and then specify the meeting location as the reminder criterion.

Here's how it works:

1. **On the left side of the Reminders screen, tap the list you want to use to store the reminder.**

2. **On the right side of the screen, tap the first empty line in the list.** Reminders creates a new reminder.

3. **Type the reminder text and then tap the More Info icon (*i*).** The Details dialog appears.

4. **Tap the Remind Me at a Location switch to On.**

5. **Tap Location and then tap Current Location or an address that appears in the list.** You can also use the Search box to specify the address of the location you want to use and then tap the location when it appears in the search results.

6. **To have the reminder appear when your iPad or iPad mini first comes within range of the location, tap When I Arrive.** If you prefer to see the reminder when your tablet goes out of range of the location, tap When I Leave instead.

7. **Tap Details and then follow steps 8 to 11 from the previous section to fill in the reminder details.**

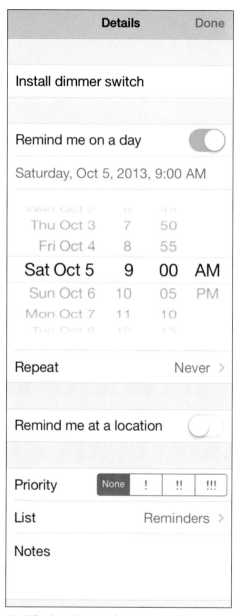

12.7 The Details dialog for a reminder.

Creating a new list and setting the default list

The Reminders app comes with three preset lists that you can use: Reminders, Home, and Work. The default is Reminders, but you can also select a different list if it's more suitable or if you want to keep your personal and business reminders separate. If none of these three prefab lists is exactly right for your needs, feel free to create your own list by following these steps:

1. **In the Reminders app, tap Add List.** If you have multiple reminders-compatible accounts on your tablet, tap the account you want to use. Reminders creates the new list.

2. **Type the name of your list.**

3. **Tap Done.** The Reminders app adds the list to the left pane.

The default list is the one that Reminders uses when you don't specify a particular list when you create a reminder. Follow these steps to set a particular list as the default:

1. **On the Home screen, tap Settings to launch the Settings app.**

2. **Tap Reminders.** The Reminders screen appears.

3. **Tap Default List.** The Default List screen appears.

4. **Tap the list you want to use as the default.**

Completing or deleting a reminder

When a reminder is complete, you don't want it lingering in the Reminders list (or whatever list it's in), cluttering the screen and making it hard to look through your remaining reminders. To avoid that, once the reminder is done, tap the radio button beside it. This tells Reminders that the reminder is complete, and the next time you display the list, you won't see the reminder (although you can always tap Show Completed at the bottom of the list to see your completed reminders).

If you no longer need a reminder, it's a good idea to delete it to keep your reminder lists neat and tidy. To delete a reminder, follow these steps:

1. **In the Reminder app, tap the list that contains the reminder you want to delete.** Reminders displays the list's reminders.

2. **Tap Edit.** Reminders opens the list for editing.

3. **Tap the red Delete button to the left of the reminder you want to delete.** Reminders asks you to confirm.

4. **Tap Delete.** Reminders deletes the reminder.

Setting reminders with Siri voice commands

You can also create reminders via voice using the Siri app. Time-based reminders use the following general syntax: Remind me to *action* at *when*. Here, *action* is the task you want to be reminded to perform, and *when* is the date and time you want to be reminded (as described earlier in the chapter when I discussed creating calendar events using Siri). See the following examples:

- "Remind me to call my wife at 5."
- "Remind me to pick up Greg at the airport tomorrow at noon."
- "Remind me to bring lunch."

Location-based reminders use the following general syntax: Remind me to *action* when I *location*. Again, *action* is the task you want to be reminded to perform; *location* is the place around which you want the geofence set up (including either "get to" or "leave," depending on whether you want to be reminded coming or going). Review the following examples:

- "Remind me to pick up milk when I leave here."
- "Remind me to call my husband when I get to La Guardia airport."
- "Remind me to call my sister when I get home."
- "Remind me to grab my sample case when I arrive at Acme Limited."

For the last of these, you can assume that "Acme Limited" is a company name defined (with an address) in your Contacts list.

How Can I Navigate My World with iPad?

Dedicated GPS (Global Positioning System) devices have become gasp-inducingly popular over the last few years because it's not easy finding your way around in a strange city or an unfamiliar part of town. Deciphering hastily scribbled directions or a possibly out-of-date map is hard and error prone. However, dedicated devices, whether they're music players, e-book readers, or GPS receivers, are being replaced by multifunction devices that can do it all, including display maps. In this chapter, I cover how to take advantage of the iPad or iPad mini's multifunction prowess using the amazingly useful Maps app.

Finding Your Way with Maps and GPS

When you're out in the real world trying to navigate your way between the proverbial points A and B, the questions often come thick and fast: *Where am I now? Which turn do I take? What's the traffic like on the highway? Can I even get there from here?* Fortunately, the answers to these and similar questions are now just a few finger taps away.

That's because the iPad and iPad mini come loaded not only with a way-cool Maps app, but they also have a built-in GPS receiver. Now your tablet knows exactly where it is (and so, by extension, do you), and it can help you get where you want to go. However, just to be clear about it your tablet only has GPS if you have the cellular model. Fortunately, Wi-Fi-only iPads can still use Maps and other location services because the tablet uses the locations of nearby Wi-Fi hotspots to get an approximate fix on your current whereabouts.

To get Maps on the job, tap the Maps icon in the Home screen, and the initial Maps screen appears, as shown in Figure 13.1. (If you see a dialog letting you know that Maps would like to use your current location, say "But of course!" and tap OK.)

Getting info about a destination

When you want to locate a destination using Maps, the most straightforward method is to search for it. Follow these steps to do so:

1. **Tap inside the Search box in the upper-right corner of the screen.**
2. **Type the name, address, keyword, or a phrase that describes your destination.**
3. **In the on-screen keyboard, tap Search.** Maps locates the destination, moves the map to that area, and drops a pin on it, as shown in Figure 13.2.

Now that you have pinpointed your destination (literally!), you can read the map to find your way by looking for street names, local landmarks, nearby major intersections, and so on. You also can use Maps to get specific directions; I show you how that works later in this chapter. You can also rotate the map. For example, if you're facing east, you can rotate the map so that it also faces east and more easily get your bearings. To rotate the map, place two fingers on the screen and rotate either clockwise or counterclockwise.

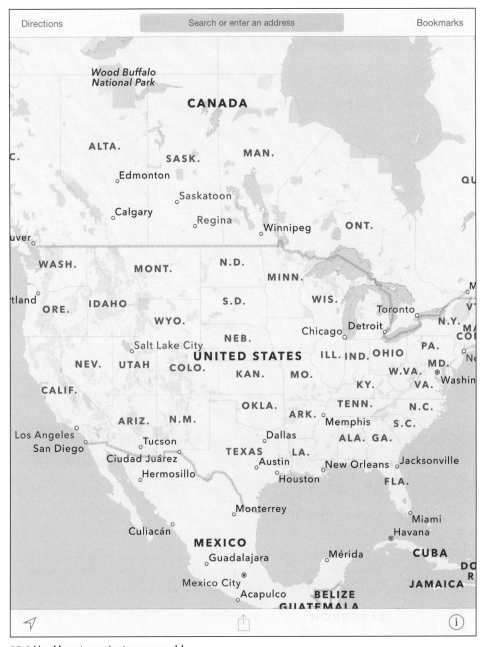

13.1 Use Maps to navigate your world.

Genius

The version of Maps in iOS 7 is an update to the version that debuted in iOS 6 to a lukewarm, sometimes even hostile, reception. Yes, Maps came with some great features, such as Flyover and turn-by-turn navigation, but it wasn't quite fully baked, and some locations were missing or displayed names that were incorrect or misspelled. The latest version is a big improvement, but caveat viator (traveler beware).

Quick Directions button

13.2 When you search for a destination, Maps displays a pin to mark its location on the map.

Knowing where a destination is located is a good thing, but you might also want to find out more about that destination. Maps has you covered there as well, because it not only provides you with general info, such as a phone number, street address, and website address, but it also ties into Yelp, a service that offers user-generated content — particularly ratings, reviews, and photos — of millions of locations around the world.

Genius If you have a Yelp account, you can add your own content about the destination. In the Reviews tab, tap Check In to let your Yelp friends know you're at the destination or tap Write a Review to post a review. You can also tap the Photos tab and then tap Add Photo to post your own pic of the destination.

Tap the destination's blue Info button and Maps opens the Location dialog. As you can see in Figure 13.3, the Location dialog offers three tabs — Info, Reviews, and Photos — that you can tap to get tons of data about the destination.

Flying over your destination

When someone says he is getting *a bird's-eye view*, he is speaking metaphorically about seeing an overview of something. With the new Maps app, however, that phrase comes about as close to being literal as you can get without actually jumping into a plane or helicopter (or somehow transforming yourself into a bird). That's because Maps comes with a feature called Flyover that gives you an interactive, three-dimensional aerial view of a destination. What use is that? Well, not much, I suppose, but it *is* jaw-dropping.

Follow these steps to enable Flyover for a destination:

1. **Search for the destination to get its location on-screen.**

2. **Tap the More (i) icon in the lower-right corner of the Maps screen to display the map options.**

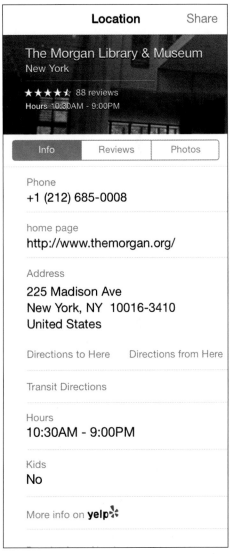

13.3 Tap the Info button to open the Location dialog and gain access to information about the destination, as well as Yelp ratings, reviews, and photos.

3. **Tap Satellite.** Maps switches from Standard view to Satellite view.

4. **Tap the Flyover button, pointed out in Figure 13.4.** Maps switches to Flyover mode. Figure 13.4 shows Maps in Flyover mode featuring New York's Chrysler Building. Flyover mode is best for tall buildings and structures; it's not much good for street-level views.

Flyover icon

13.4 Bird's-eye view, indeed; Maps in Flyover mode.

Once you have Flyover on the go, you can use the following techniques to interactively fly around your destination:

- **Spread two fingers to zoom in or pinch two fingers to zoom out.**
- **Swipe down to fly past the destination and swipe up to fly back.**

- **Swipe right to pan to the left and swipe left to pan to the right.**

- **Rotate two fingers (clockwise or counterclockwise) to fly in a circle.**

- **Simultaneously spread two fingers and slide up to reduce elevation; simultaneously pinch two fingers and slide down to increase elevation.**

Displaying your current location

When you arrive at an unfamiliar shopping mall and you need to get your bearings, your first instinct might be to seek out the nearest mall map and look for the inevitable *You Are Here* marker. This gives you a sense of your current location with respect to the rest of the mall, so locating Pottery Barn shouldn't be all that hard.

When you arrive at an unfamiliar part of town or a new city, have you ever wished you had something that could provide you with that same *You Are Here* reference point? If so, you're in luck because you have exactly that waiting for you right in Maps. Tap the Tracking button in the lower-left corner of the screen (see Figure 13.5). If this is the first time you've used the Tracking button, Maps asks for permission to use your current location, so be sure to tap OK.

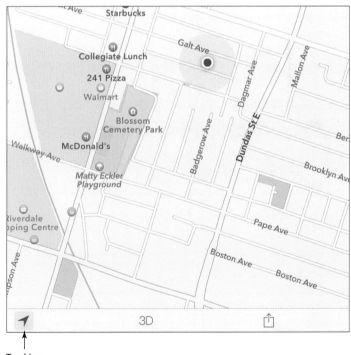

Tracking
icon

13.5 Tap the Tracking icon to see your precise location as a blue dot on the map.

That's it! Your tablet examines Wi-Fi hotspots and (if your iPad is cellular-equipped) GPS coordinates with nearby cellular towers to plot your current position. When it completes the necessary processing and triangulating, Maps displays a map of your current city, zooms in on your current area, and then adds a blue dot to pinpoint your current location, as shown in Figure 13.5. Amazingly, if you happen to be in a car, taxi, or other moving vehicle, the blue dot moves in real time.

Genius

Knowing where you are is a good thing, but it's even better to know what's nearby. Suppose you're in a new city and you're dying for a cup of coffee. Tap in the Search box, type **coffee**, and then tap Search. Maps drops a bunch of pins on nearby locations that match your search. Tap a pin to see the name, and tap the blue Info button to see the location's phone number, address, and website.

Displaying a map of a contact's location

In the old days (that is, a few years ago), if you had a contact located in an unfamiliar part of town or in another city altogether, visiting that person required a phone call or an e-mail asking for directions. You'd then write down the instructions, get written directions via e-mail, or perhaps even get a crudely drawn map faxed to you. Those days, fortunately, are long gone thanks to myriad online resources that can show you where a particular address is located and even give you driving directions to get there from here (wherever *here* may be).

Even better, your tablet takes it one step further and integrates with Maps to generate a map of a contact's location based on her address. So, as long as you've typed (or synced) a contact's physical address, you can see where she is on the map.

To display a map of a contact's location, follow these steps:

1. **In the Home screen, tap the Contacts button to open the Contacts application.**

2. **Tap the contact that you want to map.** The Contacts app displays that person's data.

3. **Tap the address that you want to view.** Your iPad or iPad mini switches to Maps and drops a pushpin on the contact's location.

Note

You also can display a map of a contact's location by using Maps itself. In the menu bar, tap Bookmarks, tap Contacts, and then tap the contact you want to map. Maps displays the contact's location.

Mapping an address from an e-mail

Addresses show up in all kinds of e-mail messages these days. Most commonly, folks include their work or home addresses in their e-mail signature at the bottom of each message. Similarly, if the e-mail is an invitation, your correspondent almost certainly includes the address for the event somewhere in the message.

If you need to know where an address is located, you might think that you need to copy the address from the message and then paste it into Maps. That does work, but it's way too much effort! Instead, follow these steps:

1. **In the Mail app, display the message that includes the address.** If your tablet is in portrait mode, tap Inbox to see the messages.

2. **Tap and hold on the address in the message to display a list of actions.** If the address is displayed as a link (that is, underlined in a blue font), it means Mail has recognized it as an address, so you can just tap the address and skip the next step.

3. **Tap Open in Maps.** Maps opens and drops a pushpin on the address.

Saving a location as a bookmark

If you know the address of the location you want to map, you can add a pushpin for that location by opening Maps and running a search on the address. That is, you tap the Search box in the menu bar, type the address, and then tap the Search button.

That's no big deal for one-time-only searches, but what about a location you refer to frequently? Typing that address over and over gets old in a hurry, I assure you. You can save time and tapping by telling Maps to save that location on its Bookmarks list, which means you can access it, usually, with just a few taps.

Follow these steps to add a location to Maps Bookmarks list:

1. **Search for the location you want to save.** Maps marks the location with a pushpin and displays the name or address of the location in a banner above the pushpin.

2. **In the banner, tap the location's name or address.** Maps displays the Location dialog.

3. **Tap the Info tab (if it exists; if not, never mind) to see the following details about the location:**

    - If the location is in your Contacts list, you see the contact's data.

    - If the location is a business or institution, you see the address as well as other data, such as the organization's phone number and web address.

    - For all other locations, you see only the address.

4. **Tap Add Bookmark.** Maps displays the Add Bookmark dialog.

5. **Edit the name of the bookmark if you want to, and then tap Save.** Maps adds the location to the Bookmarks list.

To map a bookmarked location, follow these steps:

1. **Tap Bookmarks in the menu bar.** Maps opens the Bookmarks dialog.

2. **Tap the Bookmarks tab.**

3. **Tap the location you want to map.** Maps displays the appropriate map and adds a pushpin for the location.

Genius

The Bookmarks dialog also comes with a Recents tab, which displays a list of your last few searches, locations entered, and driving directions requested. To get Maps to run any item again, just tap it.

Specifying a location when you don't know the address

Sometimes you have only a vague notion of where you want to go. In a new city, for example, you might decide to head downtown to look for a coffee shop or restaurant. That's fine, but how do you get downtown from your hotel in the suburbs? Your iPad or iPad mini can give you directions, but it needs to know the endpoint of your journey and that's precisely the information you don't have. Sounds like a conundrum, for sure, but there's a way to work around it. You can drop a pin on the map in the approximate area where you want to go. Maps can then give you directions to the dropped pin.

Follow these steps to drop a pin on a map:

1. **In Maps, display a map of the city with which you want to work in one of the following ways:**

- **If you're in the city now, tap the Tracking button in the lower-left corner of the screen.**

  - **If you're not in the city, tap the Search box, type the name of the city (and perhaps also the name of the state or province), and then tap the Search button.**

2. **Use finger flicks to pan the map to the approximate location you want to use as your destination.**

3. **Tap Info (i) in the lower-right corner of the screen.** Maps displays a list of map options.

4. **Tap Drop a Pin.** Maps drops a purple pin in the middle of the current map.

5. **Tap and hold the purple pin until it's released, and then drag the pin to the location you want.** Maps creates a temporary bookmark called Dropped Pin that you can use when you ask Maps for directions (as described next).

Getting directions to a location

One possible navigation scenario with Maps is to specify a destination (using a contact, an address search, a dropped pin, or a bookmark) and then tap the Tracking button. This gives you a map that shows both your destination and your current location. Depending on how far away the destination is, you may need to zoom out (by pinching the screen or tapping it with two fingers) to see both locations on the map. You can then eyeball the streets to see how to get from here to there.

Eyeball the streets? Hah, how primitive! Maps can bring you into the twenty-first century not only by showing you a route to the destination but also by providing you with the distance and time it should take and by giving you street-by-street, turn-by-turn instructions, whether you're driving or walking. It's one of the sweetest Maps features, and it works in the following way:

1. **Use Maps to add a pushpin for your destination.** Use whatever method works best for you: the Contacts list, an address search, a dropped pin, or a bookmark.

2. **Tap Directions in the menu bar.** Maps opens the Directions dialog. As shown in Figure 13.6, you should see Current Location in the Start box at the top of the dialog and your destination address in the End box.

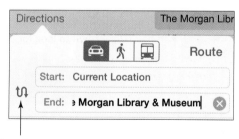

Swap icon

13.6 Use the Directions dialog to specify the start and end points of your trip.

283

3. **If you want to use a starting point other than your current location, tap Current Location in the Start box.** Next, type the address of the location you want to use.

Genius

Instead of getting directions to the destination, you might need directions *from* the destination. No sweat! When you map the destination, tap the banner, and then tap Directions From Here. If you're already in the Directions dialog, tap the Swap icon (pointed out in Figure 13.6). Maps swaps the locations.

4. **Tap the button for the type of directions you want: Car, walking, or transit.**

5. **Tap Route.** Maps figures out the three best routes and then displays them on the map in the Overview screen, which also shows the trip distance and approximate time.

Genius

If you have your destination pinned, you can get immediate directions to it from your current location. That is, you can compress steps 2 through 5 into a single step by tapping the Quick Directions icon in the information banner (see Figure 13.2).

6. **Tap the route you prefer to take.** Note that you select a route by tapping the trip time banner that appears beside the route.

7. **Tap Start.** Maps displays the directions for the first leg of the journey.

Maps features turn-by-turn directions for driving and, in the iOS 7 version, walking. This means that as you approach each turn, Siri tells you what to do next, such as "In 400 feet, turn right onto Main Street." Maps also follows along the route, so you can see where you're going and which turn is coming up. You can see your estimated time of arrival, remaining travel time, and distance remaining by tapping the screen.

Note

In iOS 7, you can also configure Maps to make driving or walking your default for directions. Open Settings, tap Maps, and then in the Preferred Directions section tap either Driving or Walking.

After tapping the screen, you can also tap Overview to see the entire route. Instead of seeing the directions one step at a time, you might prefer to see them all at once. Tap the screen and then tap the List button in the middle of the menu bar at the bottom of the screen.

Note

To switch between standard and metric distances, tap Settings, tap Maps, and then tap either In Miles or In Kilometers.

Getting live traffic information

Okay, it's pretty darn amazing that your iPad or iPad mini can tell you precisely where you are and how to get somewhere else. However, in most cities, it's the getting somewhere else part that's the problem. Why? One word: traffic. Maps may tell you the trip should take 10 minutes, but that could easily turn into a half hour or more if you run into a traffic jam.

That's life in the big city, right? Maybe not. If you're on a highway in a major North American city, Maps can most likely supply you with — wait for it — real-time traffic conditions. This is really an amazing tool that can help you avoid traffic messes and find alternative routes to your destination. The new Maps app can also show you traffic construction spots, and it gathers real-time information from Maps users to generate even more-accurate traffic data. If you're in the middle of turn-by-turn directions, Maps will even recognize an upcoming traffic delay and offer an alternative route around it!

To see the traffic data, tap More (i) in the lower-right corner of the screen, and then tap Show Traffic. As shown in Figure 13.7, Maps displays an orange dotted line to indicate traffic slowdowns, a red dashed line to indicate very heavy traffic, and Roadwork icons to indicate construction sites.

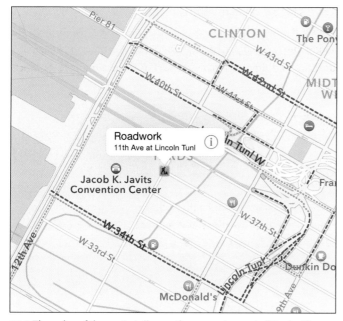

13.7 The color of the route tells you the current speed of the traffic.

285

Controlling Maps with Siri voice commands

You can use the Siri voice-activated assistant to control Maps with straightforward voice commands. You can display a location, get directions, and even display traffic information. Tap and hold the Home button (or press and hold the Mic button of your Apple headphones or the equivalent button on a Bluetooth headset) until Siri appears.

To display a location in Maps via Siri, say "Show *location*" (or "Map *location*" or "Find *location*" or "Where is *location*"), where *location* is an address, a name, or a Maps bookmark. Similarly, to get directions from Siri, say "Directions to *location*," where *location* is an address, a name, or a Maps bookmark. To see the current traffic conditions, say "Traffic *location*," where *location* can be a specific place or somewhere local, such as "around here" or "nearby." To get your current location, you can say "Where am I?" or "Show my current location."

Genius

Siri generally ignores extra terms you say that aren't relevant to the task at hand. You can say something like "Give me directions to Hoover Dam," and Siri won't miss a beat. Also, the location you specify can be based on Contacts data, such as "Show my wife's work" or "Directions to my sister's home."

Configuring Location Services

Location Services refers to the features and technologies that provide apps and system tools with access to location data. This is a handy and useful thing, but it's also something that you need to keep under your control because your location data, particularly your current location, is fundamentally private and shouldn't be given out willy-nilly. Fortunately, your tablet comes with a few tools for controlling and configuring location services.

Turning off Location Services

The next couple of sections show you how to turn off Location Services for individual apps, as well as individual system services. That fine-grained control is the best way to handle Location Services, but there may be times when you prefer a broader approach that turns off Location Services altogether. For example, if you're heading to a secret rendezvous (how exciting!) and you're bringing your iPad or iPad mini with you, you might feel more comfortable knowing that no app or service on your tablet is tracking your whereabouts.

On a more mundane level, Location Services uses up battery power. If the device's battery is getting low (or if you just want to maximize the battery for a long bus ride, for example), then follow these steps to turn off Location Services:

1. **On the Home screen, tap Settings.** The Settings app appears.

2. **Tap Privacy.** The Privacy settings appear.

3. **Tap Location Services.** The Location Services settings appear.

4. **Tap the Location Services switch to the Off position.** If you have Find My iPad activated (see Chapter 14), the Settings app asks you to confirm the new setting.

5. **Tap Turn Off.** The Settings app shuts off all Location Services.

Controlling app access to GPS

When you open an app that comes with a GPS component, the app displays a dialog like the one shown in Figure 13.8, asking your permission to use the device's location hardware to determine your whereabouts. Tap OK if that's just fine with you; tap Don't Allow if you think that your current location is none of the app's business.

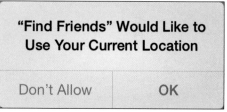

13.8 When you first launch a GPS-aware app, it asks your permission to use your current location.

However, after you make your decision, you might change your mind. For example, if you deny your location to an app, that app might lack some crucial functionality. Similarly, if you allow an app to use your location, you might have second thoughts about compromising your privacy.

Whatever the reason, you can control an app's access to GPS by following these steps:

1. **In the Home screen, tap Settings.** The Settings app appears.

2. **Tap Privacy.** The Privacy settings appear.

3. **Tap Location Services.** The Location Services screen appears, as shown in Figure 13.9.

Current location services status

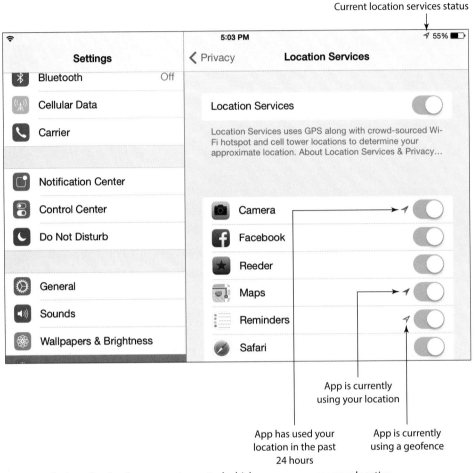

App is currently
using your location

App has used your
location in the past
24 hours

App is currently
using a geofence

13.9 Use the Location Services screen to control which apps can access your location.

4. **Configure app access to GPS as follows:**

- **If you want to deny your current location to all apps, tap the Location Services switch to Off.**

- **If you want to deny your current location to specific apps, for each app tap the On/Off switch to Off.**

Note that the Location Services screen uses the following three icons (see Figure 13.9) to indicate which apps are using Location Services and how they're using them:

- A gray Location Services icon tells you that the app has used your location in the previous 24 hours.

- A solid purple Location Services icon tells you that the app is currently using your location.

- An outlined purple Location Services icon this tells you the app has set up a geofence around your location. See Chapter 12 to learn how a geofence works.

The active Location Services status also appears in the status bar to the left of the battery status (see Figure 13.9).

Enabling or disabling Location Services

Your tablet also provides Location Services to various internal services so they can perform tasks, such as setting the time zone or serving up iAds that change depending on your location. If you don't want your tablet providing any of these services, you can turn them off in the following way:

1. **On the Home screen, tap Settings to open the Settings app.**

2. **Tap Location Services.** The Location Services screen appears.

3. **Tap System Services.** The Settings app displays the System Services screen.

4. **For any system service that you don't want to provide access to location data, tap its switch to Off.**

Sharing Map Data

If you want to show someone where you live, where you work, or where you want to meet, you could just send the address, but that's so last century. The more modern way is to send your friend a digital map that shows the location. With your iPad or iPad mini this is a snap — you can send a map via e-mail or text message, or post a map on Twitter.

Follow these steps to send someone a map:

1. **Use Maps to add a pushpin for the location you want to send.** Use whatever method works best for you: the Contacts list, an address search, a dropped pin, or a bookmark. If you want to send your current location, display it, and then tap the blue dot.

2. **Tap the location banner.** Maps displays the Location dialog for the location.

3. **Tap Share.** Maps displays a list of ways to share the map.

4. **Tap the method that you want to use to share the map: Message, Mail, Twitter, or Facebook.** Maps creates a new text message, e-mail, tweet, or post that includes a Maps link to the location.

5. **Fill in the rest of your message and send it.**

Alternatively, if the other person is nearby (that is, within 30 feet or so) and is running iOS 7 on an iPhone 5s, 5c, or 5; a fourth-generation iPad or later; an iPad mini; or a fifth-generation iPod touch or later, you can use AirDrop to exchange the location wirelessly. Here's how it works:

1. **Use Maps to add a pushpin for the location you want to send.** Use whatever method works best for you: the Contacts list, an address search, a dropped pin, or a bookmark. If you want to send your current location, display it, and then tap the blue dot.

2. **Tap the location banner.** Maps displays the Location dialog for the location.

3. **Tap Share.** Maps displays a list of ways to share the location.

4. **In the AirDrop section, tap the icon for the person with whom you want to share the location.** The other person sees a dialog asking for permission to share the location, and when she taps Accept, her version of Maps loads and displays the location.

How Do I Protect or Fix My iPad or iPad mini?

Your iPad or iPad mini is a tablet, but that humble word doesn't begin to do it justice. After all, you can use it to surf the web, send and receive e-mail, manage contacts and schedules, shoot pictures and videos, and much more. This remarkable versatility also means that your iPad is jammed with tons of information about you. Although you might not store nuclear launch codes on your device, chances are what *is* on there is pretty important. Therefore, you should take steps to protect your iPad and fix it should anything go wrong.

Protecting Your Tablet with a Passcode

When your iPad or iPad mini is asleep, it is locked in the sense that tapping the touchscreen or pressing the volume controls does nothing. This arrangement prevents accidental taps when the device is rattling around in your backpack or handbag. To unlock the device, press either the Home button or the Sleep/Wake button, and then drag across the screen and you're back in business.

Note If you have an Apple Smart Cover for your iPad 2 (or later) or iPad mini, you can also lock or unlock your tablet by opening the Smart Cover. If you find that you frequently remove the Smart Cover without wanting to unlock your iPad or iPad mini, you can turn off the automatic lock. Tap Settings, tap General, and then tap the Lock/Unlock switch to Off.

Unfortunately, this simple technique means that anyone else who gets his mitts on your tablet can also be quickly back in business — *your* business! If you have sensitive or confidential information on your device, or want to avoid digital joyrides that run up massive roaming or data charges, you need to truly lock your iPad or iPad mini.

You do that by specifying a passcode that must be typed before anyone can get to the Home screen. You can set either a simple four-digit passcode, or a longer, more complex one that uses any combination of numbers, letters, and symbols.

Note Yes, having a passcode hoop to jump through before using your iPad is a hassle. To minimize the bother, turn off the passcode when using your tablet at home, and only turn it on when you take your device out in public.

Follow these steps to set up your passcode:

1. **On the Home screen, tap Settings.** The Settings app appears.

2. **Tap General.** The General screen appears.

3. **Tap Passcode Lock.** The Passcode Lock screen appears.

4. **If you prefer to set a complex passcode, tap the Simple Passcode switch to Off.**

5. **Tap Turn Passcode On.** The Set Passcode screen appears.

6. **Tap your passcode.** For security, the characters appear in the passcode box as dots.

7. **If you're typing a complex passcode, tap Next.** The Settings app prompts you to reenter it.

8. **Tap your passcode again.**

9. **If you're typing a complex passcode, tap Done.**

With your passcode now active, Settings displays the Passcode Lock screen, as shown in Figure 14.1. You can also get to this screen by tapping Settings in the Home screen, tapping General, tapping Passcode Lock, and then typing your passcode.

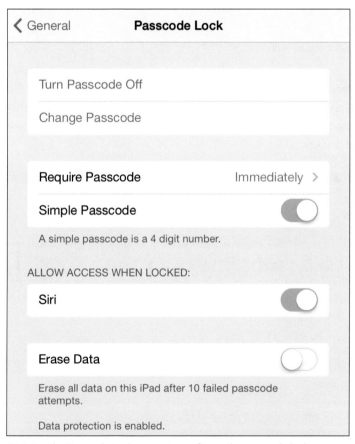

14.1 Use the Passcode Lock screen to configure the passcode lock.

Caution

You really, really need to remember your passcode. If you forget it, you're locked out of your own device and the only way to get back in is to use iTunes to restore the tablet's data and settings from an existing backup (which is described later in this chapter).

This screen offers the following options:

- **Turn Passcode Off.** If you want to stop using your passcode, tap this button, and then type the passcode (for security; otherwise an interloper could just shut off the passcode).

- **Change Passcode.** Tap this button to type a new passcode. Note that you first need to type your old passcode, and then type the new one.

- **Require Passcode.** This setting determines how much time elapses before the tablet locks the device and requests the passcode. You can choose from the following options:

  - The default setting is Immediately, which means that you see the Enter Passcode screen as soon as you finish dragging Slide to Unlock.

  - The other options are After 1 minute, After 5 minutes, After 15 minutes, and After 1 hour. Use one of these if you want to be able to work with your tablet for a bit before getting locked out. For example, the After 1 minute option is good if you need to quickly check e-mail without having to type your passcode.

- **Simple Passcode.** Use this to toggle between a simple four-digit passcode and a complex one.

- **Allow Access When Locked.** This section displays an On/Off switch for each app that you can use when your tablet is locked (in a default setup, only Siri appears). When any of these settings are On, you can use the associated app, even when your iPad or iPad mini is locked. For example, if the Siri switch is On, you can search the web and perform other voice-related tasks in lock mode. If you change any of these settings to Off, you can no longer use the associated app when your tablet is locked.

With the passcode activated, when you bring the iPad or iPad mini out of standby, you drag across the screen as usual, and then the Enter Passcode screen appears (see Figure 14.2). Type your passcode (and tap Done if it's a complex passcode) to unlock the tablet.

14.2 This is the screen you see when using a simple passcode to unlock your iPad or iPad mini.

Configuring Your Tablet to Sleep Automatically

You can put your iPad or iPad mini into Standby mode at any time by tapping the Sleep/Wake button once. This drops the power consumption considerably (mostly because it shuts off the screen), but you can still receive incoming notifications and text messages. Also, if you have the Music app running, it continues to play.

However, if your tablet is on but you're not using it, the device automatically goes into Standby mode after 2 minutes. This is called Auto-Lock, and it's a handy feature because it saves battery power and prevents accidental taps when your iPad is just sitting there.

It's also a crucial feature if you've protected your tablet with a passcode lock, as described earlier, because if your device never sleeps, it never locks either unless you shut it off manually.

To make sure that your iPad or iPad mini sleeps automatically, or if you're not comfortable with the default 2-minute Auto-Lock interval, you can make it shorter, longer, or turn it off altogether. Follow these steps to do so:

1. **On the Home screen, tap Settings.** The Settings app appears.

2. **Tap General.** The General screen appears.

3. **Tap Auto-Lock.** The Auto-Lock screen appears.

4. **Tap the interval that you want to use.** You have five choices: 2 Minutes, 5 Minutes, 10 Minutes, 15 Minutes, or Never.

Backing Up Your Tablet

When you sync your tablet with your computer (using either a USB or Wi-Fi connection), iTunes automatically creates a backup of your current data before performing the sync. Note, however, that iTunes doesn't back up your entire iPad or iPad mini. This is because most of what's on your device — music, photos, videos, apps, and so on — is already on your computer. Instead, iTunes only backs up data unique to the tablet, including your text messages, web clips, network and app settings and data, Safari history and cookies, and so on.

However, what if you've configured iTunes not to automatically sync your iPad or iPad mini? Is there a way to back up your tablet without performing a sync? You bet there is — follow these steps to make it happen:

1. **Connect your tablet to your computer.**
2. **Open iTunes if it doesn't launch automatically.**
3. **In the Devices list, click your iPhone.**
4. **Click the Summary tab.**
5. **Click Back Up Now.** iTunes backs up the device data.

If you have an iCloud account, you can also control where your iPad or iPad mini gets backed up: to your computer or to iCloud. To configure this, connect your tablet to your computer and then click it when it appears in the Devices list. In the Summary tab's Automatically Back Up section, select either iCloud or This Computer.

If you chose iCloud, you can then follow these steps to back up your data to iCloud directly from your iPad or iPad mini:

1. **In the Home screen, tap Settings.** The Settings app appears.
2. **Set up your iCloud account, if you haven't already done so.** See Chapter 4 for the details.
3. **Tap iCloud.**
4. **Tap Storage & Backup.**
5. **Tap the iCloud Backup switch to On.** Settings warns you that you'll no longer be able to use iTunes for backups.
6. **Tap OK.**
7. **Tap Back Up Now.** Settings backs up its data to your iCloud account.

Configuring Parental Controls

If your children have access to your iPad or iPad mini, you probably don't want them installing or deleting apps, or editing your account settings. Similarly, if they have tablets of their own, you may be a bit worried about some of the content they might be exposed to on the web, on YouTube, or in iTunes. You also might not want them giving away their current location.

For all those and similar parental worries, you can sleep better at night by activating the parental controls. Follow these steps to set these controls, and restrict the content and activities that kids can see and do:

1. **On the Home screen, tap Settings.** The Settings app appears.

2. **Tap General.** The General screen appears.

3. **Tap Restrictions.** The Restrictions screen appears.

4. **Tap Enable Restrictions.** Settings displays the Set Passcode screen for you to specify a four-digit code that you can use to override the parental controls. (Note that this passcode is not the same as the passcode lock covered earlier in this chapter.)

5. **Tap the four-digit restrictions passcode, and then retype the code.** Settings returns you to the Restrictions screen and enables all of the controls, as shown in Figure 14.3.

6. **In the Allow section for each app or task, tap the On/Off switch to enable or disable the restriction.**

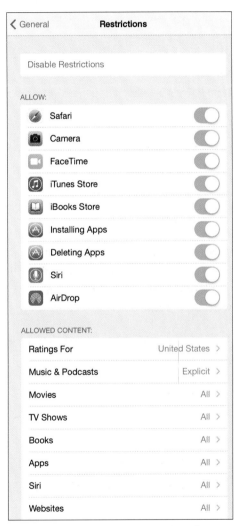

14.3 Use the Restrictions screen to configure the parental controls that you want to use.

7. **Under Allowed Content, tap Ratings For, and then tap the country with the ratings that you want to use.**

8. **For each of the content controls — Music & Podcasts, Movies, TV Shows, Books, Apps, Siri, and Websites — tap the control, and then tap the highest rating you want your children to use.**

9. **If you don't want your children to be able to make purchases within apps, tap the In-App Purchases switch to Off.** If you leave this setting on, consider tapping Require Password, and then tapping Immediately. This ensures that your children must type a password before they can make in-app purchases. If you leave the Require Password setting at 15 minutes, it means your kids can make in-app purchases without a password for up to 15 minutes after the initial purchase of the app.

10. **If you don't want your children to make changes to certain settings, tap the corresponding setting types in the Privacy section, and then tap Don't Allow Changes.**

11. **If you don't want your children to make changes to the current Mail, Calendar, or Contacts account settings, tap Accounts under Allow Changes, and then tap Don't Allow Changes.**

12. **If you don't want your children to adjust the maximum volume limit you've set (as explained in Chapter 9), tap Volume Limit, and then tap Don't Allow Changes.**

13. **In the Game Center section (which appears at the bottom of the Restrictions screen), tap the On/Off switches to enable or disable multiplayer games, and to enable or disable adding friends.**

Locating and Protecting a Lost iPad

Depending on how you use your iPad or iPad mini, you can easily end up with a pretty large chunk of your life residing on it. That sounds like a good thing, I know, but if you happen to lose your tablet, you've also lost that chunk of your life. You've also opened up a gaping privacy hole because anyone can now delve into your data. (I'm assuming here that you haven't configured your device with a passcode lock, as described earlier.)

If you've been syncing your tablet with your computer regularly, then you can probably recover most, or even all, of that data. However, I'm sure you'd probably rather find your iPad or iPad mini because it's expensive — and there's just something creepy about the thought of some stranger flicking through your stuff.

The old way of finding a device consisted of scouring every nook and cranny that you visited before losing it and calling up various lost-and-found departments to see if anyone's turned it in. The new way to find your iPad or iPad mini is by using a great app (it's also an iCloud feature) called Find My iPhone (yes, the app is called Find My *iPhone*, even on the iPad and iPad mini).

Caution

In previous versions of iOS, the one drawback to Find My iPhone was that someone who found your iPad could easily turn off the feature and disable it. The solution was to turn on the passcode lock as described earlier in this chapter. That's still a good idea, but a new iOS 7 feature called Activation Lock makes this less crucial. That's because Activation Lock means that a person can only turn off Find My iPhone by entering your Apple ID password.

Find My iPhone uses known Wi-Fi hotspots (as well as the GPS sensor and cellular antenna if you have a cellular iPad or iPad mini) to locate the device. You can also use Find My iPhone to play a sound on your tablet, remotely lock it, or send a message. In a real pinch, you can also remotely delete your data. The next few sections provide the details.

Activating Find My iPad

Find My iPhone works by looking for a particular signal that your iPad or iPad mini beams out into the ether. This signal is turned off by default, so you need to follow these steps to turn it on if you ever plan to use Find My iPhone:

1. **Add your iCloud account as described in Chapter 4 if you haven't already done so.**
   When you add the account, be sure to tap OK when iCloud asks if it can use your location.

2. **On the Home screen, tap Settings.** The Settings app appears.

3. **Tap iCloud.** Your iCloud account settings appear.

4. **Tap the Find My iPad switch to On.** Settings asks you to confirm.

5. **Tap OK.** Settings activates the Find My iPad setting, as shown in Figure 14.4.

14.4 In your iCloud settings screen, tap the Find My iPad switch to On.

Locating your iPad or iPad mini on a map

With Find My iPad now active on your tablet, you can use the Find My iPhone app or iCloud to locate it at any time. The next two sections show you how to do this using the app and iCloud.

Using the Find My iPhone app

Follow these steps to see your lost iPad or iPad mini on a map using the Find My iPhone app:

1. **On an iPad, iPad mini, iPhone, or iPod touch that has the Find My iPhone app installed, tap the app to launch it.** Find My iPhone prompts you to type your Apple ID.

2. **Tap your Apple ID and password and then tap Sign In.** Note that you must use the same Apple ID that you used to activate the Find My iPad setting on your tablet.

3. **If the app asks whether it can use your current location, tap OK.**

4. **If you're using Find My iPhone on an iPad or iPad mini, tap Devices.**

5. **In the list of devices, tap your lost iPad or iPad mini.** The Find My iPhone app locates the device on a map, as shown in Figure 14.5.

6. **To see if the location has changed, click the Refresh Location button (the circular arrow).**

14.5 In the list of devices, tap your iPad or iPad mini to locate it on a map.

Playing a sound on your iPad or iPad mini

If you misplace your iPad or iPad mini, the first thing you should try is using Find My iPhone to play a sound on your tablet. This sound plays even if your tablet is in silent or airplane mode, and it plays loudly — even if your tablet has its volume turned down or muted.

Follow these steps to do so:

1. **Tap or click Devices.** The My Devices list appears.

2. **Tap or click your iPad or iPad mini in the devices list.** Find My iPhone locates your tablet on a map.

3. **Tap or click Play Sound.** Find My iPhone begins playing the sound on your tablet and displays the alert shown in Figure 14.6.

Find My iPad Alert

OK

14.6 While the sound plays, Find My iPhone also displays this alert on your iPad or iPad mini.

Remotely locking your iPad or iPad mini

If you can't find your iPad or iPad mini right away by playing a sound, your next step should be to ensure that some other person who finds the device can't rummage around in your stuff. You do this by putting your tablet into lost mode, which remotely locks the tablet using the passcode that you set earlier (or a new passcode, if you haven't set one).

You can also provide a phone number where you can be reached and send a message for whoever finds your device. Follow these steps to put your iPad or iPad mini into lost mode:

1. **Tap or click Devices.** The My Devices list appears.

2. **Tap or click your iPad or iPad mini in the Devices list.** Find My iPhone locates your iPad or iPad mini on a map.

3. **Tap or click Lost Mode.** If you've already set a passcode on your tablet, Find My iPhone displays the Lost Mode dialog shown in Figure 14.7. In this case, skip to step 6.

4. **If your tablet isn't already protected by a passcode, tap or click the numbers in the keypad to enter a four-digit passcode.**

5. **Reenter the four-digit passcode.** Find My iPhone asks you to enter an optional phone number where you can be reached.

6. **Type your phone number, and then select Next.** Find My iPhone prompts you to type a message that will appear on the tablet, along with the phone number.

7. **Type the message, and then tap or click Done.** Find My iPhone remotely locks the iPad or iPad mini, and displays the message, as shown in Figure 14.8.

Remotely deleting the data on your tablet

If you can't get the other person to return your tablet, and it contains sensitive or confidential data (or just that big chunk of your life I mentioned earlier), you can use the Find My iPhone app or the iCloud Find My iPhone feature to take the drastic step of remotely wiping all data from the device. Follow these steps to do so:

1. **Tap or click Devices.** The My Devices list appears.

2. **Tap or click your iPad or iPad mini in the My Devices list.** Find My iPhone locates your iPad or iPad mini on a map.

3. **Tap or click Erase iPad.** Find My iPhone asks you to confirm.

4. **Tap or click Erase.** Find My iPhone prompts you for your Apple ID password.

14.7 To prevent anyone from messing with your lost iPad or iPad mini, you can remotely apply a passcode lock.

14.8 After you remotely lock your lost tablet, Find My iPhone displays your message on the lock screen.

5. **Type your password, and then tap or click Next.** Find My iPhone asks you to enter an optional phone number where you can be reached, which will appear on the iPad after it has been erased.

6. **Type your phone number, and then select Next.** Find My iPhone prompts you to type a message that will appear on the tablet, along with the phone number, after it has been erased.

7. **Type the message, and then tap or click Done.** Find My iPhone remotely wipes all data from the tablet.

General Troubleshooting Techniques

If your iPad or iPad mini is behaving erratically, it's possible that a specific component inside the device is the cause. In that case, you don't have much choice but to ship your tablet back to Apple for repairs. Fortunately, most glitches are temporary and can often be fixed by using one or more of the following techniques:

- **Restart your iPad or iPad mini.** By far the most common solution to most problems is to shut down and restart the device. Rebooting the tablet reloads the entire system, which is often enough to solve many problems. To restart your iPad or iPad mini, press and hold the Sleep/Wake button for a few seconds until you see the Slide to Power Off screen (at which point you can release the button). Drag the Slide to Power Off slider to the right to start the shutdown. When the screen goes completely black, the device is off. To restart, press and hold the Sleep/Wake button until you see the Apple logo, and then release the button.

- **Reboot the hardware.** When you restart your iPad by pressing and holding Sleep/Wake for a while, what you're really doing is rebooting the system software. If that still doesn't solve the problem, you may need to reboot the hardware as well. To do that, press and hold the Sleep/Wake and Home buttons. Keep them pressed until you see the Apple logo (it takes about 8 seconds or so), which indicates a successful restart.

Genius

The hardware reboot is also the way to go if your iPad or iPad mini is really stuck, and holding down the Sleep/Wake button doesn't do anything.

305

- **Recharge your iPad or iPad mini.** It's possible that the battery is completely discharged. Connect your tablet to your computer or the dock. If it powers up and you see the battery logo (note that this may take a minute or two), then it's charging just fine and will be back on its feet in a while.

- **Shut down a stuck app.** If your iPad or iPad mini is frozen because an application has gone haywire, you can usually get it back in the saddle by forcing the application to quit. Press and hold the Sleep/Wake button until you see the Slide to Power Off screen, and then press and hold the Home button for about 6 seconds. Your iPad or iPad mini shuts down the application and returns you to the Home screen. If an app is frozen but your tablet still works fine otherwise, double-press the Home button to display the multitasking screen, scroll right or left as needed to bring the app's thumbnail screen into view, and then drag the app thumbnail up to the top of the screen. iOS sends the thumbnail off the screen and shuts down the app.

- **Check for iOS software updates.** If Apple knows about the problem you're having, it will fix it (eventually) and make the patch available in a software update. I tell you how to update your iPad or iPad mini a bit later in this chapter.

- **Check for app updates.** It's possible that a bug in an app is causing your woes, so you can often solve such problems by updating the app. Fortunately, app updates are automatic in iOS 7, so this should never be much of a problem. To confirm that your apps are updating automatically, open Settings, tap iTunes & App Store, and make sure the Updates switch is On.

- **Erase and restore your content and settings.** This may seem like drastic advice, but it's possible to use iTunes to perform a complete backup of everything on your iPad or iPad mini. You can then reset the tablet to its original, pristine state, and then restore the backup. I explain this rather lengthy process later in the chapter.

- **Reset your settings.** Sometimes your iPad or iPad mini goes down for the count because its settings have become corrupted. In that case, you can restore it by resetting its original settings. If iTunes doesn't recognize your device, then the backup-and-restore option is out. However, you can still reset the settings on the tablet. Tap Settings in the Home screen, tap General, tap Reset, and then tap Reset All Settings. When Settings asks you to confirm, tap Reset.

Genius

If resetting your iPad or iPad mini doesn't get the job done, it could be some recalcitrant bit of content that's causing the problem. In that case, tap Settings in the Home screen, tap General, tap Reset, and then tap Erase All Content and Settings. When Settings asks you to confirm, tap Erase.

Troubleshooting connected devices

You can connect devices to your iPad or iPad mini in only a few ways: Using the headset jack, the Lightning connector, or Bluetooth. So, although the number of devices you can connect is relatively limited, that doesn't mean you might never have problems with those devices.

If you're having trouble with a device attached to your tablet, the good news is that a fair chunk of those problems have a relatively limited set of causes. You may be able to get the device back on its feet by attempting a few tried-and-true remedies that work quite often for many devices. If it's not immediately obvious what the problem is, then your hardware troubleshooting routine should always start with the following very basic techniques:

- **Check connections, power switches, and so on.** Some of the most common (and embarrassing) causes of hardware problems are the simple physical things, so make sure that the device is turned on and that the cable connections are secure. If you can't access the Internet through the tablet's Wi-Fi connection, make sure that your network router is turned on, and that the cable between your router and the ISP's modem is properly connected.

- **Replace the batteries.** Wireless devices, such as headsets, really chew through batteries. If such a device is working intermittently or not at all, always try replacing the batteries to see if that solves the problem.

- **Turn the device off, and then on again.** You *power cycle* a device by turning it off, waiting a few seconds for its innards to stop spinning, and then turning it back on. You'd be amazed how often this simple procedure can get a device back up and running. For a device that doesn't have an On/Off switch, try either unplugging it from the power outlet, or removing and replacing the batteries.

- **Reset the default settings for the device.** If you can configure a device, then perhaps some new setting is causing the problem. If you recently made a change, try returning the setting to its original value. If that doesn't do the trick, most configurable devices have some kind of Restore Default Settings option that enables you to quickly return them to their factory settings.

- **Upgrade the device's firmware.** Many devices come with *firmware*, a small program that runs inside the device and controls its internal functions. For example, all routers have firmware. Check with the manufacturer to see if a new version exists; if it does, download it and see the manual for the device to learn how to upgrade the firmware.

Updating the iPad or iPad mini operating system

iOS should update itself from time to time when you connect it to your computer (provided that the computer has an Internet connection). This is another good reason to sync your iPad or iPad mini regularly. The problem is, you might hear about an important update that adds a feature you're really looking forward to or perhaps fixes a gaping security hole. What do you do if iTunes isn't scheduled to check for an update for a few days? In that case, you take matters into your own hands and check for updates yourself.

You can check for updates right on your tablet by following these steps:

1. **On the Home screen, tap Settings to open the Settings app.**
2. **Tap General.** Settings displays the General screen.
3. **Tap Software Update.** Settings begins checking for available updates. If you see the message "Your software is up to date," then you can move on to bigger and better things.
4. **If an update is available, tap Download and Install.** Settings downloads the update, and then proceeds with the installation, which takes a few minutes.

Caution Your tablet will only go through with the update if it has more than 50 percent battery life through the entire update operation. To ensure the update is a success, either plug your tablet into an AC outlet or only run the update when the battery is fully charged.

Follow these steps to update your iPad or iPad mini via iTunes:

1. **Connect your tablet to your computer.** iTunes opens and connects to your device.
2. **Click your iPad or iPad mini in the Devices list.**
3. **Click the Summary tab.**
4. **Click Check for Update.** iTunes connects to the Apple servers to see if any iOS updates are available. If an update exists, you see the iPad Software Update dialog, which offers a description of the update.
5. **Click Next.** iTunes displays the Software License Agreement.
6. **Click Agree.** iTunes downloads and installs the software update.

Restoring data and settings

Sometimes your iPad or iPad mini goes down for the count because its settings have become corrupted. In that case, you can restore the tablet by restoring its original settings. The best way to go about this is to use the Restore feature in iTunes, because that enables you to make a backup of your settings. However, it does mean that your tablet must be able to connect to your computer and be visible in iTunes.

If that's not the case, see the instructions for resetting that I covered earlier in this chapter. Otherwise, follow these steps to restore your iPad or iPad mini:

1. **On your iPad or iPad mini, turn off Find My iPad, if it's turned on.** You do this by opening Settings, tapping iCloud, tapping the Find My iPad switch to Off, and then entering your Apple password.

2. **Connect your tablet to your computer.**

3. **In iTunes, click your iPad or iPad mini in the Devices list.**

4. **Click Sync.** This ensures that iTunes backs up your iPad or iPad mini, and has copies of all of the data.

5. **Click the Summary tab.**

6. **Click Restore iPad.** iTunes asks you to confirm that you want to restore.

7. **Click Restore.** iTunes downloads the software and restores the original software and settings. When your device restarts, iTunes connects to it and displays the Welcome to Your New iPad screen, as shown in Figure 14.9.

8. **Select the Restore from this backup option.**

9. **If you happen to have more than one device backed up, use the list to choose yours.**

10. **Click Continue.** iTunes restores your backed-up data, restarts your tablet, and then syncs it.

Caution   If you have confidential or sensitive data on your iPad or iPad mini, that data becomes part of the backup files and could be viewed by a snoop. To prevent this, select the Summary tab's Encrypt local backup check box, and then use the Set password dialog to specify your decryption password. Then click Back Up Now.

Welcome to Your New iPad

Would you like to set up this iPad as a new iPad or restore all of
your information from a previous backup?

○ Set up as new iPad

◉ Restore from this backup: [Paul's iPad – Aug 28, 2013, 9:48 AM ⇕]

Last Backed Up: 7/29/13, 10:54 AM

[Continue]

14.9 When your factory-fresh iPad or iPad mini restarts, use iTunes to restore your settings and data.

11. **Go through the tabs and check the sync settings to make sure they're set up the way you want.**

12. **If you made any changes to the settings, click Apply.** This ensures that your iPad or iPad mini has all of its data restored.

Taking Care of the Battery

Your tablet comes with a large lithium-ion battery. Apple claims that the iPad and iPad mini give you up to 10 hours of continuous usage, and hold a charge in standby mode for 30 days. Those are impressive times, although count on getting less in the real world (particularly if you have a cellular model and you're surfing the web over a cellular connection).

The biggest downside to the battery is that it's not, in Apple parlance, a *user-installable* feature. If your battery dies, you have no choice but to return it to Apple to get it replaced — all the more reason to take care of it and try to maximize its life.

Tracking battery usage

Your iPad or iPad mini doesn't give much battery data, but you can monitor both the total usage time (this includes all activities: Surfing, reading eBooks, gaming, playing media, and so on) and standby time (when your tablet was in Sleep mode). Follow these steps to do so:

1. **On the Home screen, tap Settings.** The Settings app appears.

2. **Tap General.** Settings displays the General screen.

3. **Tap Usage.** Settings displays the Usage screen.

4. **Tap the Battery Percentage On/Off switch to the On position.** Your iPad or iPad mini now displays the percentage of battery life left in the status bar beside the battery icon, as shown in Figure 14.10.

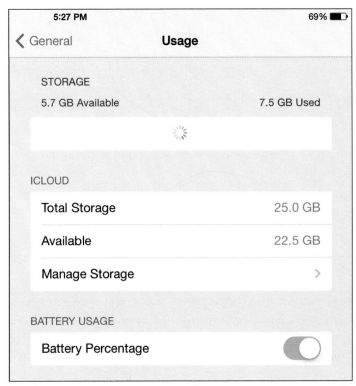

14.10 Turn on the Battery Percentage option to monitor battery life in the status bar.

Extending battery life

Reducing battery consumption as much as possible on the iPad or iPad mini not only extends the time between charges, but also extends the overall life of your battery.

311

To reduce your tablet's battery consumption, consider the following suggestions:

- **Dim the screen.** The touchscreen drains lots of battery power, so dimming it reduces that power. Flick up from the bottom of the screen to display the Control Center (or tap Settings and then tap Brightness & Wallpaper), and then drag the brightness slider to the left to dim the screen.

- **Cycle the battery.** All lithium-based batteries slowly lose their charging capacity over time. If you can run your iPad or iPad mini on batteries for 8 hours today, later you'll only be able to run it for 6 hours on a full charge. You can't stop this process, but you can delay it significantly by periodically cycling the battery. *Cycling* — also called reconditioning or recalibrating — a battery means letting it completely discharge, and then fully recharging it. To maintain optimal performance, you should cycle the battery every one or two months.

Genius

Paradoxically, the less you use your iPad or iPad mini, the more often you should cycle its battery. If you often go several days or even a week or two without using your tablet (I can't imagine!), you should cycle its battery at least once a month.

- **Slow the auto-check on your e-mail.** Having your e-mail poll the server for new messages eats up your battery. Set it to check Hourly, if possible. Ideally, set it to Manual check if you can. Tap Settings, tap Mail, Contacts, Calendars, and then in the Fetch section, tap Manually.

- **Turn off push.** If you have an iCloud or Exchange account, consider turning off the push feature to save battery power. Tap Settings, and then tap Mail, Contacts, Calendars. Tap Fetch New Data, tap the account, and then tap Manual.

- **Minimize your tasks.** If you aren't able to charge your tablet for a while, avoid background chores (such as playing music) or secondary chores (such as organizing your contacts). If your only goal is to read all of your e-mail, stick to that until it's done because you don't know how much time you have.

- **Put your iPad or iPad mini into Sleep mode manually, if necessary.** If you're interrupted — for example, the pizza delivery guy shows up on time — don't wait for your tablet to put itself to sleep because those few minutes use up precious battery time. Instead, put your device to sleep manually by pressing the Sleep/Wake button.

- **Avoid temperature extremes.** Exposing your tablet to extremely hot or cold tempera-tures reduces the long-term effectiveness of the battery. Try to keep your iPad within a reasonable range of temperatures.

- **Turn off Wi-Fi if you don't need it.** When Wi-Fi is on, it regularly checks for available wireless networks, which drains the battery. If you don't need to connect to a wireless network, turn off Wi-Fi to conserve energy. Tap Settings, tap Wi-Fi, and then tap the Wi-Fi setting to Off.

- **Turn off cellular if you don't need it.** If you have a cellular iPad or iPad mini, it con-stantly looks for nearby cellular towers to maintain the signal, which can use up battery power in a hurry. If you're surfing on a Wi-Fi network, you don't need cellular, so turn it off. Tap Settings, tap Cellular Data, and then tap the Cellular Data setting to Off.

- **Turn off Location Services if you don't need them.** When Location Services is on, the iPad exchanges data with the Wi-Fi and GPS systems regularly, which uses up battery power. If you don't need Location Services for the time being, turn them off. Tap Settings, tap Privacy, tap Location Services, and then tap the Location Services switch to Off.

- **Turn off Bluetooth if you don't need it.** When Bluetooth is running, it constantly checks for nearby Bluetooth devices, which drains the battery. If you aren't using any Bluetooth devices, turn off Bluetooth to save energy. Tap Settings, tap Bluetooth, and then tap the Bluetooth switch to Off.

Genius

If you don't need all three (or four, if you have cellular) of the tablet's antennae for a while, a faster way to turn them off is to switch your iPad or iPad mini to airplane mode. Either tap Settings and then tap the Airplane Mode switch to On, or swipe up from the bottom to reveal the Control Center and then tap the Airplane Mode icon.

Solving Specific Problems

The generic troubleshooting and repair techniques that you've seen so far can solve all kinds of problems. However, specific problems always require specific solutions. The rest of this chapter takes you through a few of the most common of these.

The screen won't respond to taps

Every now and then, your iPad might freeze, and no amount of tapping, swiping, or threatening can get it to respond. The most likely problem is that the touchscreen has become temporarily stuck. To fix it, press the Sleep/Wake button and put the tablet to sleep. Press Sleep/Wake again to wake it, and then drag across the screen. In most cases, you should now be able to resume normal operations.

If that doesn't work, then it's possible that the app you're using has crashed, so you need to shut it down as I described earlier in this chapter.

The battery won't charge

If you find that your battery won't charge, consider the following possible solutions:

- **If the iPad or iPad mini is plugged in to a computer to charge via the USB port, it may be that the computer has gone into standby.** Waking the computer should solve the problem.

- **The USB port may not be transferring enough power.** For example, the USB ports on most keyboards and hubs don't offer much in the way of power. If your iPad or iPad mini is plugged into a USB port on a keyboard or hub, plug it into a USB port on your Mac or PC.

- **Attach the USB cable to the USB power adapter, and then plug the adapter into an AC outlet.**

- **Double-check all connections and make sure that everything is plugged in properly.**

- **Try another Lightning cable if you have one.**

If you can't locate the problem after these steps, you may need to send your iPad or iPad mini in for service. A replacement battery (if you live in the United States) costs $99 plus $6.95 shipping.

Note To get your iPad or iPad mini repaired, you can take it to an Apple store or send it in. Visit www.apple.com/support and follow the prompts to find out how to send your device in for repairs. Remember that the memory comes back wiped, so be sure to sync with iTunes, if you can. Also, if you have a cellular iPad or iPad mini, don't forget to remove your SIM card before you send it in.

You can't access a Wi-Fi network

Wireless networking adds a whole new set of potential snags to your troubleshooting chores because of problems such as interference and device ranges. The following list includes a few troubleshooting items that you should check to solve any wireless connectivity problems you're having with your iPad or iPad mini:

● **Make sure that the Wi-Fi antenna is on.** Tap Settings, tap Wi-Fi, and then tap the Wi-Fi switch to the On position.

● **Make sure that the tablet isn't in Airplane mode.** Tap Settings, and then tap the Airplane Mode switch to the Off position (or swipe up from the bottom to get to the Control Center, and then tap the Airplane Mode icon).

● **Check the connection.** The iPad has a tendency to disconnect from nearby Wi-Fi networks for no apparent reason. Tap Settings. If the Wi-Fi setting shows as Not Connected, tap Wi-Fi, and then tap your network in the list.

● **Renew the lease.** When you connect to a Wi-Fi network, the access point gives your tablet a Dynamic Host Control Protocol (DHCP) lease that allows it to access the network. You can often solve connectivity problems by renewing that lease. Tap Settings, tap Wi-Fi, and then tap the blue More Info (*i*) icon to the right of the connected Wi-Fi network. Tap the DHCP tab, and then tap Renew Lease, as shown in Figure 14.11.

● **Reconnect to the network.** You can often solve Wi-Fi network woes by disconnecting, and then reconnecting to the network. Tap Settings, tap Wi-Fi, and then tap the blue More Info (*i*) icon to the right of the connected Wi-Fi network. Tap the Forget This Network button to disconnect, and then reconnect to the same network.

● **Reset the iPad or iPad mini network settings.** This removes all stored network data and resets everything to the factory state, which might solve the problem. Tap Settings, tap General, tap Reset, and then tap Reset Network Settings. When Settings asks you to confirm, tap Reset.

‹ Wi-Fi	**LogophiliaB**	
Forget this Network		
IP ADDRESS		
DHCP	BootP	Static
IP Address		192.168.2.40
Subnet Mask		255.255.0.0
Router		192.168.2.1
DNS		192.168.2.1
Search Domains	no-domain-set-bellcanada	
Client ID		
Renew Lease		

14.11 Open the connected Wi-Fi network settings, and then tap Renew Lease to get a fresh lease on your Wi-Fi life.

● **Reboot and power cycle devices.** Reset your hardware by performing the following tasks in order: Restart your iPad or iPad mini, reboot the tablet hardware, power cycle the wireless access point, and then power cycle the broadband modem.

● **Look for interference.** Devices such as baby monitors and cordless phones that use the 2.4 GHz radio frequency (RF) band can play havoc with wireless signals. Try either moving or turning off such devices if they're near your tablet or wireless access point.

● **Check your range.** If you're getting no signal or a weak signal, your tablet could be too far from the access point. If you have an 802.11n access point, the theoretical range is about 230 feet. If you have an older access point (such as 802.11g), you usually can't get much farther than about 230 feet (for an 802.11n Wi-Fi network; 115 feet for 802.11a/b/g networks) away from it before the signal begins to degrade. Either move closer to the access point or turn on the access point range booster feature, if it has one. You also could install a wireless range extender.

● **Update the wireless access point firmware.** The wireless access point firmware is the internal program that the access point uses to perform its various chores. Wireless access point manufacturers frequently update their firmware to fix bugs, so you should see if an updated version of the firmware is available. See your device documentation to learn how this works.

● **Reset the router.** As a last resort, reset the router to its default factory settings (see the device documentation to learn how to do this). Note that if you do this, you have to set up your network from scratch.

Caution

You should keep your tablet and wireless access point well away from microwave ovens, which can jam wireless signals.

iTunes doesn't see your iPad or iPad mini

When you connect your tablet to your computer, iTunes should start, and you should see the iPad or iPad mini in the Devices list. If iTunes doesn't start when you connect your device, or if iTunes is already running but the tablet doesn't appear in the Devices list, it means that iTunes doesn't recognize your iPad. The following are some possible fixes:

● **Check the connections.** Make sure that the USB and Lightning connectors are fully seated.

● **Try a different USB port.** The port you're using may not work, so try another one. If you're using a port on a USB hub, trying using one of the built-in USB ports on the computer.

● **Restart your iPad.** Press and hold the Sleep/Wake button for a few seconds until the tablet shuts down, and then press and hold Sleep/Wake until you see the Apple logo.

- **Restart your computer.** This should reset the computer's USB ports, which might solve the problem.

- **Check your iTunes version.** You should be using at least iTunes version 10.7 to work with an iPad or iPad mini.

- **Check your operating system version.** On a Mac, your iPad or iPad mini requires OS X 10.6.8 or later. On a PC, it requires Windows 8, Windows 7, Windows Vista, or Windows XP Service Pack 3 or later.

You have trouble syncing your tablet

Syncing is a crucial operation because it's the easiest way to load your iPad or iPad mini with your contacts, calendars, e-mail accounts, music, videos, and more. So, if you can't sync your tablet, that's a big problem. The following are a couple of solutions to try:

- **iTunes won't sync your iPad or iPad mini.** If iTunes sees your tablet but you can't get it to sync, you probably need to adjust some settings. See Chapter 4 for some troubleshooting ideas related to syncing. Another possibility is that your device is currently locked. That's not usually a problem for iTunes, but it is sometimes confused by a locked iPad or iPad mini. The easy remedy is to unplug the tablet, unlock it, and then plug it in again.

- **You have trouble syncing music or videos.** The most likely culprit here is that your files are in one of the following formats, which the iPad can't read: WMA, MPEG-1, MPEG-2, and others. First, convert the files to a format that the tablet does understand using converter software. Then put them back on iTunes and try to sync again. The iPad and iPad mini support the following audio formats: AAC, HE-AAC (V1 and V2), and Protected AAC; AIFF; Audible formats 2, 3, and 4, and Audible Enhanced Audio; Apple Lossless; MP3; MP3 VBR; and WAV. The iPad and iPad mini support the following video formats: H.264, MPEG-4, and Motion JPEG.

Your tablet doesn't recognize your SIM

Follow these steps if you have a cellular iPad or iPad mini, and your tablet doesn't detect your SIM:

1. **Eject the SIM tray from the side of your iPad or iPad mini using a SIM tool (if you have one), or a paper clip or pin.** Gently press the tool into the little hole on the tray, and then pull it out.

2. **Make sure the SIM is free of dirt and debris.**

3. **Reseat the SIM in the tray, and then slide the tray back in.**

If this doesn't solve the problem, then your problem is a larger one, and you need to contact Apple or your cellular provider.

An app is taking up too much space

The iPad and iPad mini are so useful and so much fun, it's easy to forget that they have limitations, especially when it comes to storage. This is particularly true if you have a 16GB model. However, even a big 64GB tablet can fill up in a hurry if you've stuffed it with movies, TV shows, and tons of magazine subscriptions.

You can tell how much free space is available on your device by either connecting it to iTunes or tapping Settings, then General, and then Usage. The Usage screen not only shows you how much storage space you have available, it also shows you how much space each app is using, as shown in Figure 14.12.

If you see that your tablet is running low on space, check the apps to see if any of them are taking up more than their fair share of hard drive real estate. If you see a hard drive hog, you can delete its data in one of the following ways, and give your iPad some room to breathe:

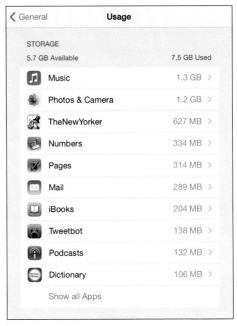

14.12 The Usage screen tells you how much storage space remains on your iPad or iPad mini.

- **Delete a third-party app.** For an app you picked up via the App Store, tap the app, tap Delete App, and then tap Delete App when your tablet asks you to confirm.

- **Delete a built-in apps.** For an app that came with your iPad or iPad mini (such as Music or Video), tap the app to display a list of the data it's storing on your tablet, and then tap Edit. This puts the list in edit mode, as shown in Figure 14.13. To remove an item, tap the red Delete button to the left of it, and then tap the Delete button that appears.

14.13 You can free up storage space by deleting individual items from some of the built-in apps.

Glossary

3G A third-generation cellular network that includes the *HSPA*, *HSPA+*, and *DC-HSDPA* standards. It is supported in the cellular models of the iPad 2 and later, and the iPad mini for data delivery over the cellular network.

4G See *LTE*.

802.11 See *Wi-Fi*.

accelerometer The component inside the iPad that senses the device's orientation in space and adjusts the display accordingly (such as switching Safari from portrait view to landscape view).

access point A networking device that enables two or more devices to connect over a Wi-Fi network and to access a shared Internet connection.

Activation lock An iOS security feature that prevents anyone from activating your iPad or iPad mini without knowing your Apple ID and password.

AirDrop A service that enables your tablet to share information, such as links, photos, and maps, wirelessly via Bluetooth connection.

Airplane Mode An operational mode that turns off the transceivers for the cellular iPad, Wi-Fi, and Bluetooth features, which puts the device in compliance with federal aviation regulations.

AirPlay A wireless technology that enables you to stream iPad video or audio to an Apple TV device, and see or hear it on your TV or audio receiver.

AirPrint A wireless technology that enables you to send a web page, e-mail message, or other text from your iPad or iPad mini to a printer.

alert A notification message that pops up on the screen and must be addressed before you can resume what you were doing.

app An application that is designed for and runs on a specific device (such as an iPad or iPad mini), or a set of related devices (such as an iPad, iPad mini, iPhone, and iPod touch).

authentication See *SMTP authentication*.

Auto-Capitalization A keyboard feature that automatically activates the Shift key after you tap a sentence-ending character, such as a period or question mark.

Auto-Correction A keyboard feature that automatically corrects errors as you type.

badge A small red icon that appears in the upper-right corner of an app icon to let you know that some new activity or data awaits you.

banner A notification message that appears at the top of the screen, but lets you keep working.

Bluetooth A wireless networking technology that enables you to exchange data between two devices using radio frequencies when the devices are within range of each other (usually within about 33 feet/10 meters).

bookmark An Internet site saved in Safari so you can access it quickly in future browsing sessions.

cloud The collection of iCloud-networked servers that store your iCloud data and push any new data to your iPad, Mac, or Windows PC.

Control Center A configuration screen that enables you to control settings such as Airplane Mode, Wi-Fi, Bluetooth, brightness, and volume. Swipe up from the bottom of the screen to display the Control Center.

cropping Removing unneeded or distracting elements from a photo.

cycling Letting the battery completely discharge, and then fully recharging it again.

data roaming A cellular provider feature that enables you to perform activities, such as checking for e-mail, when you're outside of your provider's normal coverage area.

DC-HSDPA (Dual-Carrier High Speed Downlink Packet Access) The cellular transmission standard that supports theoretical maximum download speeds of 42 Mbps.

digital rights management (DRM) Technology that restricts the usage of content to prevent piracy.

discoverable Describes a device that has its Bluetooth feature turned on so other Bluetooth devices can connect to it.

double-tap To use a fingertip to quickly press and release the screen twice.

EDGE (Enhanced Data rates for GSM [Global System for Mobile communication] Evolution) A cellular network that's older and slower than 3G, although still supported by the iPad and iPad mini.

event An appointment or meeting that you've scheduled in the Calendar app.

filter A special effect applied to a photo.

flick To quickly and briefly drag a finger across the screen.

FM transmitter A device that sends tablet output to an FM radio frequency, which you then play through your car stereo.

GPS (Global Positioning System) A satellite-based navigation system that uses wireless signals from a GPS receiver — such as the one in the cellular models of the iPad and iPad mini — to accurately determine the receiver's current position.

group A collection of contacts in Contacts. See also *Smart Group*.

headset A combination of headphones for listening and a microphone for talking.

Home screen The main screen on your iPad or iPad mini, which you access by pressing the Home button.

Home Sharing An iTunes feature that enables you to share the iTunes library on your Mac or PC with your iPad or iPad mini.

HSPA (High Speed Packet Access) The cellular transmission standard that supports theoretical maximum download speeds of 3.1 Mbps.

HSPA+ (Evolved High Speed Packet Access) The cellular transmission standard that supports theoretical maximum download speeds of 21 Mbps.

IMAP (Internet Message Access Protocol) A type of e-mail account where incoming messages, as well as copies of messages you send, remain on the server. See also *POP*.

Internet tethering See *tethering*.

keychain A list of saved passwords on a Mac or in iCloud.

Location Services The features and technologies that provide apps and system tools with access to location data.

LTE (Long-Term Evolution) The cellular transmission standard, which supports theoretical maximum download speeds of 73 Mbps, and is supported by the third- and fourth-generation iPad and the iPad mini. LTE does not meet the full specifications of the 4G standard, so it is often referred to as 3.9G.

magnetometer A device that measures the direction and intensity of a magnetic field.

Mbps Megabits per second, or millions of bits per second; a unit of data transmission speed.

memory effect The process where a battery loses capacity over time if you repeatedly recharge it without first fully discharging it.

mirroring Displaying your iPad or iPad mini screen on your TV.

multitouch A touchscreen technology that can detect and interpret two or more simultaneous touches, such as two-finger taps, spreads, and pinches.

notification Data sent by an app that lets you know it has recent activity for you to check.

pair To connect one Bluetooth device to another by typing a passkey.

pan To slide a photo or other image up, down, left, or right.

passcode A four-digit code used to secure or lock an iPad or iPad mini.

piconet An ad hoc wireless network created by two Bluetooth devices.

pinch To move two fingers closer together on the screen. See also *spread*.

playlist A collection of songs that you create using iTunes.

POP (Post Office Protocol) A type of e-mail account where incoming messages are only stored temporarily on the provider's mail server. When you connect to the server, the messages are downloaded to your tablet and removed from the server. See also *IMAP*.

power cycle A method of rebooting your iPad or iPad mini in which you turn off the device, wait a few seconds for its inner components to stop spinning, and then turn it on again.

preferences The options, settings, and other data that you configure for your Mac via System Preferences.

private browsing A web browsing mode in which Safari doesn't add sites to the History list, doesn't store site data in the cache, and doesn't save searches or passwords.

push To send data immediately without being prompted.

Reader A Safari feature that removes ads and other distractions from a web page.

ringtone The sound that plays on a cell phone when an incoming call is received.

Side switch The sliding switch that appears on the side of your iPad or iPad mini beside the volume rockers.

silent mode An operational state in which the iPad or iPad mini plays no sounds except alerts set with the Clock application.

slide To drag a finger across the screen.

Smart Group A collection of contacts in which each member has one or more things in common. Contacts adds or deletes members automatically as you add, edit, and delete contacts. See also *group*.

SMS (Short Message Service) A wireless messaging service that enables the exchange of short text messages between mobile devices.

SMTP (Simple Mail Transfer Protocol) The set of protocols that determines how e-mail messages are addressed and sent.

SMTP authentication The requirement that you must log on to a provider's SMTP server to confirm that you're the person sending the mail.

SMTP server The server that an Internet service provider uses to process outgoing e-mail messages.

spread To move two fingers apart on the screen. See also *pinch*.

SSID (Service Set Identifier) The name that identifies a network to Wi-Fi devices.

swipe To briefly slide a finger left, right, up, or down on the iPad or iPad mini screen.

synchronization (syncing) A process that ensures that data (such as contacts, e-mail accounts, and events) on your computer is the same as the data on your iPad or iPad mini.

tap To use a fingertip to quickly press and release the screen.

tethering Using an iPhone's Internet connection on a device (such as an iPad or iPad mini, Mac, or Windows PC), when the iPhone is configured as a personal hotspot.

text shortcut A short sequence of characters that represents a longer phrase.

touchscreen A screen that responds to touches such as finger taps and finger slides.

transceiver A device that transmits and receives wireless signals.

trim To edit the start and/or endpoints of a video recording or voice memo.

two-fingered tap To use two fingertips to quickly press and release the screen.

undock To move the keyboard to a more convenient part of the screen.

user-installable A component that an end user can remove and replace.

vCard A file that contains a person's contact information.

VCF (.vcf) The file extension used by a vCard.

wallpaper The background image you see when you unlock your iPad or iPad mini.

web clip A Home screen icon that serves as a link to a web page and preserves the page's scroll position and zoom level.

Wi-Fi (Wireless Fidelity) A wireless networking standard that enables wireless devices to transmit data and communicate with other devices using radio frequency signals that are beamed from one device to another.

Index